The County Books Series
GENERAL EDITOR : BRIAN VESEY-FITZGERALD

SUSSEX

THE COUNTY BOOKS SERIES

A series comprising 58 volumes. It covers every county in England and there will be four books on the mainland of Scotland, two each on the Hebrides, Ireland and Wales, and one each on Orkney, Shetland, the Isle of Man and the Channel Islands

THE FOLLOWING FIFTY-EIGHT VOLUMES HAVE NOW BEEN PUBLISHED

PLEASE WRITE TO THE PUBLISHERS FOR FULL DESCRIPTIVE PROSPECTUS

SUSSEX

ESTHER MEYNELL

Illustrated and with a Map

LONDON
Robert Hale & Company
63 Old Brompton Road, S.W.7

First Edition March 1947
Second impression June 1947
Third impression August 1948
Fourth impression March 1949
Fifth impression January 1950
Sixth impression March 1962
Seventh impression August 1966
Eighth impression February 1972

ISBN 0 7091 2617 4

PRINTED IN GREAT BRITAIN BY
LOWE AND BRYDONE (PRINTERS) LIMITED, LONDON

FOREWORD

THIS book is an impression of the history and topography of Sussex. The topography is entirely personal, for I felt it was better to write of those parts of Sussex I knew really well, than to attempt to give, from other people's books, or from cursory visits, an account of the whole county. Guide-books provide all that kind of information. The thing I have tried to do is to give some of the reasons why Sussex is different from her neighbouring counties, and was for so long a "secret kingdom."

I have deliberately refrained from any allusions to the changes and accidents of the recent war in Sussex—troops and searchlights on the Downs, aerodromes, damage done by enemy bombs. These things will pass. Sussex will absorb them into her long history, but they cannot take their place in that history till they have receded into the past.

Because this book is dedicated to the Sussex Archæological Society, it must not be assumed that the Society is in any way responsible for it. Any errors and mistakes it contains are on my own head. I would not dare to call myself an archæologist: I am but a beginner, an amateur—which means a lover—of the subject. The dedication is nothing but a small sign of gratitude for the immense amount of interest and pleasure I have gained all the years I have been a member of the Society.

E. M.

DEDICATED

To the President, the Council,
and my fellow Members of the
Sussex Archæological Society

CONTENTS

ILLUSTRATIONS

ix

ILLUSTRATIONS

ACKNOWLEDGMENTS

The illustrations above, numbered 2, 3, 5, 6, 7, 8, 9, 10, 11, 13, 14, 15, 16, 17, 20, 21, 23, 24, 25, 26, 28, 29, 32, 34, 35, 37, 41, 43, 44, 45, 48 and 49 are reproduced from photographs by Mr Will F. Taylor of Reigate. The remaining 17 illustrations are reproduced from photographs supplied by Mr T. Edmondson of Folkestone.

CHAPTER I

THE SUSSEX SCENE

1

SUSSEX, like every other English county, is a palimpsest wherein one writing lies upon the top of another—the writing first of God, and then of man. The earth itself, its structure out of nothingness and chaos, out of water and fire, is God's handwriting. The first writing of man—so dim to our imagination unless a little archæological training is brought to bear upon it—is vast and yet elemental, written with such poor implements, a deerhorn pick, a sharpened flint, yet more enduring than any other work of man. Time, fire, destruction of war, may overwhelm and obliterate noble buildings in stone and in brickwork, may wipe out great libraries and great paintings, but when the Old Stone Age Man and the New Stone Age man dug in the chalk with his imperfect implements—the vastness of the results compared with the inadequacy of the means, completely staggers our mechanical and conceited age—his writing is indestructible and defies all that time can do. If so obliterated by farming operations as to be invisible from the earth's surface, then it can be seen, bold and challenging from the sky, as though that earth-bound Neolithic Man raised a saluting hand across incredible centuries to the airman flying above his ancient encampments. This is what the chalk does, holds the records perdurably. That is why Sussex, whose most memorable and lovely geologic feature is the chalk hills called the South Downs, is so notable a repository and storehouse of the writings of Early Man. The Downs, so large and simple and peaceful in their outline against the sky, so mysterious and unchanging through all their mutations of atmosphere, of sea and cloud and sea-mist, are haunted—haunted by the men who first found their home and their sepulture there.

It is surprising how many people think scenery just happened, and believe a landscape is a permanent thing and that what it is to-day it always has been and always will be. This idea is palpably absurd, more so in those who are dwellers in the coastwise counties of England, for on the seashore the writing of time and change is more plainly visible than anywhere else. Mountains, which exist by very reason of their rocklike nature and hardness, may with some truth be called eternal. But round the English coast the sea restlessly and unceasingly mumbles and mouths, wearing away even the ironlike granite cliffs of Cornwall. Where England meets the Channel with a margin of sand, shingle, or chalk cliffs, the results of sea-erosion are dramatic, and have changed not only the aspect of the coast, but the history of England itself.

In no county is this more visible, of no county is this more true, than of Sussex. Kent and Sussex, each as bold as fair, have always stood in the forefront of English history. But though Kent is nearer to the continent of Europe than Sussex, it was not to Kent that Cæsar came, nor William the Conqueror, but to Sussex, because the physical conformation of that flat coast round Pevensey was favourable to invasion.

The English as a nation are fairly obstinate and stubborn, whether they come from Lincolnshire or Dorset, from Essex or Yorkshire; maybe there was some special arrangement of Providence in causing the two most prominent of our conquerors to step ashore on Sussex soil. William of Normandy tripped and fell as he did so, and with a swift wit turned the disconcerting experience, as he rose with his hands full of Sussex mud crying, "I have taken seizin of England!"

Actually he had taken seizin of Sussex, and Sussex, had he but known it, has always been a kingdom by itself—obstinate, cut off, slow, unchanging, with a vast looming background of pre-history. These things were so because of the geological structure of the county—which, again, formed the nature of the inhabitants, their ways and customs and vernacular-building. When you have said the words "Chalk" and "Flint"—

and they must be said in capitals—you have said a great deal
about the history of Sussex.

How many times in museums has one seen a listless, bored
face peering down at a collection of flint implements in a glass
case—curiously edged lumps of dull or bright surface,
covered with meaningless marks, some sharp, some smoother.
By the side of them are little curling and often faded paper
labels, on which are written things like "Flint Axe : Paleolithic. St. Achuel II."

"How very dull and depressing it all is ! Let's go and get
some tea. We did not come to Sussex to look at flint implements, we came"—so might have been said by any visitor
in any year up to the year 1939—"to walk on the Palace
Pier at Brighton and sniff the fishy breezes; to ride on the
curious and temperamental little electric railway (quite a
chance of being stuck above the mumbling waves) under the
Kemp Town cliffs to Black Rock; to picnic on Beachy Head;
or scramble among the ruins of the Conqueror's Castle at
Hastings."

But if there had been none of those flint implements in the
glass cases it is highly probable there would have been no
Brighton and no Hastings, not to speak of Bognor Regis
and Worthing, of Chichester and Arundel and Lewes, of
Winchelsea and Rye. With those shapen lumps of flint Early
Man first began to make things, and so to make himself. Fire
and knapped flints were what first distinguished him from
the animals.

Sussex is not a very large county—much longer, of course,
than wide—but in its extent of mileage it contains an astonishing variety of scenery and types of building. All these qualities derive originally from the fundamental earth from which
all things come and to which all things return. Geology is
the foundation of history, and all the changing beauty of the
Sussex scene is due to the varieties of geological formation.

In its most outstanding feature Sussex is a chalk county,
and Hilaire Belloc says of chalk in his *Old Road* :

". . . its lovely breadths delight us when the white clouds
and the flocks move over them together; when the waves
break it into cliffs they are the characteristics of our shores
and through its thin coat of whitish mould go the thirsty

roots of our three trees, the beach, the holly, and the yew."

Chalk and flint belong together, and the importance of flint in the early history of man can hardly be exaggerated. Of all the English counties that boast the chalk in their structure, Sussex is the richest in flint, and that great chalk hill called Cissbury, at the back of Worthing—a glorious hill, a Hill of the Dawning, in outlook and position and meaning—is the greatest repository of flint-knapping in England, except for that place called Grime's Graves in Norfolk. It should be called Grime's Cradle, not his grave, for it was on those flints and the flints of Sussex that Neolithic Man cut his teeth.

The flint-knapping industry is dead in Sussex—dead for many thousands of years. But in Suffolk, at Brandon, it is still in actual existence (or was a few years ago), a faint and fading pulse of what was once so vital and alive. And still in this day, as in that remote past, it is purely a matter of human skill—the human hand and eye dealing with what would seem a most intractable material.

Pick up a lump of flint from a whitish ploughed field on a shoulder of the Downs—the Sussex farmer will plough a field with an almost vertical plough, so that his horses look something like a hay-carting team in the Luttrell Psalter— and examine its chalk-encrusted shapelessness, the clumsy nodules, not unlike the contortions of that root vegetable called artichoke. Few objects could look more unpromising. It is hard, it is unbeautiful—though sometimes there are caves of sparkling crystals within these flints, as any Downland child can tell you. Imagine yourself—if you can—in a world in which this lump of flint was your sole possession, all that stood between you and starvation, or a violent and unpleasant death. It is extraordinarily difficult to imagine this—there is something ridiculous about it : as the saying is, the mind "boggles" at it. Then you see, lying in the furrow, another lump of flint, very like the lump in your hand, except that it has been split open by the blow of a steel-shod hoof, or the crushing of a wagon-wheel. Inside the greyish chalk incrustations the flint is seen to be black, of a hard, almost glistening, surface, with a texture resembling glass—it will take a blue tinge from the bright sky above. One of the nodules of this flint is split at a different angle so that a sharp edge is left. Why, you think, it should be possible to cut with that edge—you try it on your hand, undoubtedly you could draw blood with it quite nicely. And there is that branch of wayfaring berries you have half pulled from the tree, but cannot quite manage to sever the tough resistant fibres, and you have no knife with you. What about this sharp flint edge? A little sawing, the branch yields, and the coveted berries are in your hand. You look at the flint knife with interest—yes, the flint knife!

You have made the discovery that was made ages ago by Neolithic Man—the New Stone Age Man—and dimly, behind him, by Paleolithic Man—the Old Stone Age Man. The discovery—beside which all our boasted modern inventions are flimsy as thistledown—of Flint as weapon and tool.

The flint, so valuable and indispensable to the progress and existence of Early Man, was formed at a much later time than the period when the chalk itself was made with incredible slowness in the bed of the sea. The bands of flint in the chalk came into existence after the chalk rose from the sea in which it was formed, both before and after the folding which took place in mid-Tertiary times. Some geologists hold that flints are still forming—an opinion in which the Sussex farm-labourer would heartily agree, for he is convinced that flints "grow." How otherwise explain the fact that when an arable field has been cleared of flints a fresh crop invariably appears?

Among other things to be found on Sussex soil are those fossilized sea-urchins known as "shepherd's crowns," which from the time of the Bronze Age till nowadays have been regarded as a symbol of good luck. Many a fine specimen can be seen carefully and superstitiously cherished on farmhouse and cottage mantelshelf.

Other fossil discoveries that have been made in Sussex at different times suggest a strange, remote world. There was a mollusc seven feet long, the whorls of whose shell if straightened out would have stretched to sixty feet—a curious "object of the seashore." Also some fossilized eggs of great size exist, which, it is thought, may have been the eggs of the Iguanodon.

The mention of that obsolete reptile will bring to the mind of any geologically inclined Sussex inhabitant the name of Dr Gideon Mantell, who discovered the fossilized remains of that early monster of the Weald, the Iguanodon. Dr Mantell, who was born at Lewes in 1790, was a physician and surgeon in his native town, who thought nothing of visiting forty or fifty patients a day, many of them suffering from such dreadful diseases as typhus and smallpox, and he did not hesitate to bleed a patient to the extent of forty ounces at a time. But in spite of his busy medical life he had a consuming passion for the geology of his native county—some of the natives believed that he ground up the fossils he found in the chalk to make his medicines—and his contributions to geological knowledge were outstanding. He was the first geologist to point out the fresh-water origin of the Wealden strata, and to him fell the thrill of discovering in the sandstone of Tilgate Forest the Dinosaur, that gigantic lizard who was about twenty-five feet in length, and with his equal height and extensive neck could comfortably crop the herbage of the trees on which he supported his apparently harmless existence. To Mantell it must have been the high spot of his life when he found those fossil bones telling to him their exciting tale. He had in the course of years made a magnificent collection of the fossils of the chalk, but it was this gift of the Iguanodon's bones from another stratum of Sussex which made his name universally known.

3

These bones, and others like them, of huge and uncouth creatures who once walked about Sussex, are the probable origin of all the dragon legends, of which Sussex has not a few. Remote folk-memory of stumbling upon fossilized imprints—for, of course, no man, not even Early Paleolithic Man, had ever actually encountered such creatures—would account for this.

Deep and "fathomless" pools were also a source of dragon legend. There is one at Lyminster, near Arundel, called the Knucker Hole (or Nuck Hole, there are variants in spelling) which never freezes in the most severe winters and was in early days reputed to be the haunt of a dragon, whose fiery breath would naturally keep any foes at bay. This dragon used to prey upon the unfortunate inhabitants of those regions, as well as upon their cattle, carrying the victims off to the swampy regions of the Arun to consume them. At last a champion arrived who destroyed him. In proof of the truth of this story the tomb of the dragon-slayer may be seen at Lyminster Church, and on the coffin slab is carved a representation of his sword lying across what may be regarded as the ribs of the monster.

In the beautiful Swanbourne Lake in Arundel Park there is a curious suggestion of a dragon lying asleep beneath the water, shimmering in hues of greenish blue—quite vivid enough to give rise to a dragon story, though I have never heard that it has done so. There is no mention of it in any guide-book and maybe only a few people have noticed it.

A famous Sussex dragon-slayer was St. Leonard, after whom St. Leonard's Forest—then the haunt of a very pernicious dragon—is named. The legend says that wherever the saint's blood was spilt in his encounters with the dragon a host of lilies-of-the-valley sprang up. These lilies continue to flourish in the Forest. In these regions is also a place called Dragon's Green.

The Lyminster dragon and that of St. Leonard are early monsters, but according to a seventeenth-century pamphlet another dragon or serpent had appeared in St. Leonard's Forest "in this present month of August, 1614." About this dragon the author quaintly says he "would send better news if he had it." He describes the forest as "a vast unfrequented place, full of unwholesome shades and hollows." He also describes the "serpent" in great detail, "shaped almost in the form of an axel-tree of a cart—a quantity of thickness in the middest, and somewhat smaller at both ends." The scales were "blackish along the back and red under his bellie." On either side, he says, are what appear to be incipient sprouting wings, "but God, I hope, will defend the poor people in the neighbourhood that he may be destroyed before he growe to fledge. He is of countenance very proud, and at

7

the sight or hearing of men or cattell, will raise his necke upright, and seem to listen and looke about with great arrogancy."

It must be left to the seventeenth-century reader to decide whether the author is displaying accurate observation or a vivid imagination—but the Loch Ness monster of our own days should check undue scoffing.

4

But Dr Gideon Mantell would have been shocked at such inaccurate and wild imaginings. His Iguanodon was a definite and actual reptile, whose bones may be handled and measured and inspected. From these bones the creature has been reconstructed. His tail was long and thick, a kind of rudder, and so was his neck; he walked upright upon his powerful hind legs; his forelegs being short and used like arms. A very good idea of a dragon, this Dinosaur, only lacking the wings to give him the proper heraldic appearance. But in reality he was a harmless reptile, in spite of his earth-shaking tread, for he lived principally upon leaves. In the Mesozoic times in which the Iguanodon flourished, a portion of the Weald was an extensive fresh-water lake, and these huge reptilian creatures spent part of their time in the water and part on the higher land. Crushed under their heavy feet were the winkles which were to form the Sussex marble, or "winklestone," and in sandstone, then soft, there is here and there the impress of the Dinosaur's footmark.

There was little to suggest the Sussex we know in this strange, subtropical world in which the Iguanodon and his kind paddled through existence—however long his days may have been, doomed to extinction when the mammals came along, owing to his slow and clumsy body and his minute brain. But the one who lay down to die ages ago in Tilgate Forest was to rise again to fame when his remains were found by Dr Mantell.

Besides discovering and naming this reptile of the ancient world, Mantell wrote several valuable books on Sussex geology, including *The Fossils of the South Downs, The*

Geology of the South-East of England and *The Geological Structure of the South-East Part of Sussex.*

The house at the foot of the Castle Keep at Lewes where he lived for so many years still exists, though for a time he removed to Brighton, and his geological collections—which were eventually purchased by the British Museum for £4,000—were also to be seen there. A certain gentleman who described himself as Horace Smith, Esq, was moved by the sight of this geological museum to poetry, and addressed Gideon Mantell as

> Columbus of the subterranean world!
> Star of Geology! Whose rays enlighten
> What Nature to her darkest depths had hurl'd—
> Mantell! We proudly welcome thee to Brighton.

There are fourteen more stanzas, but none quite equal to the opening one.

5

A comparatively recent geologic past is quite far enough to go in order to obtain a reasonably comprehensive picture of the Sussex scene. The long line of the Downs which makes the seaward rampart of Sussex from the borders of Hampshire to Beachy Head is the most definitely Sussex thing of all, the natural feature that marks out Sussex from her "nine and thirty sisters fair." Other counties have chalk downs—but they are not like the Sussex Downs. Even the Sussex Downs have definitely different characteristics in the western and eastern halves of the county. "Each to his choice," but an East Sussex man or woman will always feel a greater nobility and simplicity about the almost treeless Downs which range from Truleigh Down and Wolstonbury and Ditchling Beacon toward the sun-rising, past that noble spreading group of Firle—whose thrusting profile is so notable from many aspects—and Caburn, wherein is cupped the jewel of Lewes; on towards that mysterious Long Man of Wilmington, swelling and sinking to the heights of Beachy Head, and then falling away to the flats and levels, the odd little hills,

9

like a child's toys, whereon are set Winchelsea and Rye. Then comes Pevensey Level, and that Romney Marsh which is as much Sussex as it is Kent—though a Kentish man would no doubt deny this—and perhaps is neither, for, as the saying has it, "There's Europe, Ashy, Africa, America—and Romney Marsh."

The aspects of the Downs are amazingly varied, according to the position from which they are viewed, or passed at a motoring speed. It is as though they themselves were moving in a ritual manner, from a procession to magnificent groups in which Downs remote and strange peer over the nearer shoulders. It is necessary to know your Downs well to recognize them from all angles—the similarity of rounded and moulded form does not preclude an astonishing variety of aspect. The direction of each Sussex road, whether going straight from the north southwards, or going from east to west, or diagonally, will give an amazingly different picture. For intimate and enchanting beauty the ancient road or lane that runs from east to west close under the very spring of the Downs from the Weald, is unsurpassable, but it gives no vista save sideways, no glimpse of the Downs crowding and shouldering together like mysterious creatures of the Dawn.

However one may feel about the more elemental and austere quality of the eastern Downs, yet the westward-sailing hills are possessed of a soul-satisfying beauty. Chanctonbury Ring is known wherever the name of Sussex is known. The moulded perfect shape, the forward thrust which makes it a kind of castle, the crown of beeches, give Chanctonbury a special eminence in the great sweep of the Downs. It holds the imagination and the memory as though it brought all that downland beauty together in its bosom. From so far to the east as Firle Beacon beyond Lewes, a glimpse can be caught of Chanctonbury. And from Chanctonbury itself the views are marvellous—once its summit is attained. So steep and sudden is the slope that standing on the crest one can see but a portion of the downward sweeping curve. To climb straight up the slippery turf is an arduous proceeding. I have recollections of doing so as a child, with other children, and between the slipperiness, the steepness, and the howling wind which seemed as though it would pluck us by the hair and hurl us from our foothold, we were reduced to crawling up on hands and knees, to our own great satisfaction and amusement.

But once the crest of Chanctonbury is reached it is a great view that lies around. To the northwards can be seen Box Hill and Leith Hill and the Hog's Back—a mere backcloth, as it were, of Surrey for the Sussex scene. Close below is the village of Washington, and beyond is Arundel Castle and the slender spire of Chichester Cathedral. On the eastward Downs the Devil's Dyke hill stands out and marches on to Wolstonbury, which swings outwards as though to look at beech-crowned Chanctonbury, and below Wolstonbury is the old village of Poynings with its fine cruciform church. The ancient and enchanting little town of Steyning lies in full view of Chanctonbury Ring, and beyond that the fanged ruin of Bramber Castle, with attached village, wet in winter, dusty in summer, but still of considerable charm. To the south of the Ring is Cissbury, and beyond that on the southward horizon lies the sea. It is a great Sussex view, but the view from Chanctonbury must always miss one essential Sussex beauty, and that is the prospect of Chanctonbury itself.

Each Sussex man or woman has one particular place or aspect in the county that above all others means Sussex. For me, in spite of a personal preference for the Eastern Downs, it is Chanctonbury, but Chanctonbury from far away. It was that blue view of Chanctonbury which gave me in childhood my first conscious feeling of the beauty of the visible world and the mystery of the invisible. Standing in the rough matted grass of a neglected field, looking westward, with the great line of the Downs sweeping towards a sunset sky where the headland of Chanctonbury floated like something of another world, beauty took hold of me, consciously and inescapably —the curious ache of it, and the troubling for the first time laid on the young resilient heart.

Years later an old Sussex countrywoman, looking on nearly the same scene with time-worn eyes, said to me : "It doos something to you."

It does.

The Downs are a rampart—beyond them the sea, behind them the Weald, the Hollow Land. In the remote geologic ages the whole outline and shape of this Sussex was different. The chalk Downs stretched, like an inverted bowl, across the whole county, from the South Downs to the North Downs. The Downs that we see now are but the rim, as it were, of that bowl, worn down by rain and wind and weather of all kinds, by the action of frost, the denudation of rivers—and by glaciers too, as some geologists hold—to the semblance we now know.

Few English counties can claim a more interesting and varied geologic history than Sussex—and Sussex may also claim as remarkable a record in pre-history as in recorded history.

We are apt to think, owing to the inadequacy and limited outlook of the majority of the history books on which we were brought up, that the history of a country—and the history of a county is but the same thing on a smaller scale—is caused and created by the men who inhabited it, by its kings and heroes. That is a most lopsided idea, as a certain number of people are beginning to perceive. Geology, except to its devoted students, has a somewhat dull and difficult air, with a memory of the lifeless aspect of "specimens" in glass cases, all neatly labelled and conveying little to the uninstructed eye. But geology is really the foundation of everything—"Dust we are, and unto dust we return." Out of that dust, out of the Chalk and the Greensand and the Gault Clay was Sussex formed. Because of these geological formations Sussex scenery—so varied and so different in different parts of the county—was created by time and weather, and upheavals of the earth's crust, and sinkings under the sea. There the men who were to be Sussex men, little as they knew it in their dim and dawning days, discovered that they could live a precarious existence in certain parts of Sussex and not in others : that water was to be found in certain places and not in others; that the springs "broke" at certain times—though they knew nothing of a "watertable"—that dry stream-beds became "winterbournes."

Early Man had three primary necessities—water, food, and a moderate safety (he could never know security) from his enemies, whether human or animal. Certain places in what was to be the county of Sussex gave him these needs. There he settled, and there he dug his earthworks—his incredibly large earthworks—and where he dug them in the chalk not Time itself wipes out his handiwork. Seeing those earthworks, such as the great circumvallum of Cissbury—that and the Devil's Dyke being the largest in the county—and listening to the learned elucidations of the archæologists, I confess at times to a sense of incredulity. The thing itself and the explanation hardly seem to fit—the vastness of the work and the inadequacy of the tools, the flint implement and the deer-pick. But this, of course, is heresy. One cannot fail to be impressed by the infinite patience and skill and integrity of the modern field archæologist, whose work is based on what the spade digs up, and who sifts and ponders with such a carefulness of actual investigation. Yet even on concrete evidence there is room for a difference of interpretation as to the *meaning* of the evidence.

Man, whether Paleolithic or later, always brings trouble when he enters upon the scene. There is a certain peacefulness in considering for a while a Sussex where he had not begun his activities.

7

It is no use going so far back in geological time as to the period when there was no Sussex at all. What we want to think of and imagine if we can is a Sussex that had arisen from the sea, and was, in that part of it exposed to the sky, largely composed of a substance formed under the sea—chalk.

This chalk stretched in a great curve from what we now call the South Downs to the North Downs. The Wealden clays and greensands, and what was ages later to be the great Wealden forest, were hidden beneath this dome of chalk—some geologists believe it may have been 5,000 feet high. We should have had considerable difficulty in recognizing our Sussex then. Between Chanctonbury Ring in the west and

13

Mount Harry in the east, a great depth of chalk, what is called the Senonian, the chalk-with-flints, has been eroded away, and instead of the original mountainous curve, we have all the gracious shapes and forms now known to us.

It gives a faint idea of the immensity of time that has been needed to denude and wear away this chalk mass if we recall the puny heights—in spite of the majestic effects—of certain points on the Downs which are now the most elevated. The greatest height is reached by Littleton Down in the very west, which is 837 feet. Ditchling Beacon, in the middle part of the county, is 813 feet. Chanctonbury is 783 feet, and Beachy Head round about 500 feet. Yet in spite of these very moderate elevations Gilbert White was right when he spoke of "this majestic chain of mountains." More majestic, in all probability, than the originally much greater heights of the undenuded chalk when it stretched right across what is now Sussex, for that would have looked—had there been any eye to behold it—like an elevated plain.

We do not, if we are Sussex people living in daily sight of the Downs, think of chalk as a stone. Its crumbling and malleable nature, its lack of cragginess, its flowing form, seem to deny it that harsh appellation. But geologists call it a stone, a limestone, though admitting that it is a peculiar one. In fact, among all the sedimentary rocks there is nothing quite like chalk. The reason for this is because it is largely formed from the shells of minute creatures called *foraminifera*, which lived and died at the bottom of the sea for uncounted ages, till those living particles, like white dust, had formed the hundreds of feet of chalk which we now know as Ditchling Beacon or Duncton Down. That Milky Way of *foraminifera* is quite as astounding to the mind of man as the one in the midnight sky. The Downs are so completely covered in turf that the casual eye does not always realize their structure— in past times the chalk pits, which are still there but grassed over, made this more visible. But anyone who wishes to realize chalk in the mass and depth should go to the Chalk Pit Inn on the road running under the Downs into Lewes. Behind that small roadside inn is a vast excavated chalk pit, with sheer walls that tower to the sky in an astonishing manner. That chalk pit is the work of man; but across the road, as it draws near to Lewes, the chalk drops again almost as sheerly, down to the water-levels and the Ouse Valley. That steep drop, it is surprising to realize, is the work of that small and sluggish river.

In winter and wet springs the waters of the Ouse spread over these levels and give a curious magic to the setting of Lewes. We see the little hill city as it must have looked in earlier, undrained days, and we realize the times when Mount Caburn was practically an island between the Ouse and the Glynde Reach.

None of the Sussex rivers in this day have a wild and torrential character—they crawl gently along through peaceful stretches of meadowland, past willows and rushes and cows pasturing on their banks, with the fool's-cap shingled spire of some little Sussex church rising now and again from a hump of slightly higher ground where a hamlet clusters, keeping its feet out of the winter floods. Anyone looking down from High-and-Over on the wide valley of the Cuckmere can hardly believe that valley was carved through the chalk barriers by that gentle thread of river.

To realize how it was done, and done not only by the Cuckmere in the east of Sussex, but by the Arun in the west, and the Adur and the Ouse in the middle, it is needful to go back to the time when the chalk extended across Sussex, curving north and south, and thus forming two watersheds down which the rivers rushed, southwards direct to the sea, northwards more circuitously to the sea by means of the Thames estuary. The force of the rivers of these steeper slopes would obviously be much greater, and the greater the force and spread of water the greater the denuding power—especially when to the power of water was added the grinding force of those Tertiary beds, which originally lay on the top of the chalk. Those scattered stones called sarsens found stranded or partially buried on the Downs are remains of the Tertiaries.

The name "sarsen," by which these stones are almost universally called in Sussex, is something of a mystery. I have heard it suggested that the word comes from "saracen," which was used (perhaps from the time of the Crusades) to denote a stranger. Certainly these partly crystallized blocks of sandstone are "strangers" to the chalk.

There is also discovered in parts of Sussex what is known as Sussex marble. It is found in the Wealden clay in the beds of shelly limestone. It is composed of the shells of a fresh-water periwinkle—the Sussex people often call it winkle-stone. It will take a fine polish, is grey in colour, and decorative, as the winkle-shells, all crammed close together, are cut across at all the angles in which they lie, and so show a great variety of shape and form. The petrified periwinkles are set in a kind of cement of crystallized limestone.

8

Chalk is very porous. It soaks up water, and the water sinks down and down till it comes to some non-porous stratum like clay, and it is where this junction occurs that the springs gush out, as they do at Clayton and at the little Downland village of Fulking, where that marvellous water comes rushing in an endless, life-giving, radiant flow. It is because of these springs that there is that long string of little villages at the northward foot of the Downs—not man's first habitation in Sussex, but very early.

The porousness of chalk partly accounts for those water-less high valleys—combes they are called—with which the Downs are moulded and shaped. Once long ago, when the water-table was higher and the climate wetter, there were streams in these combes; in fact, the combes were made by the streams. But the streams were not strong enough to cut their way through to the sea, as the surviving Sussex rivers did; they sank and died, the thirsty chalk swallowed them up. They disappeared as rivers and emerged again from below as springs, and sometimes as winterbournes—rivers which only run when the hills are saturated with water, which is naturally not in summer.

Through long periods of geological time, through sinkings and upheavals, through water and ice and storms, Sussex, in something the shape we know it, came into being.

Roughly speaking Sussex is a succession of strips running

16

from east to west. First against the sea is the rich alluvial land, early cultivated, which lies to the southward of the Downs, wider in the western end of the county and fading away towards Brighton and on to Beachy Head, where the chalk cliffs step down to the seashore. Behind this lies the long sweep of the Downs themselves, falling in gentle, though often steep, curves to the level clays of the Weald. That word means wood, and in early times and indeed up to the period of Elizabeth and the Sussex iron-forges, the Weald was largely covered by dense forests—the Andredsweald. Clay is the mother of oak trees, long-lived and enduring. Sussex oak has ever been famous for its quality.

The Wealden clay and the Wealden forests together made a tolerably impenetrable barrier to the north. Beyond the Weald comes what is known as the Forest Ridge, a lighter and more barren land, home of gorse—great golden sheets of it—and heather and pine trees : the least authentically Sussex of all the strips.

Then just to stop any "foreigner" getting into Sussex at either end, at the east and at the west, to keep out the Kentish men and those from Hampshire, there was a vast area of marsh—still the most difficult of obstacles to movement when it is undrained.

So it is small wonder that Sussex remained a "secret kingdom"; that people who were inside Sussex could not get out—and very few of them wanted to—and that people who were outside could not get in. The only way to enter the county in the early days was by sea. It was by sea the invaders came, the Angles and the Saxons and the Danes, Cæsar and Norman William and after him those French pirates who used to come by night and set the tocsin ringing in Watchbell Street at Rye. But if Rye flamed to the midnight sky, the men of Rye built the town up again and took their vengeance on the Frenchmen. It is the motto of a Sussex man that he "wun't be druv."

Chanctonbury Ring

9

These various geologic strips that run across Sussex from sunrise to sunsetting, and which lie roughly parallel, though with certain turns and breaks in direction, are also divided in another way. They are cut across from north to south by four principal rivers, as though severed by a knife of water. These four rivers are the Arun, the Adur, the Ouse and the Cuckmere, all of which have cut themselves a way through the chalk Downs to the sea. The sea is the natural and inevitable outlet of these rivers—and as a consequence these rivers are the natural and inevitable ingress to invaders, who always, when they cast eyes on England, must come by sea. So it was obvious to those who at different times held and guarded Sussex that they must put a lock and key on each of these four rivers to keep the invaders out. This they did by building castles at points which commanded those waterways. So the lock and key on the Arun is Arundel Castle— very plain and clear to see at this present day, looking directly down from its height to the river and the first bridge across it. The Adur and its first bridge is now guarded by nothing but a jagged fang of Bramber Castle, of broken and clotted flint, tangled with ivy and briar, but its strategic position is still formidable. The shell of the keep and the two great gateways of Lewes Castle still look down on the Ouse and the bridge which is the first to cross it. The Cuckmere, being unnavigable, has not needed the same protection. But in the further east is Pevensey Castle, the most imposing of all the fortresses, though not set upon a height like the others, because the heights have gone, the Downs are ended at Beachy Head, and we are now in that strange and shifting Sussex country which has within historic time been changed by the sea, where harbours have silted up and land that once held human habitations now lies beneath the waves.

There is a curious uncertainty of feeling about the eastern end of Sussex, as though that low line of sea crawling towards the low shore, withdrawing and crawling in again—whispered in the lisp of its waves of change—change still to come. There is none of the serenity and security given by the chalk hills. Once they were under the sea, but now they look very competent to keep the sea out from drowning the villages and farmsteads of the Weald. The devil, so they say in Sussex, once tried his hand at it when he cut that remarkable cleft in the Downs called the Devil's Dyke, to let the sea through to drown all the Wealden churches, the sight of which and the multitude of which annoyed him. But the cunning of an old Sussex countrywoman and of a Sussex cockerel was sufficient to defeat his plan—he mistook a candle behind a sieve for the rising sun and fled, leaving his Dyke unfinished.

It is an odd thing how very gullible is the devil in all the legends—a child could get the better of him.

10

But what the devil failed to do, the Sussex rivers have achieved—they have cut through the chalk hills to the sea. They have made a way for themselves from the county where they rose—our Sussex rivers are not of that impressive variety of waterway that wanders through many counties and gathers tribute from many hills and valleys—to the sea which is their bourne. But in so doing they inevitably opened a way to the invader, and broke down that rampart of Downland which would have been so formidable an obstacle. Also they offered almost the only means of transport in a county which right up to the end of the eighteenth century was notorious for the badness or the non-existence of its roads.

It is an accepted Sussex story that an eighteenth-century traveller, on one of the tracks of adhesive clay then known as roads, saw in his way a hat; surprised at the sight he picked it out of the mud to find beneath it a man—and beneath the man a horse. In the same century a distinguished visitor from London found himself by mischance in Sussex, and was horrified to observe the lady of the manor in her coach slowly proceeding to church, drawn with immense labour by a team of eight plough-oxen. Ploughland or so-called road, there was not much to choose between them.

Even so the genuine Sussex spirit objected to any improvement. When it was at last proposed to make a proper turnpike road through the parish of Mayfield, the cost of it to be paid by turnpike dues, all the important inhabitants rose up in protest. "One farmer," said a clerical historian of the parish, "called it an idea not only ruinously extravagant, but also absurd, 'for how,' he asks of the meeting, 'can a wagon stand upright if it has no ruts to go in?'"

It used to be said that Sussex women were as long-legged as storks from the exercise they got in pulling their legs out of the heavy clay.

It is therefore obvious that rivers, where navigable, offered a much easier mode of progress than roads. So the Sussex rivers, though not impressive or comparable to many of the other rivers of England, have had an important share in her history.

Anyone looking at the convolutions of the rivers on a map of Sussex must be struck with the way which they restrict themselves to the confines of the county. The depth of Sussex, from the north to the south, is not very extensive, but the Sussex rivers, with commendable local patriotism, a strong sense of the *genius loci*, however near to alien borders they may rise, are plainly determined to remain on Sussex territory. The course of the eastern Rother (there are two Rothers in Sussex) is particularly noticeable. It rises at Rotherfield—that great Sussex antiquary and historian, Mark Antony Lower, records the curious and interesting fact that "the River Rother rises in the cellar of the mansion called Rother House in the parish of Rotherfield"—and swings due eastward through Etchingham straight to the borders of Kent, but there makes a sharp turn and with an angle like an elbow flows down to Rye and enters the sea below Winchelsea. A river most obviously determined to remain in Sussex. The Ouse and the Adur are faithful to the same ambition, and the Arun twists and turns like a snake to contain her waters in the narrow stretch, but half the depth of Sussex, between her junction with the western Rother and her meeting with the sea at Littlehampton. Only one famous river rises in Sussex and then deserts the county, and that is the Medway.

Sussex rivers are not noted for striking beauties—no gorges, rocks or waterfalls adorn them, and the waters of East Sussex are inclined to be muddy. There is a certain modesty in their scenic claims. But the Arun offers enchanting pictures to memory, running under overhanging beech-woods, or clear in the sunshine, or—perhaps most magical of all—as seen from the high bluff of Burpham, meandering along amid a thick embroidery of reeds and rushes and willow herb, with the romantic towers of Arundel Castle beyond. This is the Old River Arun, and owes its lazy afternoon charm to the fact that the main stream has been diverted to a more direct course.

Such a river scene is as different as possible from the Ouse at Piddinghoe, with the broad slow stream washing the muddy banks, some barge-like vessel lying at anchor, the whole plain, peaceful look of the country thereabouts. Above this rises the little eminence on which is set the enchanting round-towered church of Piddinghoe, of whose "begilded dolphin" Kipling speaks—only the weather-vane is not a dolphin, but a salmon-trout; it must be admitted that Kipling's version sounds much more poetical. Southover near by has the same round thirteenth-century tower and the same weather-vane. The Ouse was a salmon river once.

The western Arun and the eastern Ouse, in the differing quality of their aspect and character, typify the richness of West Sussex and the austerity of East Sussex.

11

In the matter of bridges the Sussex rivers are fortunate—they have many noble bridges. It seems as though men displayed some of their best qualities when they built bridges—perhaps because in the old religious days it was regarded as one of the major works of piety to build a bridge, coming only second to the building of a church. Indeed, the two were often combined, for an important bridge frequently had a little chapel in its structure, so that the returned or departing traveller might offer prayers for the perils of the journey behind or before him.

Stopham Bridge over the Arun is one of the most notable in Sussex, and in its massiveness and its solidity, the rightness of its proportions, gives that sense of the inevitable which belongs to noble building. It marks an important point in the progress of that river which in its pleasant windings cannot be considered more than a stream till it reaches Alfoldean Bridge. The great bridge at Stopham marks the furthest limit to which the tide reaches, and it is just below Stopham that the western Rother joins the Arun and together they flow past Pulborough, an interesting wandering place, long of importance in the history of the county, as the Roman Stane Street crosses the Arun there. The bridge at Stopham has seven arches, with magnificently massive cutwaters, and the parapet is indented with little recesses in which one may stand in safety from the traffic and look down at the continual fascination of moving water. Rooted in the ancient stones of the bridge there grows a sturdy little yew tree, flourishing in air and on air, as it would seem. In early times there was a wooden bridge, and the then parson of Pulborough was the moving spirit in the erection of this great stone bridge. This was about 1423. Near that date was also the building of another noble Sussex bridge, that of Trotton, which spans the western Rother. The five ribbed arches are of beautiful proportions, and originally the parapet had recesses over the buttresses—the original builders knew that men should have time to "stand and stare." But modern hurry and the dangers of the highway have removed these retiring-places. Nevertheless, that hero of Agincourt, Thomas, Lord Camoys, who built this bridge, and who is buried in an altar tomb in the adjoining church, can still recognize and be proud of his bridge if he ever crosses it in the glimpses of the moon.

The river names of Sussex are old—most river names are, for rivers are things that primitive man can neither ignore nor do without. But old as the names are, each river had an older one, now forgotten save by a few archæologists and peerers into the past. The Arun was once the Tarrant—a name recalled by a street in Arundel. To the westward the river which parts Sussex from Hampshire at its coastal end, now called the Ems, was the Westbourne. Going eastward across Sussex the Adur was the Sore; the Ouse the Mid-Wynd; the Cuckmere the Wandelmestrow—a delightful river name; while the eastern Rother was called the Lymney. The old name of the western Rother was the Scire, which means bright, or clear. The western rivers in Sussex are more sparkling than the eastern ones.

12

Before a river can run to adorn and fertilize the face of the country, there must be a spring, a source, some means by which the underground waters, fed from the rainfall, can reach the surface again. Sussex, owing to its geological structure, is a somewhat peculiar county in this respect—lavish with water in some places, niggard in the extreme in others. The reason that large stretches of the Weald were so long uninhabited was not only due to the forests—and forests in the old use of the word do not always mean dense woodlands —but to the absence of water. Clay is not kind in that respect.

The long string of old villages at the northern foot of the Downs—so close tucked under that winter sunset comes early to them—owe their existence to the fact that there the watersprings break out in generous abundance at the junction of the chalk and the upper greensand. The chalk is a great sponge to absorb the rainfall. When it reaches the greensand it is held, and bursts out in springs where the two strata meet, as they do at the base of the Downland. Hence these old villages, to drink of the life-giving water, built in the times when man settled by his water, instead of bringing the water to where he was settled. The useful and in these days necessary pipe can never give the pure and vital feeling of water as does that lavish spring which breaks rejoicing from the hill at Fulking and pours its limpid stream without pause for the refreshment of the generations of men.

Alice Meynell, in an essay on "Wells," emphasizes what we miss of the beauty of natural water :

"A very dull secret is made of water, for example, and the plumber sets his seal upon the floods whereby we live.

23

They are covered, they are carried, they are hushed, from the spring to the tap. . . . The springs, then, the profound wells, the streams, are of all the means of our lives those which we should wish to see open to the sun, with their waters on their progress and their way to us; but, no, they are lapped in lead."

The names scattered on the Sussex map, and the water-mills—it should be remembered that the water-mill is much older than the windmill, Domesday Book is full of water-mills, but has no windmills—show where water was abundant. Names which no longer bear to modern ears any watery suggestion had originally that meaning, as Wish Field, which means a wet field, or the Gote (often modernized to Goat), which means a watercourse. Many farms are named by water, as Tulley's Wells Farm—Tulley's being itself a corruption of St. Olave's—near Lewes, while the Wales Farm, where is the East Sussex Agricultural College, may easily be a corruption of Wells Farm. The name of Arundel most probably is a partly water name and is Celtic —Aran, a high place, and Dôl, a water-meadow. No other syllables could better describe the situation and appearance of that romantic town.

Water is the first need of man. In his early stages of life on the chalk Downs he had a greater abundance of water from the sky than he has nowadays. Examination of Iron Age wells has shown that the bottom of them was a long way above the level of the present water-table.

Into the vexed question of Neolithic and later dewponds it is not proposed to enter—it is a specialist discussion, and the specialists do not agree. It is enough for the ordinary lover of the Downland, without much learning as to their age or methods of construction, to enjoy the attractions of that shallow, saucer-shaped depression, reflecting the mood of the sky in its water—the only water to be seen on the summit of the swelling chalk hills, where our early Sussex ancestors lived their bare lives and buried their dead in those barrows whose simple outlines have outlasted the "gnawing tooth of Time," and are eloquent of a past piety and a past race— those prehistoric peoples who looked upon scenes that we still look on almost unchanged when we walk among the slopes of the deep Downs. Whatever changes and chances may come, the Downs will always be essential Sussex, and always be haunted by the people who so long ago lived there, as John Masefield has written :

> Something passes me and cries as it passes
> On the chalk Downland bare.

Chapter II

EARLY MAN IN SUSSEX

1

HE was a very early man indeed, and part of his skull was found at a retired little place called Piltdown. People who have never set foot in Sussex, people in other continents, have heard of Piltdown because of that bit of skull.*

The finding of the oldest known human skull depended on Mr Charles Dawson—who was a keen geologist and a Fellow of the Geological Society, as well as of the Society of Antiquaries—taking a walk in the neighbourhood of Piltdown one day in the early part of this century. Piltdown is near Fletching and about seven miles north of Lewes. In the course of this momentous walk he saw some labourers digging for gravel, and the eye of a geologist being always attracted by any fracture of the earth's surface, he stopped to look. He asked the men if they had found anything interesting in the way of fossils or bones, and told them if they should discover anything to keep it for him. He was later handed a small piece of remarkably thick skull-bone and then discovered—with what horror may be imagined—that the men had found what they thought was a cocoanut, and like ignorant children had deliberately smashed it up. One can imagine the scene : the labourers stopping for a pull at their bottles of cold tea, kicking the gravel-stained "cocoanut" about, and one of them playfully bringing down a heavy pick to smash the skull of that very early Sussex ancestor of theirs.

When Mr Dawson began to guess what the fragment of bone might be, he immediately set up a careful search and in course of time, aided by Sir Arthur Smith-Woodward, discovered other pieces of the skull. Part of the right half of the lower jaw was found, part of the ridge of the left eyebrow, part of the back of the skull, and a few other fragments :

* Publisher's Note – The author died before the Piltdown skull had been shown to be a fake. Ironically she unconsciously told the truth when she described it as "the mixture of the skull of a man and a monkey".

26

enough to enable a conjectural model to be made of the bony structure of the head of this Eoanthropus, Dawn Man, as Sir Arthur Smith-Woodward christened him, who lived in so remote a time as a geological period, the Early Pleistocene. A model of this head of Piltdown Man (or woman, as some authorities consider) may be seen in the museum of the Sussex Archæological Society at Barbican House in Lewes. It is not surprising that it is not a very attractive countenance —though there is something rather curiously pathetic about it—for it is the mixture of the skull of a man and a monkey. The jaw is chinless and simian, the teeth are not quite human, but the eye-sockets and forehead have the look of humanity, though the brain capacity is very small, and the brain case very thick. But it is thought, from careful tests of the moulding and shape of the skull, that this inhabitant of Sussex had the power of speech and the ability to remember names.

With the skull were also found bones of the now extinct creatures who wandered about that Paleolithic world which is so difficult for us to realize in this gracious Sussex where we now live. Some idea of the length of time that stretches between us is given by the geological fact that the River Ouse is now eighty feet below what was once its gravel bed where the bones were found.

There is a little story which always comes to my mind when I walk past the charming old house within the Barbican Gateway at Lewes where Charles Dawson was living at the time of the discovery of the Piltdown skull. Apparently he did not at first fully realize the significance of the first fragment of bone. He washed it free of the gravel deposit and put it out in the sun to dry on the thick yew-hedge surrounding his garden—so there was the precious bone at the mercy of wind or dog or any idle boy. However, it survived the risk, and with the later recovered portions of the skull was eventually delivered to the hands of the Trustees of the British Museum, and so—suitably, even if regrettably— removed from its native Sussex soil.

A few years ago a memorial was erected to the finder of the Piltdown skull on the spot where he made his discovery. On the monolith are inscribed the words :

"Here, in the old river gravel, Mr Charles Dawson,

F.S.A., found the fossil skull of Pilt Down Man, 1912–13. The discovery was described by Mr Charles Dawson and Sir Arthur Smith-Woodward in the quarterly journal of the Geological Society, 1913–1915."

2

Having made the acquaintance of the Dawn Man, we can now move on to survey something of the life of his descendants of the Old Stone Age and the New Stone Age who lived in Sussex, and of the very surprising things they did with their only tool, the flint.

There is not space or need here to attempt even an outline history of the flint in the hands of early man—it is a specialized and detailed subject. It is sufficient to say that the importance of flint can hardly be exaggerated, and it is by means of flint—so satisfactorily indestructible—that archæologists have learned much of what they know of the life of Early Man. It is by what is called the patination of flints that the comparative age of specimens is told, according to the circumstances of their finding. If one wanders over a ploughed chalky field, picking up a handful of different flints, most of them will be whitish, but some will show a greyish or blue stain through the white, and a newly broken flint will be a slightly iridescent black, encased in a skin, as it were, of the chalky white. A thickly patinated flint, one that looks as if it might be a lump of hard chalk, is older, has been longer exposed to the conditions that produce patination, than one that is only filmed over the black core.

Now one of the things that Neolithic man—Paleolithic man, as was inevitable, has left fewer traces of his existence in Sussex—found out for himself was that the flints he picked up lying about on the surface of the ground, which would be those with which he first began, did not flake so well, because they were tougher, as those he dug out below the surface. And so, in course of time, he came to develop regular flint-mines, with shafts sunk and galleries branching off, to work the seams of flint. Sussex has many of these mines.

Dr E. Cecil Curwen—to whom, and to his father, Dr Elliott Curwen, Sussex archæology owes an immense debt—

describes in his valuable book, *Prehistoric Sussex*, the personal experience of entering one of those flint mines when it was being explored and opened, of treading where the last foot had been that of a Neolithic miner :

"Slowly and with awe one of the excavators creeps into the gallery, candle in hand, noticing everything and careful to disturb nothing. He is acutely conscious that he is the first human being to enter this underground workshop for some four thousand years. Suddenly he catches sight of a row of holes, clearly punched in the chalk wall, with a second row below and nearly parallel with it, while on the floor close by is a pick made from the antler of a red deer. By means of these two rows of holes a miner had been about to split out the intervening block of chalk when for some reason he dropped his pick and left. And there the holes look as if they had only been made yesterday, fresh and clean-cut, with the chalk burred a little at the lip by the pressure of the pick. . . . Here and there on the walls or roof a black mark is seen. This is actually the soot from the old miners' lamps, still there, and looking perfectly fresh after the lapse of four thousand years."

Some of the lamps used by these prehistoric flint miners have also been discovered—they are rough kind of cups hollowed out of lumps of chalk, in which some sort of wick floated in grease. It is a solemn thought how long the things that man has made with his hands remain, defying the disintegration of time, while he himself vanishes, leaving but a shadow behind.

The principal flint mines in Sussex are Cissbury, the most famous of all; Blackpatch Hill, Harrow Hill, Stoke Down, Bow Hill, Tolmere Pond, Lavant Caves, and Windover Hill. All these mines, except the last, circle round about Worthing, Findon and Chichester, in the western half of Sussex. Windover Hill is in the Eastbourne direction, the hill on which the mysterious Long Man of Wilmington, carved in the chalk, "looks naked towards the shires."

Cissbury Ring is a glorious place. On a memorable summer day some years ago it was visited by a gathering of the members of the Sussex Archæological Society. It was a brilliant morning of May, and the great grass-grown circle of some sixty acres—it is a walk of a mile and a half round the vallum—which is still in places nearly forty feet above the fosse—was partly covered with golden gorse and surprising patches of violets growing abundantly in that unshaded place. From the ground it is not easy to see the depressions that indicate the filled-in shafts of the flint mines—filled in by the Neolithic miners themselves as they opened fresh shafts —but in photographs taken from the air they are easily visible.

Cissbury is encircled by a great earthwork, ditch and rampart, which is of a later date than the flint mines. Grass-grown, it makes a noble promenade, in which half Sussex seems to swing round the walker. From different parts of the rampart it is possible on a clear day to see the Seven Sisters beyond the mouth of the Cuckmere with their feet in the waters of the Channel. These Seven Sisters have each got a name, and beginning from the Birling Gap end the names are Went Hill Brow—from this runs an ancient trackway— Baily's Hill, Flagstaff Point, Bran Point, Rough Brow, Short Brow, Haven Brow. To the westward from Cissbury the Isle of Wight can be seen, and nearer to view the dark hump of Chanctonbury's crown of beeches, and Truleigh Hill, and Wolstonbury which looks down on Hurstpierpoint. How strange to remember that these ancient miners, when they came up from their chalk shafts, would look upon the very same views as we behold, practically unchanged, except that Chanctonbury would be bare of its cap of beech trees. The Downs, by reason of their height, their lack of water, are great resisters of change, and—most happily—the despair of the speculative builder.

Having dug up his flints the Neolithic miner then proceeded to knap them into the shapes of his need, whether as implements or weapons. Cissbury was a great workshop of this kind, and is littered with flint chippings, flakes and cores. Flint knapping was brought to a very high state of craftsmanship, and flint implements continued to be made and used long after what is called the Bronze Age had begun. In the early Bronze and Iron Ages it was only the wealthy and important who had weapons of metal—just as nowadays there are still many country places which have only lamps

and candles, though for long electricity has been the common
necessity of towns.

It would take a modern man a long time to make a perfect
flint implement—the delicate precision of the blows on a leaf-
like arrow-head, even of the late Paleolithic period, has to
be seen to be appreciated. In all flint knapping it is not
strength, but judgment and balance that counts. Anyone who
has watched the flint-knappers of Brandon in Suffolk at work
will realize this, though theirs is but coarse and everyday
work compared to the achievements of their Paleolithic and
Neolithic ancestors.

Flint, in the history of Early Man, is vital, for it and the
wood which has perished were the only tools of the Old
Stone Age people, though their civilization had advanced
considerably towards the close of their period. But in Paleolithic times England was not an island, and the Paleolithic
people were hunters and wanderers—in Sussex to-day (if one
can speak of Sussex in those remote ages), in Brittany or
Belgium to-morrow. The Paleolithic slowly merged into the
Neolithic—there were no sharp-edged divisions of periods—
but there are two clear-cut things which mark out the two
cultures from each other. The Old Stone Age people belonged
to the continent of Europe, and were hunters, not husbandmen; the New Stone Age people were increasingly pastoral
and agricultural—and it was in their period that England
became an island.

So, after Piltdown man, who, without doubt, resided in
Sussex and died here, we can regard the Neolithic people as
the first natives of Sussex about whom we know very much.
Really, owing to the researches of the archæologists and to
the work done by their meticulous spades, we know quite a
lot about the way our New Stone Age ancestors lived and
died in Sussex—elsewhere, also, of course, but what is outside the county of Sussex is not our concern here.

At the end of the Old Stone Age the people of that period
were using not only flint, but bone and ivory, and their cave-
paintings were remarkable. But these things were in Europe,
not here. Then when the New Stone Age began man very
slowly advanced in the arts of living. He began to scratch
the surface of the earth and to grow a poor sort of corn—

five of his rare and beautifully knapped flint sickles have been found in Sussex, with a faint shine and iridescence on the blade edge from the silica in the wheat straw. He domesticated the dog; he began to make pottery and to weave; to grind stone; to polish his flints. He buried his important dead in chambered long barrows, and he used cremation. He raised the great megalithic temples—though not in Sussex. And at the end of this period the first date in prehistory appears, for the beginning of the Bronze Age is roughly dated at two thousand years before Christ.

4

By comparison with the remoteness of the early periods, it is possible to feel quite intimate with Neolithic and Bronze Age man. It is on the Downs that he has left us such an indelible impression both of his living and his dying. The remains of his living are less visible to the uninstructed eye than the relics of his death—though when the light of the sun is low, at rising or setting, certain strange and significant lines appear upon the surface of the Downs speaking of things past, of early agricultural activities written in these lynchet tracings. The burial mounds, the long barrows and the round barrows, which are scattered about the Downs in Sussex to the number of nearly a thousand, can hardly be overlooked, even by the most careless, and the solitude and silence of their setting, the simplicity of their outline, make them among the most impressive monuments that man has ever left behind to speak of his existence. The beauty of the South Downs is acknowledged everywhere, but had they never been inhabited by man, had they known no life save that of the lark and the wheatear, the wild orchis, the gorse, and the juniper bush, they would not be the Downs we know, with a strange awe and magic behind their visible loveliness. As it is they are haunted by memories of that dark and small race which still dwells in the remoter edges of Britain. In the dusk of evening it is easy to imagine, with an English poet, that

> The Downs are peopled then;
> Fugitive low-browed men
> Start from the slopes around.

A Bridge near Balcombe
Beddingham

One of the strangest combinations of mystery and science is the way that photography from the air has revealed the haunts and habitations of early man, so that fields which are dumb at the close approach, reveal their secrets from the air either as "shadow-sites" or "soil-sites" or "crop-sites." But, of course, the oldest implement of all in the hand of the archæologist, and still the most important, is the spade.

Few things more enthralling, to those whose tastes lie that way, can be imagined than an archæological "dig" on the Downs. Field archæology has become the pursuit and hobby of the active, of those who can walk for miles, and dig all day in the hot unshaded sun with an unrelaxing eye on the smallest things the spade may turn up. Such exertions are not for the purblind, dusty, bearded old archæologist of popular imagination.

An early Sussex archæologist who certainly did not deserve the epithet of "dusty" was that Dr Gideon Mantell whose fame as the discoverer of the bones of the Iguanodon has already been mentioned. He was a very spruce and well-groomed-looking person, judging from his portrait, and his keenness and activity in all geological and archæological matters was notable. But his methods of excavating a barrow make the modern archæologist shudder. His *Journal* has been recently edited by Dr Cecil Curwen, and the following extract will show the careless methods of the early nineteenth-century digger. The date is the July of 1818, and Dr Mantell wrote :

"About this time I had eight tumuli dug open near Mount Caburn. In one of them was deposited a skeleton of a warrior, having a large urn on each side of it near the pelvis; one urn contained burnt human bones only; the other contained calcined bones also, and a necklace of beads of various forms and materials. Some were flat and large; these were of jet, some were of amber, and resembled our common beads, and others were composed of green porcelain; some of these last were united, three or four together like a pulley. A beautiful green porcelain amulet was also found among the bones, of this form but twice as large."

Before field archæology became a science it was the excavator's way to open a barrow, pick out a few objects which struck him as interesting or curious, without taking any par-

D

Cuckmere Valley
Fairlight

ticular note of the position of such things, and then, curiosity satisfied, fill in the barrow again. It is realized now that the finds of the archæological spade are all of importance, though naturally they are not all equally spectacular. The only way to get a proper idea of modern methods is to attend a "dig" on the Downs, and watch the care and the patience, and share the excitement when something interesting is sifted out from the spadefuls of earth. Such small finds most of them may seem—a flint arrow head, flint flakes from the knapping floor, a small heap of fire-darkened flints which had been made red-hot and then dropped into the cooking vessels (themselves not strong enough for direct flame) to heat water in which to "seethe" the meat.

It was on the Downs near Lewes that I first saw these things, and as it was a Bronze Age habitation site there were found a few fragments of bronze, bits of a broken axe, a bronze knife much corroded away—nothing very important, but then many so-called Bronze Age people may never have set eyes or hands on the valuable metal. There were also broken pots of a coarse gritty paste, but, where the pieces were large enough to be patched together, of a fine shape. It is always a matter of amazement how admirable are the forms and the decorations—even when done with nothing but a fingernail or a twisted cord—of these early pots. The tall beakers of the so-called "Beaker" people are of a quality to enchant the eye.

The pots found up on the Downland heights were made there in those primitive hut circles, looking out on the glorious and almost unchanged scene (a miracle of time standing still) that we behold. Maybe the swelling lines, the curves and mouldings of the Downs suggested to the potters the simple and noble shapes they used.

The potters are generally supposed to have been the women, as they were also the spinners (their spindle whorls, often hollowed from pieces of chalk, are frequently found) and the weavers. In the Barbican House Museum at Lewes there is the skeleton of a young Bronze Age woman which was found complete at the Trundle near Goodwood, and now reposes in her glass case, in the position in which she was discovered. She lies on her side in an attitude that even in

34

bones has an air of grace and youth—she was only just cutting her wisdom teeth. Unlike Dr Mantell's "warrior," she was not accompanied in her burial by even a single bead of jet or amber, nor any tool or toy for the next world.

5

In Sussex soil has been discovered one of the most beautiful objects ever yielded by the distant past. This is a cup shaped out of a single lump of red amber. When Hove, now the glittering extension of Brighton, was a little hamlet, it had a Bronze Age tumulus on which the local children always played special games on Palm Sunday and Good Friday. But in the middle of last century the builders stole this hillock from the children, and when it was levelled and dug into, a rough coffin hollowed out of an oak tree was found. The coffin crumbled away at the touch of the air, and revealed fragments of decayed bones, and in the centre of the bones was the lovely cup, together with a brooch, a bronze dagger, a stone axe-head, and a whetstone. The cup holds about half a pint, and has, with its projecting handle, been turned from a single piece of amber. It has a slightly out-curved rim, and below the rim a band of close-set raised lines. The proportions are so exactly right and beautiful that no artist of any age could improve it. And think of the ancient faith and affection that devoted an object so rare and treasured to the tomb. Only one other amber cup has ever been found in Britain, and that came from Wessex.

This was a rich treasure to come from the tumulus on which the children played their Easter games, where is now the back of Palmeira Avenue at Hove.

But if we are thankful to have recovered undamaged from the shades the Hove amber cup, there is much archæological treasure the loss of which has to be mourned—mostly lost through simple unadulterated ignorance. There is the almost incredible tale of what is known as the Mountfield Hoard. Mountfield is a wooded district about four miles north of Battle, and the scene of the story is a farm known as Taylor's on the eastern bank of the Darwell. In 1863, on the 12th of

January, a ploughman named William Butchers was ploughing the Barn Field on Taylor's Farm. He found his ploughshare entangled with a long piece of brass, as he thought it. He then saw there was a square-shaped hole in the ground from which he collected a number of other brass objects. He showed them to the farmer, who was not in the least interested, and said the ploughman could keep them. So Butchers endeavoured to sell them, but found nobody wanted to buy such useless and odd things. Eventually he managed to dispose of them—they were eleven pounds in weight—at sixpence a pound. Still, with a wage probably of twelve shillings a week, five and sixpence was quite a little windfall. Then a man from Hastings recognized that this heap of old brass was in reality gold and a Cheapside firm of refiners bought the lot for £550. This hoard, the buried treasure of some Bronze Age chieftain, never came into the hands of any archæologists, who would have realized that its value was far above rubies, and almost in its entirety was melted down—two small fragments of what was found by that poor Sussex ploughman are now in the British Museum.

Of Long Barrows, belonging to the Neolithic period, Sussex has only seven. One is on Cliffe Hill, Lewes—its impressive lonely outline can be seen by anyone standing in a certain part of the busy High Street. Another is near Piddinghoe, and one on Firle Beacon. Alfriston parish has another called the Long Mound, and Windover Hill has its Long Burgh, while Wilmington Hill has the Hunter's Burgh, and the seventh Long Barrow is at Stoughton. It will be seen that all these Neolithic burial mounds are in the eastern half of the county.

The Round Barrows of the Bronze Age are many and scattered all over the South Downs. They are often in groups, like those on the Race Hill at Lewes, at the Devil's Jumps on Treyford Hill, and Bow Hill near Chichester; while on Heyshott Down there is a group of eight, showing the different forms of bell, bowl, and ring barrows. The best impression of these barrows as a whole can be got from the remarkable air photographs now available. Things invisible from the ground are writ so plain and large from the air.

Certain kinds of antiquities do not need any artificial aid
to reveal their meaning. Among these are many of the Downland forts, those that are of the nature, though not on the
scale, of the great Dorset stronghold of Maiden Castle.

One of the most eloquent in Sussex is that beautiful hill
promontory by Lewes called Mount Caburn. Its natural
shape and position alone make it notable, but to this is added
a remarkable earthwork, running round its head like a
coronet in a clear and arresting line. It must remain one of
the major archæological mysteries how early man, with his
primitive tools, achieved such large entrenchments and great
megalithic monuments as may be found most notably in
Dorset and Wiltshire. There they stand, under the sky, with
a look of eternity about them, increased by the nobility of
the setting. Even though Sussex cannot boast such works as
Maiden Castle and Avebury, it yet is a memorable experience to come upon Caburn from the hinterland behind, walking over the resilient turf, the eye full of solitude and the
swelling and sinking lines of the Down country, where it
seems as if no foot save a shepherd's had ever been before,
and then to behold the deep lines of rampart and ditch
encircling the crown of the bare, beautiful hill. Caburn is
what is known as a contour fort, as it follows the shape of
the hill it encircles. The naturally steep sides of the hill are
only encircled by one rampart, but the northern part, where
approach is easy, has a duplication of defence. There is
only one entrance, well contrived and well defended. But
careful excavation has shown that this beautiful hill-top was
not only a fortress but a village, a gathering of homes, whose
inhabitants of the early Iron Age carried on there the domestic pursuits of spinning, weaving, pottery-making and bronze
smelting. Among their long-discarded possessions were found
a beautiful bronze fibula or safety-pin brooch, a finger ring,
and some coins, as well as many rougher and earlier objects.

In early days Caburn was an island between the Ouse and
its tributary, now called the Glynde Reach. The waters
spread out as far as Fletching, very nearly joining the waters

of the Cuckmere and almost stretching to the sea which then covered Pevensey Level. A much more watery Sussex it was then, for towards the west the now inland little town of Steyning was a port, and on the extreme east and edge of the county Winchelsea and Rye rode royally with the tides lapping their cliffs.

There are twenty-three hill forts on the Downs, but of these only four, the Caburn, the Trundle, Cissbury and Whitehawk—now a somewhat depressing neighbourhood on the Race Hill above Brighton—have been excavated with any thoroughness.

The two largest earthworks in Sussex are Cissbury Ring and the Devil's Dyke, as it is now called. But the old name for the long angular enclosure, the earthwork, was the Poor Man's Wall—Poor Man being probably another synonym for the Devil. This "wall" is quite distinct from the great natural cleft in the Downs which now bears the name of the Devil's Dyke, and at which the Brighton trippers gaze for a few moments before they hurry off to the attractions of the "amusement park" so thoughtfully provided to mitigate the original noble solitude of the Downs.

Before field archæology and the study of pre-history had become a science, these Sussex hill forts were generally considered to be Roman. The Sussex native, also, faced with anything he did not understand, was inclined to ascribe it to the Romans—or the Devil, or that still older name Grim or Grime.

In his *Earthwork of England,* Hadrian Allcroft made a strong protest against that Romanizing tendency. The great view from the top of Ditchling Beacon moved him to write :

"All Sussex is spread out as in a map beneath you, and your couch is the very soil on which your forerunners lived the simple life in the wide air of the Neolithic time. For, whatever else is the matter of your dreaming, let them not be of Roman legionaries quartered here startling the eternal silence with the clash of armour and ever and again creeping stealthily down by the 'sunken road' beneath the camp upon the Weald below. These be pleasant dreams for such as be not antiquaries. This is no Roman camp, no Roman road leads to it, and no Roman mind ever planned a sunken road out of it. 'Ditchling slype' is deep enough and steep enough in all conscience, but it is just what the trampling feet of men and beasts have made it in the course of centuries. Your dreams here should be of times and peoples yet earlier than the Roman—of taller warriors clad in skins and armed with stone, and of others harnessed in bronze or helmeted with the horned casque of the iron time, but not of those terrible squat interlopers who made such play with the short sword and the *pillum*, and carried upon their shields the blazon of the thunderbolt."

CHAPTER III

ROMANS AND SAXONS

1

THE Romans marched about Sussex with their usual firmness and decision. Even the terrors of the Weald, which so bogged down later locomotion, did not stop them. From Chichester to London they built a road, the Stane Street, which Hilaire Belloc calls "the best preserved and most distinct Roman road in England," which shot northward in an arrow-like flight.

There is still a good deal of Roman work awaiting exploration in Sussex, but of the known Roman monuments the principal ones are Stane Street, the villa at Bignor adjoining it, another villa at Southwick, one at Angmering, and one at Wiggonholt, not yet fully explored. The villa at Southwick was first discovered so long ago as 1815, and at intervals pottery, mosaic and tiles were found and displayed, but no serious attention was paid to the site until over a hundred years after its discovery, and in the meantime the relics found had completely disappeared. This is rather typical of the Sussex attitude towards Roman remains until the twentieth century. The Wiggonholt villa shows the marks of destruction by fire, possibly in the "fourfold invasion" of the Saxons, Scots, Picts and Attacotti of A.D. 367–8. The best part of the villa is being preserved and roofed. But even in these more enlightened days, when a Roman villa is found on a valuable site it is often, after excavation, filled in again and built over —and this obliteration must have happened many times in the past. Bignor, now the pride of Sussex, had a narrow escape.

Only a mile or so away from the Wiggonholt villa was found in the middle of last century a hoard of 1,800 late Roman coins, packed in rows in a wooden box—buried, probably, in those troubled times of Saxon invasion.

These villas are in the western part of Sussex—but in the

eastern side of the county is the most magnificent Roman monument above ground that Sussex can boast, the fortress of Pevensey.

The Roman genius, which is stamped heavily enough on various parts of Britain, and most notably of all in that great wall of Hadrian's in the north, has always had a somewhat alien air in Sussex, which even before the Saxons came seemed more fitted by nature to be their habitation than that of the Legions. The most impressive of the Roman works always seem to be their roads, and roads do not so much suggest a people who settle as a people who march on and march away—as eventually the Romans did. Belloc, so emphatic in his admiration of what Britain owes to Rome, has to admit that when it comes to highways even Rome has to yield a little to "the rolling English road." Sussex, so quiet, but so definitely obstinate, gave the great Stane Street, which the Romans built from Chichester to London, a definite push here and there from the mathematical rigidity which the Roman engineers aimed at. In his book on Stane Street Belloc admits somewhat reluctantly, "The dead straight line normal to Roman roads is, in this country, frequently, or rather generally, modified."

So we may take a certain satisfaction in the thought that if the Romans greatly altered and impressed England, England herself, and not least Sussex, had a certain mollifying effect upon Roman rigidity. No one who has seen the remains of that great Roman villa at Bignor can doubt it, built, as Belloc says, "upon one of the most solemnly beautiful sites of South England, covering a general southern slope that looks right at the dark wall of the Downs above it."

Such a view, so noble and uplifted, which was the daily prospect from the Bignor villa, must have influenced its inhabitants, even if unconsciously. To-day the effect is oddly reversed, for on the road that skirts the swelling site of the villa, looking upwards across a plain farm field, one sees a curious little collection of low wigwams, built of rough flint and thatched with straw, which are what now represent the stately villa. A somewhat puzzled search for the lady with the keys reveals, when she permits entry, that these gnomes' houses have been erected to cover and protect from weather ravages the remarkably fine Roman pavements which are practically all that remains above ground of the villa. It is —or was—a very impressive villa, one of the largest ever found in England, and had something like sixty rooms and quarters for slaves, covering altogether several acres, with, of course, the usual luxurious Roman bathing arrangements.

Before 1811 these tessellated pavements were covered by the soil of a farm field, known as the Berry field. Once more it was the inquisitive plough which revealed this piece of British history, showing, on investigation, the ground-plan, the ornate pavements, the baths and plunge pools and hypocausts of this residence from which some Roman, or Romano-British prefect, surveyed the Sussex scene, and did not find the weather, as some Roman writers had declared, to consist exclusively of fog and rain—the site of the villa is skilfully placed to take the sun.

These tessellated pavements are beautiful in execution and design in their subdued colourings of white, red, buff, blue and green—the white of chalk, red of brick, buff of sandstone, blue and green of limestone. The subjects of these mosaics are markedly Roman—Ganymede being carried off by the eagle, the head of Medusa with snaky locks. Also the Seasons—Winter very cold and shuddering. But whether the materials of these mosaic pictures were native ones or brought, with the craftsmen who executed them, from overseas, they have a definitely foreign air. They do not belong to Sussex, though for so many centuries they have rested on Sussex soil. There is something sad, because alien, about them—perhaps Roman nostalgia still breathes from them— "the Roman and his trouble."

Rome was to be no permanent conqueror of Britain, was not to settle down and become one with the conquered, as the Saxons and the Normans were to do, and in doing so leave behind them buildings and monuments which are part of English growth and glory.

The Roman has left many signs of his habitation in Sussex—many roads, apart from the great Stane Street, most of them only recently discovered; many villas, apart from the famous one at Bignor. At that specially interesting Sussex place, Bosham, a villa with a central court was built in the reign of Antoninus. A marble head (a portrait of one of the Claudian family), a Roman bath, a small amphitheatre were also found there. Many names have also been left behind : Roman Gate and Roman Wood, and Adversane, which has a Latin air, and Coldharbours, which are said to belong to Roman roads—though strict archæologists throw cold water on this theory now—and are supposed to mean halting-places for the marching cohorts where there was neither food nor warmth provided, unlike the *mansios* or road stations, at the end of each day's march.

And the end of the final day's march is also to be found in Sussex in the form of Roman cemeteries. There is a famous and crowded one at Hassocks, close to the London-Brighton railway, but it was carelessly dug out many years ago for the rose-pink sand which abounds about there, and many valuable records were lost. Many Roman cremation urns were found there, including a few Bronze Age urns; also a few Saxon ones, which continue to puzzle antiquaries, as it was not the Saxon custom to use Roman cemeteries, or cremation. All these burials together, from Bronze Age to Saxon, cover the long period of seventeen hundred years. But this "Field of Urns" is predominantly Roman, and like most Roman cemeteries was placed by the side of the road. It is now bounded on two sides by roads, the road to Hurstpierpoint and the road up Clayton Hill that goes on to Brighton. But it is not these roads which the Romans made, but the one on the western side of the cemetery, going north and south, which at that point meets and crosses another Roman road running east and west. Just across the present road to Hurstpierpoint, opposite the cemetery, is Ham Farm and Butting Hill, which is believed to have been a Saxon moot hill. The position is very beautiful all along the ridge of Wickham Hill, with Wolstonbury looking benignly down, and a little further along suddenly standing back to reveal a further sweep of Downs and a distant prospect of Chanctonbury.

The Hassocks Roman cemetery did not yield all the treasure it would have done had it been excavated at the beginning archæologically, instead of commercially for sand.

But the burial urns had their usual accompaniment of food dishes and drink bowls and occasionally the coin to pay Charon for the passage of the Styx. Some of the bits of Samian ware may be seen in the Barbican House Museum at Lewes.

But in spite of these things the Roman is gone from Britain and from Sussex in a curious and complete way. He came, he saw, he conquered—and he went away again, utterly and finally, and after him came the Dark Age when Clio, who had just taken up her pen after the long blank of pre-history, where the only records were flints and sherds and earthworks, flung it down again, and we hear nothing save the footsteps of the Legions marching, marching away from Britain, and the grinding of the keels of the Long Ships upon the Saxon Shore.

2

But before this dim and troubled period of history there were nearly four hundred years of Roman rule, and Sussex bears still many a remembrance of that rule. The Roman conquest was not stamped upon Sussex with blood and slaughter—the troubled inhabitants, not skilled in war, surrounded by many conflicting tribes and claims, seem to have accepted the Pax Romana with relief. They may be said, symbolically, to have descended from their hill-fortress on Mount Caburn in east Sussex to trade in the Roman market-place at Regnum—now Chichester—on the western edge of the county.

The Romans were considerably interested in Sussex—though even more so in Kent—one of the reasons being that there was iron in Kent and in eastern Sussex. The real Iron Age came in with the Romans—the so-called Iron Age following that of Bronze was but a shadow of the real thing as shown by the clanking armed Legions when they marched about the known world and made their metalled roads. Actually metalled, in some cases, as was shown a few years ago, for a Roman road in Sussex, which had been partly made with waste from the iron workings, was struck by lightning in a great thunderstorm, and the fusing of the metal killed the corn which was growing above it, and thus revealed the line of a lost road.

Eastern Sussex to the Romans was iron, and their iron workings are scattered all about that region. From the time of the Romans to the time of Elizabeth, and somewhat beyond, iron was an important Sussex industry, and if the coal, which is also there on the ancient Palæozoic floor, did not lie beneath too great a thickness of Jurassic beds, happily, to render mining possible, East Sussex would no doubt now be a real "Black Country" instead of the pleasant agricultural scene it mostly is. There are parts of Sussex where the very tombstones in the churchyards are made of iron, and look oddly like the iron fire-backs for which the county is famous and with which many an old Sussex hearth is adorned. Guns also, of course, were made in large numbers of Sussex iron, smelted by Sussex charcoal, and the claim is made for a Sussex iron-master in the well-known bit of doggerel :

Master Huggett and his son John
They did cast the first cannon.

3

If the Romans found their iron needs in East Sussex, they evidently regarded West Sussex as a better place for residence, judging from the number of remains of villas that have been found there. The climate is slightly warmer, and on the plain between the Downs and the sea, widest at that side of the county, all the available sun and shelter is to be had. It is the nearest approach to their own skies that the Romans could discover in these parts, so no wonder the wealthy and important among them and among the Romanized Britons built their villas so thickly in the Chichester region.

The original Chichester was a tribal city, but as it now exists it is of essentially Roman planning, with its two main streets crossing at the centre—marked for many centuries now by the famous and beautiful Market Cross.

One of the most remarkable Roman relics in Chichester is

an inscribed stone tablet let into the wall of the Council House. This chiselled bit of history was found buried four feet down in April 1723, beneath a house at the corner of South and Lion Streets, and it goes back to the time of Cogidubnus, who submitted to Rome when the troops of Vespasian landed on the Sussex shore after conquering the Isle of Wight. In return for his malleable behaviour Cogidubnus was made a princeling under Roman control, and in this inscription is described as "By the authority of Tiberius Claudius, Cogidubnus, King, Legate of Augustus in Britain."

Belloc has a word on this subject : "Nor have we any direct history of Sussex," he says, "during the four hundred years of the Roman occupation, save in one characteristic matter at the beginning of that period. Sussex was sufficiently a unit and sufficiently cut off to have over it a local kinglet, recognized by the Empire. Sussex was already a 'kingdom.' "

This stone, which was part of a temple dedicated to Neptune and Minerva, was, according to the inscription, raised to the welfare of the Imperial Family, by the Guild of Builders at their own cost, and the site for the Temple was given by Pudens, son of Pudemtinus. Cogidubnus had a daughter named Claudia (not unnaturally, as he was King "by the authority of Tiberius Claudius"), and it has been suggested that Pudens gave this site for the temple in Chichester more from love of Claudia than of her father. From this the tale has been carried to the idea that St. Paul was once in Chichester—"in travels oft"—and that from that city he sent the greeting of Pudens and Claudia to Timothy.

Whether it is permissible or not to imagine the great Apostle walking the streets of that Sussex Regnum which was in time to become a Christian Cathedral city, it is an excellent piece of good fortune that this, one of the most remarkable Roman inscriptions in Britain, has been preserved. Sussex has a somewhat careless reputation in regard to Roman relics, and Chichester is not guiltless in this reproach, for both another Roman inscribed tablet and a pagan altar found in the city have disappeared. The Roman antiquary has full cause to gnash his teeth as he reads the record of a Roman bust, a Roman bath, and other objects found in various parts of Sussex followed by the statement, "since lost," or "now undiscoverable."

The Cathedral itself was erected over the foundations of Roman buildings, and remains of these, and of mosaic pavements, have been found within the walls.

The city walls, parts of which make such an attractive promenade under the shade of the large elm trees, are Roman in origin—recent excavations show them to have been constructed some time in the second century—though their present pleasant aspect of flint-built masonry on the outer side and grassy slopes on the inner is much later than the Roman occupation of the city of Regnum.

4

The most impressive Roman remains visible in Sussex are those of Pevensey Castle. The Romans are primarily associated with their roads in most minds, and they stamped their roads all over England, but there are two drawbacks to the investigation of Roman roads. When they are incorporated as portions of highways in actual daily use, modern metalling and upkeep destroy completely any "historic" feeling, and the only thing that speaks of Rome is their unflinching straightness—though many purely modern roads are also straight. On the other hand, when the original Roman road has sunk into swampy ground, been overgrown by scrub and gorse, or become part of a ploughed field, then much knowledge, patience and labour are needed to reveal it again. As a field sport this may surpass all others and a lifetime may joyfully be given up to it. Sussex is fortunate in having such a learned and devoted leader in the hunting of Roman roads as Mr Ivan D. Margary, whose investigations have immensely enriched our knowledge of the lesser Roman roads within the county. An example of his work is the tracing of a lost Roman road running from Barcombe Mills north of Lewes, to Streat—a Roman-betraying name—through Ditchling and Hassocks, by the Roman burial-ground. He found the indisputable road nearly as far as Storrington, where more conjecturally the road curves up through Wiggonholt, where there is a Roman villa, to join Stane Street above Pulborough. This is a long and important stretch of road, half across Sussex, running all the way on the zone of greensand which lies roughly parallel with the Downs, and it had been lost and forgotten. Its recovery and that of others, for which the county is indebted to Mr Margary, is of great importance in our knowledge of Roman Sussex.

But the discovery of lost Roman roads is a specialist's pursuit, and not for the ordinary untrained man or woman— though few of us can stand on the edge of such a bit of recovered road, open again to the sky after so many centuries of obliteration, without some stirring of imagination, some faint far vision of the cohorts swinging past.

But it does not need any imagination, any personal creative effort, to see Pevensey Castle. It is too big, too impressive, too visibly present in this our day—it cannot be overlooked. Pevensey has been added to and increased by Norman builders, but the grim strong structure of wall and semi-circular solid bastions, rising above the surrounding levels— which once were sea, even so late as the time of Holinshed, who tells us "into Pevenscie haven divers waters doo resort" —has nothing to distract from its impressiveness. Like Bodiam, not so far away, there is something astonishing about Pevensey, so that the heart misses a beat on being first confronted with this monument from the "dark backward and abysm of Time."

The Roman walls enclose a space of about ten acres, and are shown by archæological research to have been built between A.D. 250 and 300. As all the land was marshy thereabouts, and the walls were built on what was then an island —the surrounding names show other islands, as Horseye, Northeye, Chilleye, Richneye—the Roman builders were taking no risks with their foundations. They made a bed fifteen feet wide of clay and oak stakes, and above this was three feet of clay and flints. Then came heavy timbers covered with concrete. The wall that was finally built upon this was a little over twelve feet wide and twenty-eight feet high, faced with blocks of greensand, and with a rubble core. This wall has the characteristic Roman bonding courses of flat red tiles which go right through the twelve feet of thick-

Stopham Bridge
Trotton

ness. The wall was further strengthened by twelve towers or bastions, some of which are now fallen or destroyed.

Pevensey Castle—so called for convenience, though the actual castle, with the remains of a moat, is a Norman erection within the much older Roman walls—was part of the Roman defences of the Saxon Shore, which extended round the coast from northern Norfolk to western Sussex. It was one of the Roman responses to the mutterings of those Scandinavian and Teutonic peoples then just beginning to be heard. These hordes of invaders were later to sweep over this great defence and, as the *Saxon Chronicle* records, none of the people within the walls of Anderida, as Pevensey was then called, were left alive.

But the memory of that tragedy has been covered by many centuries, though still the great walls remain that the Romans built. Not so many years ago old prints showed how the walls were draped and smothered in ivy, with wild bushes sprouting between the stones, and what time and sieges had not done would have been accomplished by the frail remorseless fingers of vegetation, against which not even Roman mortar can stand. But the Castle now belongs to the National Trust, owing to the generosity of the Duke of Devonshire, and the Office of Works has put it in order, so that both the Roman and the later Norman part of it are as comely as can be, the great stretches of grass within the encircling walls as neat as a vicarage lawn. This neatness seems to put the thought of the Roman soldiers and auxiliaries rather far away, still more so the memory of that fierce massacre— "old, unhappy, far-off things" lie now like the merest shadow on the grass. But the well that supplied the garrisons can still be seen. Of this well that great Sussex antiquary Mark Antony Lower gave an interesting account when describing excavations that took place at Pevensey in the middle of the nineteenth century. This well, he says, is "of very remarkable construction. It is seven feet in diameter and steined with solid ashlar. After descending forty feet it gradually contracts and is continued to the depth of fifty, where it is further narrowed to a frame-work of solid oak of square form, and little more than two feet across . . . among other objects brought up during the emptying of this well there

E 49

Knapps Cottages, West Burton
In Ashdown Forest

were several of those large spherical masses of green sandstone—generally supposed to be catapult balls—which have so often been found in the castle, and some skulls which upon examination by competent persons have been pronounced to be those of *wolves*."

A later excavation investigated an earlier and Roman well at Pevensey. This well was much shallower and smaller in diameter and lined with large timbers. Various kinds of debris were found at the bottom, including leather sandals. The most important find was the original well-rope made of twisted strands of bark. This rope, says Mr Salzman, who records the excavations in the Sussex Archæological Society's *Collections*, "is important as being apparently the only piece of Roman cordage yet found in Britain." Other finds were the skull of a domestic cat and wood of the beech tree—thus settling the debated questions as to whether the cat and the beech existed in Britain in Roman times. And in the well were found seeds of the wild plants which roamed the country before the Romans came and after they had gone. Flax seed was in the well, and buttercup and fool's parsley, henbane and hemlock and persicaria, sheep's sorrel, stinging nettle, stitchwort, sow-thistle, blackberry, vetch, bracken and black bindweed. It sounds like an earlier and rougher edition of Perdita's offerings. Has anybody told us what plants the Romans grew in Britain?—vervain is supposed to be associated with the Romans. But perhaps they preferred a tessellated pavement to a flower garden.

5

In Sussex, apart from the walls of Pevensey, there is little Roman work left above the ground. The great villas and the smaller ones have sunk beneath the soil, having, in many cases, been burnt down by the Saxon invaders. The great roads are either re-metalled and in use, or overgrown and forgotten—though archæological skill and enthusiasm is now tracing them and laying portions open to the light of day. Devotion to the Romans in Britain is as marked in some historians as is the reverse in others. Everyone knows that

Hilaire Belloc is a great believer in Roman order, while Hadrian Allcroft is even faintly comic amid his erudition in his dislike of them. In his *Earthwork of England*, already quoted, Allcroft says, "From time to time have been found Roman keys, skeletons, a pot of coins, and all the customary rubbish which the Roman left behind him."

The unfortunate Roman, if he died here, usually had to leave his skeleton behind him. And even more usefully to future ages he left not only his bones and the remains of his buildings, but many of his coins and much of his pottery, which was usually of a noble shape. Laws, too, he left us, and some of the Latin tongue embedded in our very mixed language.

There is one relic he has left us—though its discovery does not belong to Sussex—which speaks of something not usually visible under the general hardness and efficiency we associate with the ancient Roman rule. That is the altar-stone on which is chiselled a dedication "To the genius of the British countryside." Perhaps that is the most touching thing —perhaps it is the only touching thing—which that nation of law-givers and soldiers has bequeathed us. We in Sussex cannot but feel that there is something softening and endearing in our county, and we know beyond question that Roman eyes looked out upon the prospects we love, from Gumber Corner in the west, and from the top of a then treeless Chanctonbury, from Firle Beacon and from Mount Caburn —looked out over a wild and wooded Weald across which those masterful engineers had cut their roads. Some of those who returned to Italy or to Gaul would surely remember Sussex.

But the time was fast drawing near when it was to be no longer the Kingdom of the Regni, or a Roman province, but the country of the South Saxons.

6

An historian and archæologist, S. E. Winbolt, who devoted much of his time and work to Sussex, says in one of his books :

"Vestiges of the Saxons, of many kinds, are probably more richly represented in Sussex than in any other English county. Their cemeteries have been found, among other places, at High Down, near Worthing, and at Alfriston : the churches of Worth and Sompting are famous throughout the country as living examples of Sussex architecture. Saxon place-names are thick-scattered all over the map, especially on the coastal plain."

The Roman impress on Sussex was stern and military; the Saxon was decorative and agricultural. But the great mark between the two periods is that it was in the Saxon era that Christianity came to settle in Sussex. And Sussex has one remarkable and outstanding monument of this tremendous change in the Saxon church at Worth.

As the Saxons built more with timber than with stone or flint, as they were carpenters before they were masons, it is inevitable that of their timber buildings few or none survive. There is a very fascinating little cottage at Steyning with a steep "cat-slide" roof, which is called Saxon Cottage, but its only claim to the name may lie in possible Saxon foundations, as there may have been a cottage there in Saxon times. Winbolt says of some cottages near Hardham that they "probably stand on Saxon sites." But such cottages were roughly and poorly built; even the Saxon thane's great timber hall was inevitably perishable and doomed to destruction by fire or decay. But stone and flint are another matter—bricks, of course, having vanished with the Romans, not to return for many centuries.

Worth is on the northern edge of the county in the St. Leonard's Forest region—the name of Worth indicates forest—almost on the line that divides East from West Sussex. It is a strangely impressive church. It is not necessary to know much of its history, or of ecclesiastical architecture in general, to feel the atmosphere of eld as one enters it—the massive arches, the high, small defensive windows, speak of the church as a refuge, not only spiritually, but materially. The plan is cruciform and it has one of the rare apsidal chancels—the "little, lost Down church" of Upwaltham has another. Worth is the largest Saxon church in England, and is still set about with the remains of the vast

Worth forest, where huge and misshapen beeches, crouching and lying along the ground, slumber in company with great yews whose sombre shade is lit in due season with the marvellously translucent tiny lamps of the yew berries—so beloved by thrushes. There are certain bits of forest in Sussex which in feeling, if not in fact, go back at least to Domesday, and seem to bear no sign of this present age, forests where it would seem but natural to meet the swine rootling for beech-mast or acorns in charge of an inarticulate Saxon swineherd. Such a swineherd and his wife will have attended Mass in this church of Worth into which you walk from this our day, and no amount of what is called "progress" will prevent your heart, like his, from being subdued by the solemnity of these walls. The chancel arch, which is high and very rugged and even slightly crooked, at once arrests the eye. It speaks of early building and lacks the firm compact touch of the Norman masonry which was to follow it. On either side of the chancel arch are lower arches, massive and rough, leading into the transepts, and there are also three equally rough arches now blocked up. There remain a few of the original Saxon windows. Three of these in the nave—two on the north side and one on the south—are probably unique in England. They are high up—for this church, in its time, was a refuge against the Danes—with two round-headed lights divided by a turned shaft of stone. In the north transept is another small round-headed window, which has been made smaller than it was originally built—a memory of the fear in which the Saxons, who had themselves invaded Sussex, were to live of those later invaders, the Danes.

On the outside, Worth Church bears many marks of its Saxon building. For those who are unable actually to see it, better than any photograph, to my mind, is the impression given by the etching in R. H. Nibbs' *Churches of Sussex*, which was done in 1850. The curious shape, with the high apsidal east end, held up, as it were, by the great thrusting buttresses (a much later addition), the Saxon long-and-short work at the quoins, the string course, and the odd and characteristic pilasters which run up the walls at intervals, are all well known. Nibbs' drawing of the interior of the church is also very interesting, especially as in many details it does not agree with the interior as it is now.

7

Two other Saxon churches in Sussex must be mentioned, as both are notable—Sompting and Bishopstone. Sompting has a remarkable tower, which has been depicted many times. I recall a picture, painted a number of years ago by an artist whose name I do not know, in which that aloof and somehow saintly-looking tower had a pleasant farmyard foreground. Now, that ancient bit of Saxon piety is tragically swamped in bungalows and garages and all the ungracious modern litter which so disastrously strews the Sussex coast. Sompting Church is lost there, a ghost from another world. Some places in Sussex, some parts of Sussex, even in this day, most strangely, manage to retain an unchanged air, to keep, even close to a clattering town, the feeling of their past. But Sompting Church tower, though an almost perfect and unspoiled example of Saxon work, has had its roots cut away from it by all that has invaded the scene. It is no longer growing and alive, it is a *revenant* under the moon. That is all the more pitiable, for it is a beautiful thing. The angles of the four-sided gabled tower, meeting at the apex in such sharp and yet harmonious contrast, are at once satisfying and simple. The hand of the Saxon mason is plainly visible in the characteristic long-and-short work of the quoins, the string-course and the pilaster strips that run up the centre of each face of the tower. Better than any photograph—photographs, for some reason, seem to miss its essential quality—is the impression that Nibbs again has given of this relic of our Saxon past in his etching—though there is a solitary look about his Sompting tower which is unhappily quite vanished now.

There are some Roman bricks built into the north and west sides of this Saxon tower.

The church at Worth and the tower at Sompting are almost wholly untouched Saxon work, both of them unique in the proper sense of that much-used word—unique not only

in Sussex, but also in England. The earliest work in churches
is apt to be destroyed, overlaid, or rebuilt. Therefore the
third example of Saxon church-building, that of Bishopstone, is not so complete, for Bishopstone represents at least
seven centuries of church architecture—Saxon, Norman and
Early English.

It is a singularly fascinating church, and found in an unpromising spot, in dangerous proximity to prosperous but
unbeautiful Newhaven. But if Newhaven lacks beauty it has,
at least, sense and reality, and is a busy little seaport engaged on a legitimate job, in no way to be confused with
those dreary, squalid bungalow towns, with architecture
ranging from the sham Gothic castle to the defunct railway-
carriage, which disfigure the Sussex coast.

But leaving the somewhat depressing outskirts of Newhaven and turning inland, there is a lane which runs into a
hollow of the Downs, and this lane leads to the hamlet of
Bishopstone—hidden away, untouched, apparently unconscious of this modern world.

I shall always remember my first seeing of it on a golden
May afternoon, the surprising discovery of a place that suggested the sixteenth or seventeenth century, and when one
comes to the church, centuries much earlier.

In Domesday Book it is called Biscopestone; this is very
close to the present name, over eight hundred years have
done little to alter its pronunciation. That authority on the
Sussex dialect, W. D. Parish, who in 1885 edited for the
Sussex Archæological Society a facsimile and translation of
the Sussex portion of Domesday Book, spoke amusingly of
the difficulty in identifying the names of places in Domesday
Book, owing to the extraordinary spelling.

"The spelling is, in fact, phonetic," he says, "and expresses
as nearly as possible the sounds pronounced by the natives of
villages, who, using their own local dialect, and evidently
speaking, as the Sussex rustics still speak, with closed lips,
gave answer in a shy and sulky tone to the first question of
the King's officers, 'What is the name of this place?' To
those who are familiar with the local manner of speech it
will be extremely interesting to trace in an apparently
difficult Domesday name, the exact pronunciation which still

puzzles the stranger enquiring his way on a Sussex country road."

Part of what the Domesday records says of Bishopstone is this :

"The Bishop of Chichester holds in demesne Biscopestone. In the time of King Edward it vouched for 25 hides, and now likewise. In demesne are 3 ploughs; and 30 villeins with 9 borders have 30 ploughs. There are 40 acres of meadow. Wood for pannage for 3 hogs and of 3 hogs one hog for herbage. In the time of King Edward it was worth £26, and afterwards £11. Now £20."

The large number of ploughs, with the small number of hogs, suggests that, as would be expected from its position on the Downs, there was little wood for pannage at Bishopstone.

It is little more than a manor farm, with its adjoining buildings. There is a pleasant farm-house, backed by noble barns; a few cottages; a steeply sloping village green, which was not so much a green as a sheet of solid gold covered in buttercups when I first saw it. The hedges and the ditches were frothing and creamy with cow-parsley, and there were tall elms set about in that decorative manner natural to elms. It might have been an English idyll painted by Birkett Foster, and only needed a few solid children in sunbonnets and pinafores to complete the scene.

Through the trees the grey tower of the church can be seen, and on approaching it and looking up at the tower one realizes that here is something much earlier than the sixteenth century. The church is built entirely of grey flint and has an impressive slope of roof and is set in an enchanting position, with a churchyard that even more than most village churchyards suggests peace. But the square flint tower of Bishopstone is what at once arrests one's attention. It most oddly and archaically ascends to the little conical cap in a series of four diminishing sections, divided by string courses. It needs no special knowledge, as one stands at the foot of this tower looking upwards, to realize that here is a piece of very early architecture—the massive simplicity and a certain primitive look bespeak a remote century. This primitive appearance is enhanced by the row of gargoyle heads which go round on all four sides of the tower, gazing out over the Sussex scene, worn down by time and the prevailing south-westerly winds from the sea to an expression of bland idiocy.

The tall Saxon south porch, with its long-and-short work, and the dial-plate above it carved with the name *Ead-ric*, are very notable, and there is a Saxon carved tombstone in the tower and dog-tooth moulding on some of the arches.

In the churchyard the prevailing names on the tombstones seem to be the rather odd ones of Catt and Venus. In the little churchyard of Bramber I once found a name that had a Roman air, Virgo.

Could the ancestor of that family have been some Roman legionary?

8

There are remains and fragments of Saxon building in many of the churches of Sussex. It is not needful to search them all out, for Worth and Sompting are the most outstanding and complete. But for pure historic interest the church at Bosham—and never, unless you wish to offend Sussex ears, pronounce that name as though the first syllable was Bosh; as in so many Sussex words the emphasis is on the last syllable, so it becomes on the native tongue Boz-ham—cannot be omitted, for that church is associated in a peculiar and intimate manner with the last of the Saxon kings and the coming of the Normans to rule England. In the Bayeux Tapestry we actually have a picture of the church at Bosham—to remove any possible doubt there is the word "Ecclesia" above the roof—showing Harold entering to receive the Sacrament. It is a curious-looking church, probably not more closely related to the original than a small child's conventional drawing of a house. But it has the high Saxon arched doorway and two decorations on either side of it which might be pilasters running up to small high windows.

The still existing tower of Bosham Church is Saxon, but looks the less so because of the tall steeple that has been imposed upon it. But however added or altered every visitor to Bosham should remember Mark Antony Lower's words that it is "presumably the oldest site of Christianity in Sussex."

Roman material is incorporated in the fabric of the walls and the base of the chancel arch. Under the Saxon King Adelwalch an Irish monk settled at Bosham and "lived poorly and served God."

It was Herbert de Bosham who was secretary to Thomas à Becket, and into Becket's mouth Tennyson put the words

>   Better have been
> A fisherman of Bosham, my good Herbert,
> Thy birthplace—the sea-creek—the petty rill
> That falls into it—the green field—the gray church—

9

It was from Bosham that Harold set out on his fatal visit to Normandy—he who was to be the last of the Saxon kings, he who was to bring to an end in the middle of the eleventh century that Saxon domination which had first begun as a serious menace in the middle of the fourth century, when England, especially the southern part of it, was held as a Roman province.

The slow Saxon penetration spread over many years, never as one final conquering battle like that of Hastings, stamped itself upon Sussex not only in the remaining churches, but in the names of innumerable villages, in the ancient speech, in the very name by which this county is now known, the county of the South Saxons. And also in the complexion and build of many a farm labourer who ploughs and reaps the Sussex fields to-day.

As has been shown, the Sussex coast, with its easy rivers, offered tempting access to the Saxon and Scandinavian sea-rovers, who could sail up the Ouse or the Adur—then protected by no castles—pillage and plunder, and sail away again. Only sea-power, as it is now called, could have saved Sussex after Roman strength had decayed. And Sussex had no sea-power.

The first Saxon conquest was of Regnum—Chichester is the name imposed by the Saxons—which apparently was taken by surprise and fell without much resistance. But after that it is evident that the Britons, though deserted by the Romans, defended their "secret kingdom" with courage and success, for it was eight years before the Saxons managed to get across the county from the western Chichester to the eastern Pevensey, or Anderida. There they met a stout resistance, for the Britons were not taken by surprise in this case, and they had the walls of the Roman fortress, erected for this very purpose, to fight behind.

An account of their methods of fighting shows how valiant and ingenious they were. It is Henry of Huntingdon who writes this account, which in spite of its twelfth-century date is so detailed that it suggests the persistence of folk memory —which stretches over longer periods than that. He says :

"Aella besieged Andredsceastor, a strongly fortified city. The Britons then collected like bees, and beat the besiegers in the day by stratagems, and in the night by attacks. No day, no night occurred wherein unfavourable and fresh tiding would not exasperate the minds of the Saxons; but rendered thereby more ardent they beset the city with continual assaults. Always, however, as they might assail, the Britons pressed them behind with archers and with darts thrown with thongs; wherefore quitting the walls the pagans directed their steps and arms against them. Then the Britons, excelling them in fleetness, ran into the woods, and again came upon them from behind when they approached the walls. By this artifice the Saxons were long annoyed and an immense slaughter of them was made, until they divided the army into two parts, so that while one part should storm the walls they might have behind a line of warriors arrayed against the charges of the Britons. But then the citizens, worn down by long want of food, when they could no longer sustain the multitude of assailants, were all devoured by the sword, with the women and little ones, so that not an individual escaped."

After that record of Germanic savagery it is pleasant to recall a drawing from Nibbs' *Antiquities of Sussex*, published in 1874, showing the east side of Pevensey Castle with a charming little cottage tucked in between the towers, a

small round cornstack to the side of it, and an old Sussex
woman shaking her mat against the Norman gateway. Rural
peace on the site of ancient wars.

10

The Saxons, unlike the earlier inhabitants of Sussex, did
not regard the chalk Downs as a desirable dwelling-place.
To them it was a place of the dead, thick with barrows
which would be haunted by alarming spirits—so many of
these tumuli and megalithic remains have acquired the name
of the devil, or the still older Grim or Grime. Neither did
the Saxons settle on the sites of Roman villas and farms—
they usually burnt and destroyed them. Once they decided
to become Sussex men, and not raiders from overseas, they
set to work to make clearings in the Wealden forests and to
build villages along the seaward side of the Downs, and also
along the northern foot where the water sprang between the
chalk and the greensand. They slowly abandoned the sword
and the torch for the ploughshare and the woodman's axe,
and became the first farmers of the Weald, sinking their feet
into the Sussex clay where they have more or less stuck ever
since. The earlier Celts and Britons did their light scratch
farming on the chalk uplands—signs of it may easily be seen
when the light is low and shadows lie.

It is principally by the names of the villages they established that we know of the Saxons in Sussex—of recorded
history there is little. In fact there are long stretches of darkness, when Sussex seems so cut off from the rest of England
as to be almost non-existent.

But if the Saxons were grim in their onslaught on un-
defended coasts, and dumb in their lives, they were decorative in their deaths. From the skin-clad Stone Age people
and the armoured soldiers of the Legions we come to the
coloured, bead-hung, buckled, brooched Saxon man and his
womankind. And it is from their cemeteries that we know of
their passion for personal decoration, and also for the adorn-
ing of their drinking vessels, their combs and hand-mirrors,
and other household and personal possessions. The custom

of burying with a man or woman the things that had aided
and given pleasure in life is a very old one—it began in the
Stone Age and continued right up to Saxon times. It was
Christianity that destroyed it, with the teaching that the soul
did not need such baubles in the next world. But historically
we must be thankful for so human and touching a custom,
which has given us so much of our knowledge about the ways
of the people who dwelt in this land before us. The earth is
a great preserver—fragile things laid away in graves are
discovered centuries afterwards, when the same ornaments
and utensils left in the dwellings of the living have vanished
completely away.

There was a great Saxon burial-place found near Alfriston
in East Sussex. A house was being built and a garden made
when over one hundred and fifty graves—all inhumed burials
—were discovered, and the bulk of them examined. The
skeletons were found much decayed and broken, but the
masses of objects laid in the graves were in a good state of
preservation. Many of them may be seen in the Barbican
House Museum at Lewes. There were quantities of beads,
in amber, rock crystal, coloured porcelain—green, yellow
and red—glass, some of them black glass, and a few bugle
beads. There were also gilded bronze fibulæ; pins and
brooches, silver finger rings, a bronze bowl, as well as the
warrior's shield bosses, swords and spears—almost corroded
back to the ironstone from which they were smelted. There
were also vessels of glass which in spite of their fragility had
survived the long centuries in the earth better than the iron
weapons.

Amongst all these graves there was one that stood out
from the others by certain special features. It was a woman's
grave, and she was a cripple, the thigh-bone and shin of one
leg were deformed. But, if a cripple, she was either wealthy
and important or the well-beloved of some powerful thane,
for her grave was loaded with treasure. I take this account
from the complete list of the contents of this and all the
other graves given by Mr A. F. Griffiths and Mr L. F
Salzman in the *Sussex Archæological Collections* for the year
1914.

Under the Saxon lady's head was a conical glass vase,

much crushed. On her breast was a large bronze-gilt fibula, square-headed, and another pair of bronze fibulæ as well as a "highly decorated thin silver penannula brooch," and a large bronze buckle. There were also a great number of beads of all sizes and colours and materials. Particularly interesting were the sixteen rings of silver wire strung with beads "found in such positions that they must have been arranged down the front of the dress."

I have seen these bead-strung silver rings and have always thought what an attractive decoration they must have been on the flowing Saxon feminine dress, swinging and colourful with every movement.

That is by no means all that was found in this crippled woman's grave. Let us hope that in life she found some compensation for her disabilities in these pretty things.

11

It must be a reflection occurring to all of antiquarian tastes how much more permanent man is in his burial than in his life. Out of the grave have come so many memorials of the past, and the Stone Age barrows have outlasted so many soaring structures. In famous words Sir Thomas Browne has expressed this feeling in reference to tumuli. "Time," he said, "which antiquates antiquities and hath an art to make dust of all things, hath yet spared these minor monuments."

But there is a slighter and more elusive thing than earthworks and burial barrows which bids fair to outlast even better the onslaughts of time, and that is the names of places —at least in the old and genuine country, though even in the Sussex country it is possible to find an ancient name like Wodenhaile stupidly changed to a meaningless Wood Knoll. Sussex is remarkably rich in Saxon place-names—and also in the names of many families which have kept their names and in some cases their dwelling places, unaltered, or only slightly modified, from Saxon times.

Any dweller in an old and rooted Sussex village will realize that certain family names are indigenous—names that are on the churchyard tombstones and on dignified

sepulchral slabs let into the church walls. They may now be
the names of the village blacksmith and baker and sweep,
and no longer to be found at the "Big House"—which is
likely enough in alien hands—but they are names which
belong to the village, and have belonged for an astonishing
number of centuries.

In the middle of the last century that well-known Sussex
historian, William Durrant Cooper, said "that in no part
of England has there been less change in the names of persons
and places since the days of the Heptarchy than in the county
of Sussex."

These names are predominantly Saxon. The names of
rivers and of certain prominent natural features are still
retained from the ancient British ones—these the Saxon conquerors did not alter. The Danes who came after them have
not left much impress on Sussex—its geographical position
was a little too far round the south coast to be very comfortable or safe for them. There are certain Danish-derived
names in Sussex, as Dancworth and Danny, a couple of Dane
Hills and a Dane Wood, and round Hastings there are
Danish traces.

Such a meagre list shows how small was the mark made
here by the Danes, while the name of almost any ancient
village picked at random from the map of Sussex will betray
its Saxon origin. The fabric on which all later Sussex history
was stitched is Saxon, and it persists beneath all the designs
which have been later sewn into it. Also it persists in the
physical type of numbers of the native-born. "About Chichester," says one writer, "the old South Saxon type—tall, spare,
blue-eyed and fair-haired—still meets one at every turn,
scarcely modified by the flux of a dozen centuries."

And it is not only about Chichester but in the deep Weald
and in the villages on the edge of the Downs that one may
meet a cowman, or a wagoner, or a man in the coppice
making hurdles, who is as Saxon as his ancestor who maybe
fought at Hastings. And if you can induce him to open his
slow lips for more than a brief "Good day," it will be something not far removed from Saxon speech that you will hear.
In unspoiled and remote parts, the older people still use the
Saxon form of plural, as in the famous "Three ghostesses

a-sitting on postesses." In his *Dictionary of the Sussex Dialect*
W. A. Parish said : ". . . it will be observed that most of
our words now in common use, denoting agricultural and
domestic implements, are either to be traced to an Anglo-
Saxon derivation or actually retain their original Anglo-
Saxon names in all purity of spelling and pronunciation.
From this source also nearly all the Sussex surnames and
names of villages and farms are derived."

But, unhappily, education and the wireless are killing these
ancient dialects as hard as they can. Still, though the native
speech in this present age of enlightenment may be standar-
dized away, the names of places, of villages and fields and
farms are happily tougher after so many centuries, and are
not in the same danger. It is a sign of the natural continuity
of agricultural life that, as Durrant Cooper said, "a large
proportion of the oldest enclosures hold to this day the
names given by Saxon cultivators." In a paper he wrote on
this subject in an early volume of the *Sussex Archæological
Collections* he said :

"We cannot take up an apportionment for the tithe-rent
charge in any parish without being struck with the many
Saxon names retained. . . . The Saxon language and the
Saxon names, and in the main, the Saxon blood remain in
Sussex almost unchanged in the nineteenth as they did in the
ninth century."

Eddius, a much earlier writer belonging to the eighth
century, described Sussex as a territory "which has impreg-
nably resisted the attacks of other provinces owing to the
difficulty of the terrain and the density of the woods."

There are certain terminations to place-names which show
their Saxon origin. The Norman Conquest made practically
no difference to the names of places already existent in Saxon
times—the "resistant county" resisted any change in the
names of its villages and hamlets and fields, and the Domesday surveyors accepted—though often puzzled as to the
spelling—the uncouth syllables presented to their Norman
ears. Modifications have, of course, taken place in the
passage of centuries, but it is in the termination of place-
names that the Saxon origin is generally seen. The principal
Saxon endings are *ing*, meaning a meadow, but also, and

64

more generally, the people of some Saxon leader, as Fletching, the people of Flecci; Ditchling, the people of Dicul; Poynings, the people of Puna. Sometimes to this termination was added another, as in Chiltington, which meant the people of Cilta's *tun* or enclosure. Other endings are *ingham, ington, ton, ham, field, fold, hurst, den, lye* and *worth*—the last four meaning settlements in forests.

All dwellers near the Downs are familiar with the word *borstal*, meaning a way up the Downs, and often named from the nearest village at its foot, as Ditchling Borstal or Washington Borstal. It is derived from the Saxon words *beohr*, meaning hill, and *stigele*, a steep ascent.

The origin and meaning of place-names is a fascinating study, which is only of late years receiving full and serious attention. It is not only Saxon names that are full of interest, little kernels of history, but also those of much later centuries.

12

The Saxons not only left their place-names scattered about Sussex from the earlier-settled southern parts to the later-settled wooded Weald and northern portions of the county, but in the course of the several centuries they were dominant here they dropped a considerable number of coins about. Often they are found singly—anyone digging his garden may turn up a Saxon coin—and sometimes in hoards. There is always something of tragedy in the discovery of a buried hoard, for it is so obvious that the owner, who must have buried it in fear of some disaster, never came back to claim it. The story of the finding of one Saxon hoard will suffice. It was at a farm called Chancton Farm, a mile or so to the north of Chanctonbury Ring, on land that had once belonged to King Harold's brother Earl Gurth, that the hoard was discovered a few days before Christmas, 1866. Once more it was the "useful plough" that unearthed the crock in which the coins had been buried. The coins were scattered all about, and the ploughman and other farm labourers picked them up in hundreds. As they were not current coin of the realm they were not regarded as of any value except as

F

West Dean. Church and Medieval Vicarage

curiosities, and as such for a few days, while the interest was fresh, the landlord of the Washington Inn accepted a dozen as payment for a quart of beer. But the news of the discovery got about in more educated circles, and the postmaster of Washington and the vicar of Parham rescued one thousand seven hundred and twenty coins, which proved to be pennies of Edward the Confessor and Harold. The original hoard is supposed to have been nearly double the seventeen hundred which were eventually sent to the British Museum.

Many of these coins were minted at Steyning, not far away from the scene of the discovery. There were also Sussex mints in Saxon times at Lewes, Hastings and Chichester. The pennies of Harold, minted at Steyning and Lewes, have all the air of a portrait, showing him in left profile, crowned and sceptred, with a neat curly beard and moustache and a large, though in the Lewes example, somewhat sly-looking eye. In the Steyning coinage he appears definitely kingly.

There is an odd little legend, which has all the appearance of folk-memory, in connection with these coins. So long ago as 1868 and so recently as 1925 this legend has been vouched for by responsible persons. It is that on the site of the discovery, called Gurth's Barn, though there is no barn there now, the figure of a very aged man with a long white beard has occasionally been seen, from "time-everlasting-beyond," wandering with head bent to the ground as if searching for some lost treasure.

13

The connection of Harold, the last of the Saxon kings, with Sussex, both at Bosham and at Hastings, is too well known to need describing. But an earlier king, of whom we know much more than of Harold, King Alfred, had also links with Sussex. In the eastern parts of the county, at the back of Eastbourne, there is a little lost hamlet, happily untouched by the finger of progress—that bad fairy at the christening of beauty—which has a most interesting connection with Alfred. This is West Dean—there is another West Dean in the west of Sussex, with which it must not be confused, and also two East Deans in each end of Sussex, a rather puzzling arrangement which suggests a time when the inhabitants did not wander far from their birthplaces. The story is told of a Sussex man who, having quarrelled with his wife, to mark his displeasure took the unprecedented course of going to stay with a relative a few miles away. But very soon he came back, saying that in spite of his wife's temper he would rather be at home, as he could not stand "foreign parts."

West Dean is believed to be the place where King Alfred had a manor-house, and where Asser, who was to be his biographer, saw him for the first time. Bishop Asser describes the meeting :

"In those days did the King call me unto him and I came from the uttermost part of Britain. So I set my face to go unto him through many a long mile, and came even unto the land of the Saxons who dwell to the right which in Saxon speech is called Sudsexe. And there in a town royal that is called Dene, first did I see him, and full royal was his welcome."

It is possible that the remains of the ancient manor-house there may be actually on the site of Alfred's palace.

West Dean can claim to possess in its Parsonage House one of the oldest continuously inhabited houses in the county —a thirteenth-century dwelling of stone and flint, with immensely thick walls containing a narrow spiral stairway, great beams and deeply splayed lancet windows, still possessing the oaken shutters which closed them when glass was too costly for a "pore parsoun."

As a residence it is somewhat dark and narrow, but it is good to know that it is still lived in and cared for and that within its most ancient walls books and flowers and fires still make it a home.

King Alfred held lands at Lullington and Sutton near by, and these lands and "Dene" were bequeathed in his will. He also possessed lands at Ditchling in the centre of Sussex, which he left to his nephew Osferth. The names of Court Farm and Court Gardens Farm in that village perpetuate a long-past connection with that very Christian king.

The Saxons, as Saxons, are gone, absorbed into the soil of Sussex, their blood mingled with that of earlier and later races, but their characteristics and colouring, in many cases hardly modified, are still to be seen in Sussex fields and villages. But the people who were the last to become Christians in this kingdom have left scattered about the county they named many relics in stone which are unaltered since the Saxon mason's hand fashioned them. Worth, that remarkable church, has been described and Sompting, but there are many other specimens of Saxon stonework worth a pilgrimage.

It is well to remember that when these early churches were in the building the tower was specially designed for a refuge and a stronghold, and that in later times, when the original nave and chancel were often altered, and added to, the tower was, as often as not, left untouched and so still speaks a more primitive architectural tongue than the rest of the fabric. Early Saxon towers, in order to repel attack, were often built with no external door and could only be entered from within the church. This was so at Bosham and Sompting. Sometimes the priest had his dwelling in the tower, reaching his simple cell by means of a ladder and a doorway—at Bosham and Singleton these doorways can be seen. There are some fine Saxon external doorways in Sussex and they may be found in an almost perfect condition at the churches of Bosham, Bolney, Friston, Hangleton—that strange lonely church of the Downs—Horsted-Keynes, Lurgashall, Slaugham, Stopham, Old Shoreham, Lyminster, Wivelsfield and Worth. At Lewes, against the east end wall of the ugly modern church of St. John-sub-Castro, is a beautiful Saxon doorway which was saved when the old edifice was destroyed. The design of this door is worth looking at with its moulded arch and imposts. Bolney Church has a south door and Wivelsfield a north door (not in its original position) which are fine examples of Saxon arches moulded in two orders, and so alike that they suggest the same mason's handiwork.

Saxon doorways are usually narrow in proportion to their

height, and have not the broad bowed massiveness of the
Norman archway. This can be seen clearly, as in an architectural primer, at Lyminster Church, where a Norman doorway has replaced a Saxon one, but the graceful Saxon arch
is still visible above the squatter Norman one.

Besides the notable Saxon chancel arch at Worth there
are unspoiled ones at Bosham, Botolphs, Buncton, Chithurst,
Clayton, Ford, Lyminster, Ovingdean, Selham and West
Hampnett. Rumboldswyke had a Saxon arch built entirely
of Roman bricks—shameful as it is to tell, this unique record
of two successive civilizations was completely destroyed.

Clayton Church, set in its curiously remote little village
at the foot of the Downs, under the windmills, Jack and Jill,
which are such a landmark for miles around, has a plain and
perfect Saxon chancel arch, which harmonizes austerely with
that simple, aloof little church, still set in a quiet rural scene
where nothing speedier than a cow walks the lanes, in spite
of its perilous proximity to the railway line rushing to
Brighton. Another unspoiled Saxon arch is that of the church
at Selham. Clayton is plain, Selham is ornate, but singularly
graceful with its interlaced carvings on the capitals.

These are some of the treasures our Saxon ancestors have
left us in Sussex in the "heathen kingdom" that so late
became Christian.

CHAPTER IV

SELIG SUSSEX

1

SELIG is a Saxon word meaning holy or blessed. Inevitably it has degenerated into "silly" in the course of many centuries, and has been thrown at the Sussex country people as an expression of contempt—silly Sussex. But it used to be "Holy Sussex."

The one Sussex legend known to every Brighton weekender is that the devil was so annoyed by the number of churches in Sussex that he attempted to cut his great dyke through the Downs in order to let the sea rush into the Weald to drown them.

It is true that Christianity came late to Sussex—another sign of the remote and cut-off nature of the county in early centuries—and the heathen dwellers on the Sussex coast were so ignorant both of heavenly wisdom and early common sense that St. Wilfrid found the poor creatures linking hands and wading into the sea to drown themselves, as they were starving and did not know how to fish. Like the wise man he was —the English saints from St. Cuthman to St. Thomas More have always had their feet firmly fixed on the earth, no matter how heavenly their contemplations—he first taught them how to feed their bodies, before he dealt with their spiritual salvation. The peculiarly English quality and kindliness of this early Sussex saint (for Sussex he is by adoption, though not by birth) is enchantingly conveyed in that story of Rudyard Kipling's in *Rewards and Fairies* called "The Conversion of St. Wilfrid." Eddi the priest and Padda the seal are both very real in that story. There were seals then in that region of Manhood End of Selsey—for the name means Seals' Island.

St. Wilfrid holds first place among the Sussex saints, for it was he who converted and baptized the heathen people of Sussex. St. Wilfrid is not a native of the county; at the most

70

he spent but five years of his life here, but those five years were so important to the land of the South Saxons that St. Wilfrid, who was actually Bishop of York, has come to be regarded as a Sussex saint.

His first visit to Sussex was accidental, and he was received with most discourteous violence by the heathen inhabitants. Wilfrid was returning from Compiègne, where he had been consecrated by twelve bishops, when a great storm arose and cast his ship upon the "unkind country of the South Saxons," and by an unusual ebb of the sea was left stranded there. The inhabitants rushed to the shore to plunder and slay, while one of their priests of Baal stood upon a hill to curse. Though the people with Wilfrid were but few compared with the natives, they managed to beat them off, and at the turn of the tide their vessel floated off. Eddi describes this adventure in his *Vita Wilfridi,* saying how Wilfrid ". . . prayed to the Lord his God, who immediately ordered the sea to return a full hour before its wont. So that when the heathen, on the arrival of their king, were preparing for a fourth attack with all their forces, the rising sea covered with its waves the whole of the shore, and floated the ship, which sailed into the deep. But, greatly glorified by God, and returning Him thanks, with a south wind they reached Sandwich, a harbour of safety."

Years went by and St. Wilfrid's tremendous energy in the service of God was fully employed in preaching and building in his vast diocese of York. As Father Faber said of him :

"God gave him no rest; the saint sought it not, lived it not; rest did not suit him; peace is out of place here, for if we have too much of it now we have less of it hereafter."

St. Wilfrid's life was one of toils and effort and journeys. He was pursued by strife and jealousy. He only escaped martyrdom in his youth because his persecutors thought him too beautiful to slay. He was imprisoned by one Saxon king, who would have murdered him had he dared. His bishopric of York was torn from him and dismembered, and he was finally driven forth an exile from his northern diocese. It was in his wanderings that he eventually came to Sussex, and for five years found a refuge there—perhaps the most peaceful time in all his stormy life. The roughness of his first reception was atoned.

When St. Wilfrid came to Sussex this second time the South Saxons were in a very sad way—still heathen, except for a handful of monks at Bosham, though the rest of the Heptarchy was converted to Christianity. This was, of course, partly owing to the geological manner in which Sussex was cut off from the surrounding kingdoms.

Eddi, the faithful clerk and precentor and biographer of St. Wilfrid, said that Sussex was full of woods and natural ramparts and much severed from the rest of the world.

The date of St. Wilfrid's coming to Sussex is usually given as the year 680. For some years before he came Sussex had suffered from a devastating drought, the crops were dried up and withered, the cattle dead. A great famine was over the land and the people were in such despair that in groups of fifty at a time they took hands and waded into the sea to drown themselves, or jumped from the heights of the chalk cliffs. Into this hopeless scene came St. Wilfrid to preach Christ's gospel, and as he preached a gentle healing rain began to fall. After three years of drought this was miracle enough to make the Saxons desert their hard-hearted heathen gods. But there still remained the question of feeding them, for even the beneficent rain will not produce crops till the proper processes of nature have their due time. But Sussex has a long sea-coast and in the sea are fish. St. Wilfrid found the people were so ignorant that they did not even know how to fish, save for a few poor pond eels. So this fisher of men went down to the seashore with a large net which he had caused to be made, and casting the net into the waters it brought forth a great draught of fishes—thus, in a very biblical manner showing the people that there was abundant store of food for them on their own coasts.

"By this benefit," says Bede in his *Ecclesiastical History*, "Bishop Wilfrid gained the affections of them all, and they began the more readily at his preaching to hope for heavenly goods, seeing that by his help they had received those that are temporal."

He built a monastery—St. Wilfrid was a great builder—on the peninsula of Selsey, the Island of Seals, near Bosham, on land given him by the Saxon king. This land, Bede says, was "compassed round about by the sea except on the west side, where it had an entry into it of about a stone's throw."

There he dwelt with Eddi and his four other priests who shared his exile—Eappa, Eadda, Padda and Burghelm. One of his earliest acts was to baptize and free all the slaves who went with the Selsey lands which had been bestowed upon him by the recently converted Saxon king Ethelwalch. Thus St. Wilfrid became, in Faber's words, "master of all the hearts of all the Sussex men."

He was the first Bishop of Sussex, and his cathedral of Selsey came long before the "heaven y-pointing" spire of Chichester.

But St. Wilfrid was not to end his days in Sussex. In the year 685 his patron, King Ethelwalch, was slain in battle by Ceadwalla, who thereupon became king. The fierce Ceadwalla was a pagan, but St. Wilfrid performed another miracle in converting him, and as a sign of gratitude the king conferred on the bishop as a gift the little town of Paganham in Sussex. St. Wilfrid obtained certain freedoms for his little town—that no castle should be built to dominate it, that the inhabitants should not be taxed for the upkeep of the bridges and should not be pressed for military service. In confirmation of this charter, "I," declared Ceadwalla, "have put a turf of the said ground upon the holy altar of our Saviour, and by reason of my ignorance in writing my name I have expressed and subscribed the sign of the Holy Cross."

Father Faber may be quoted in his attractive account of this demesne of St. Wilfrid's in Sussex :

"For many a year how many a mouth blessed Wilfrid in the little town of Paganham? When the lights twinkled in the windows on a winter's night, to a passing traveller those straggling streets of Paganham might look like any other town; but it was not so; the Church had touched the town, and a very chrism of pure and simple-minded happiness was outpoured upon it. No stern castle frowned with its deep machicolations from the summit of the hill, but the sheep browsed there, and the children played there, and there were the blue sky above, and the sweet unhindered breezes. No rude retainers, no debauched soldiers spread dismay and sin

73

among the peaceable inhabitants; no unmannerly officers of the king raised cruel levies for the bridges which the swollen brooks had forced away in the last rains; and the young men followed the plough and washed the sheep, and married early, and so had married sons to give a home to their grey hairs, and all because youths were not pressed for the royal army. What deep, yet hardly conscious happiness—for happiness is not deep when it is conscious—was there by the firesides of Paganham; and had you seen the children playing on the hill, where the castle *would* have been and was not, and had asked their Christian names, how many, think you, would have answered—'Wilfrid'? Not a few."

2

St. Wilfrid's cathedral has, for many centuries, been under the sea, and the fishermen, whose ancestors he first taught their skill, fish above its shattered walls. Nobody knows what the first cathedral church in Sussex was like, but Hexham in Northumberland remains to show that Wilfrid belonged to the race of great churchbuilders. Camden, in his *Britannia*, has the picturesque statement that the "ancient little citie where the bishops had their seat, hidden quite with water at every tide, but at low water evident and plaine to be seen." If so the tides have changed since Camden's day, for no tide now uncovers that ancient cathedral city, though fragments and relics have been fished up from the sea bottom. The most important of these fragments are two richly carved stone panels which are now in Chichester Cathedral. They are each about six feet square, and one shows Christ with Martha and Mary, and the other a scene from the raising of Lazarus. The carving, though early and archaic, is remarkably skilled and full of grace. Another recovered relic is a holy water stoup, now in the chapel of Arundel Castle. And there is always the possibility that the sea may yet yield some further treasure.

The sea has greatly changed all this southernmost part of Sussex that St. Wilfrid knew so well. The fishermen sail over what is still called The Park, and Seals' Island is now part of the Manhood Peninsula. Sunken church bells are said to ring from the watery depths, and when the sea mists come down and enshroud these low-lying lands which seem partly made of water, St. Wilfrid might still walk here and feel himself at home. It is a special part of Sussex, with an atmosphere and skies all its own.

St. Wilfrid's name must always be specially cherished in Sussex, as it was he—of whom Eddi said so simply that he was "affable to all, penetrating in mind, strong in body, expert at all good works, never with a sour face"—who first brought Christianity to the "unkind county" and made it into Selig Sussex.

3

Bosham, with its little colony of monks who upheld the flickering light of Christianity in the Sussex darkness before the dawn that St. Wilfrid brought, has many religious tales to tell. It has associations with King Canute, one of whose daughters, "a lady of surpassing beauty," took the veil in a convent in Bruges, while another daughter died for her faith.

But Bosham's particular link is with another daughter of Canute, who died as a child when her royal parents were residing at Bosham, and was buried in the Saxon church there. This story is particularly interesting, for it is an outstanding example of the persistence through centuries of tradition, and its final discovery to be historic truth—so deep an impress had the death of a child princess made on the minds and memories of Sussex villagers. Every visitor to Bosham has heard the story but not so many have heard the first-hand account of the finding of the coffin of Canute's daughter. This is set forth fully in an early volume (for the year 1866) of the *Sussex Archæological Collections*. The story is told by the Rev. Henry Mitchell. He says that "the fact of the interment of Canute's child within their ancient church was never for one moment doubted by the people of Bosham, and when the opportunity offered I was resolved to test the truth of the tradition."

The floor of the church was taken up near the traditional spot on August the 4th, 1865, and among the people present were Edgar Varley, an artist, and a surgeon from Chichester. "I directed the masons who were at work in the church," Mr Mitchell writes, "to sound the spot which tradition had pointed out as the site of the child's grave. The iron bar at once struck upon a stone, and on removing the mould which covered it a stone coffin was presented to our delighted gaze. The mason in raising the lid, which was firmly fixed to the coffin by concrete, broke it in two places; but when it was raised the remains of the child were distinctly visible, and Mr Varley at once made a most correct and careful drawing of the coffin and its contents. . . . From the size of the body the child must have been, as handed down by tradition, about eight years of age at the time of her decease.

"In fact tradition is verified as to the exact spot of the interment and as to the remains being those of a child; the stone coffin also corresponds in rudeness of style with coffins of Canute's period; and the piscina which still exists appears to have belonged to the altar before which masses were said on behalf of the soul of the young princess."

That is the first-hand account of the opening of the coffin of Canute's little daughter, nearly 850 years after the burial. It is sufficiently remarkable—but Sussex has an even more remarkable story of an historic coffin, which will be told in due course.

Bosham is commonly believed to be the seashore on which Canute gave his courtiers a lesson on the limitations of kingly power. Other counties may claim their coasts as the scene of this famous moral lesson, but Sussex people have no hesitation in placing it at Bosham.

4

After the life of St. Wilfrid, crowded with so many services to God, so many toils and tribulations, in contact with so many kings and prelates—his years in Sussex being almost the only ones in which his life was in any way secluded—it is a great contrast to turn to the life of another Sussex saint. St. Cuthman is as simple as a folk-tale, and has much the same quality. There is a peculiar pleasure in associating these stories with the Sussex fields, for they fit perfectly into the rural scene.

St. Cuthman had an old mother who had lost the use of her legs, and her excellent son pushed her about in a wheelbarrow—no doubt of a similar pattern to the wheelbarrows still used to hold the swept-up autumn leaves in many a Sussex garden to-day. He took his mother with him everywhere, for she was lonely when he was at his work of shepherding. One of St. Cuthman's earliest miracles was connected with sheep—when for any reason he had to leave them unguarded, he drew a circle round them with his crook and in the Holy Name charged them to remain within it.

One day when St. Cuthman was pulling his mother along the Sussex apology for a road, the ropes attached to her wheelbarrow broke just as he came by a field full of haymakers. The saint picked some twigs of elder from a bush and turned them into a rough withy. The haymakers laughed at him for this and at his queer conveyance of his mother, and because of this a great flood of rain came down and ruined the hay. Ever since then it has always rained at haymaking in that particular field, so the story tells us.

It was supernaturally conveyed to St. Cuthman that wherever his elder-withy broke he was to stay and build his church. This happened at what is now Steyning. "A place," says the old record, "lying at the base of a lofty hill, then woody, overgrown with brambles and bushes . . . enclosed between two streams springing from the hill above."

The church at Steyning is situated at the fork of two rivulets, and is probably on the actual site of the little wooden church built by St. Cuthman.

While the little wooden church was building certain constructional difficulties cropped up which somewhat discouraged the simple saint, till a stranger appeared and told him how to remedy the trouble, saying, "Nothing is wanting to those that fear the Lord." Cuthman, overcome with awe, besought the stranger to tell him whom he was. "I am He," was the answer, "in whose name thou buildest this temple."

St. Cuthman was buried in the church he had built and is regarded as the tutelary saint of Steyning. When Steyning was a port it was called Portus Cuthmanni. Not only St.

Cuthman, but King Ethelwulf, father of Alfred the Great, are buried at Steyning, and Mark Antony Lower in his *Worthies of Sussex* has this pleasing paragraph about them :

"Among the rock-work of the vicarage garden at Steyning are two stones with incised crosses of a very rude and archaic character, which were dug up some years ago from what had been the foundations of the church, to the westward of the existing portion of the structure. There is architectural proof that they must have been deposited there as mere material in the twelfth century, when the present church was erected. It may be asking too much of the reader to consider these two rough and battered old stones as memorials of an Anglo-Saxon saint and an Anglo-Saxon king; but if he should choose to regard them as the gravestones of the holy Cuthman and the royal sire of Alfred, I shall not find fault."

5

Among the Sussex saints there is the redoubtable St. Dunstan, who was not only a saint, but a craftsman and apparently possessed of that somewhat rare quality among saints, a sense of humour. It was a useful quality in dealing with that remarkably gullible personage, the devil. St. Dunstan was a skilful worker in metals; he could make a golden chalice or an iron horseshoe. He had a little forge near by the church he had built at Mayfield—that most picturesque little Sussex town set on its hilly ridge, with its long street adorned with fine timber houses with wavy old roofs and an iron pump for water on the edge of the footway halfway up the street.

The story is—a well-known Sussex story—that St. Dunstan was working one day in his little smithy when the devil, disguised as an attractive damsel, with evil intentions entered upon him. But with his usual carelessness the devil allowed a cloven hoof to be glimpsed beneath his skirt, which St. Dunstan's sharp eye immediately perceived. Without a moment's hesitation the saint picked up his tongs, which fortunately were red-hot, and clapped them firmly on the devil's nose, who, restored to his natural ugliness, fled with a howl of rage to Tunbridge Wells to cool the inflamed organ in the spring there.

These same tongs may be seen at the Convent of Mayfield. In that charming old book, Louis Jennings' *Field Paths and Green Lanes in Surrey and Sussex*, he gives rather a nice little account of inspecting these tongs of St. Dunstan's, which "may be seen," he says, "in the 'Palace' in Mayfield, now a nunnery. One of the sisters showed them to me only a few weeks ago; how could I doubt any longer? The iron is worn with time and seems still to bear traces of the desperate struggle of nine hundred years, for it is nearly as long as that since St. Dunstan lived at Mayfield.

" 'These are the tongs with which St. Dunstan worked his miracle,' said the worthy sister.

" 'I have read of the legend in my book,' said I, meaning no offence.

" 'It is not a legend,' replied the sister in a tone of slight reproof.

" 'No, no,' said I. 'I did not mean to throw any doubt upon the story.' "

Jennings says of St. Dunstan's little town :

"Mayfield is one of the haunted places of Sussex. Many are the signs and wonders which have been seen there. Ghosts are still said to appear in some of the old houses in the neighbourhood, and the stranger is half inclined to believe that the ancient forge at the entrance to the village is the very one in or near which St. Dunstan performed his famous miracle."

What is now the convent at Mayfield has but come back full circle to the hands of its ancient owners. It was the Palace of pre-Reformation Archbishops of Canterbury, but at the Reformation passed into secular possession, as did so much of the property of Holy Church. The noble chapel— and to see it a-flutter with nuns in the incomparable dignity of habit and veil on such an occasion as the Good Friday Stations of the Cross is to have a lovely memory—was once a banqueting hall and then fell to partial ruin and was un-roofed to the sky, and ivy and moss clambered and clung on what are now once more internal walls, and weather left stains on the ashlar which still show rather strangely against the embroidered hangings and vestments in the soft light of candles.

6

From the beauty and dignity of the Palace of the Arch-bishops of Canterbury, it is a far cry to the humble abodes of the pre-Reformation celibate priests scattered here and there still visible about the villages of Sussex, in some cases merely a sparse room in the church tower. At Lindfield there is such a one, and still preserved there is a dried-up mummified sod of grass which was the priest's kneeling cushion.

At Alfriston there is a very famous Priest's House. This old and humble house was on the very edge of final decay, full of holes where birds and vegetation crept through, its thatch fallen, its beams exposed, when it was rescued. It was bought by the National Trust—it was the first property pur-chased by the Trust after its incorporation in 1907. It was bought for the absurd sum of £10, but £350 was spent on restoring it—and well spent. It is "an ancient vicarage of post and panel, a specimen of the lowly abodes with which our pre-Reformation clergy often contented themselves."

When Louis Jennings went to visit it during his Sussex pilgrimage he found an old woman living there by herself who gave him the surprising historical information that she "had heard say that the Popes of Rome did use to live here."

This thirteenth-century Clergy House is particularly in-teresting as, unlike so many buildings of an early date, it has not been altered from its original construction by the addi-tion of a second story. It still retains its humble clay floor, and the roof timbers are still blackened by the hearth soot. To stand under those sooty timbers at dusk, in that bare earthen-floored little house-place, is to be conscious of a curiously close contact with the past.

The lines written by Bishop Hall at the beginning of the fifteenth century about a labourer's dwelling would not be

80

very out of scale if applied to many a priest's house of the same, or an earlier, period :

Of one bay's breadth, God wot ! a silly cote,
Whose thatched sparres are furr'd with sluttish soot
A whole inch thick, shining like blackmoor's brows,
Through smok that down the head-less barrel blows.

But even less luxurious were the dwellings of anchorites, and of these Sussex had several, both men and women, immured in their cells adjoining the church of their choice; in many cases their only communication with the world a little window where food was handed to them, and the window or "squint" through which they beheld the altar. This was for the sterner type of anchorite—some of the anchoresses, though cutting themselves off from the world and never leaving their dwellings clinging to the walls of the church, yet lived there in some comfort and even had the attendance of a maid—such was the anchoress whose cell and whose bones were discovered in the course of some alterations to St. Anne's beautiful church on the hill at Lewes. Her existence was known because St. Richard, Bishop of Chichester, made her a gift in his will. But it was not till the recent alterations to the vestry of St. Anne's that the discovery of her grave, close to the squint through which she beheld the high altar and heard Mass, was made.

Another Lewes anchorite was the mysterious Magnus, whose story in stone may be seen set into the walls of the ugly, modern church of St. John-sub-Castro. The old church of that name, as Camden tells us, was "a little one, desolate and overgrown with brambles." But that church, as Mark Antony Lower, writing in 1865, says, was "an edifice of high antiquity, which modern necessities and modern bad taste have replaced by a hybrid structure—half-castle, half-barn." It was only owing to Lower's urgent efforts that the Magnus stones were saved from destruction and built into the walls of the present unattractive church bearing the old name of St. John-sub-Castro, so called from being sunk close below the steep of Lewes Castle. Sussex owes a great debt to her mid-nineteenth-century archæologists and antiquaries—with-

The Church, Lullington. This is the Chancel of the original Church

out them we should have been robbed of much that we now cherish.

The translation of the inscription cut upon the two half-circles of stone says :

"Here is immured a Soldier of the Royal Family of Denmark; whose name, Magnus, indicates his distinguished lineage : Relinquishing his greatness, he assumes the deportment of a lamb, and exchanges for a life of ambition that of a humble anchorite."

Nobody knows who Magnus really was, and probably from that ignorance sprang the legend that he was the son of Harold slain at Hastings, or even—based on the statement of Giraldus Cambrensis that Harold survived the battle —that here the last Saxon king immured himself until his death.

7

Anyone who goes down the steep natural hill on which Lewes stands, crowned by the artificial mounds of the Keep and the Brack Mount, and proceeds to Southover, that gracious old suburb of the county town, and then walks along a little way past St. John's fine red-brick tower and turns to the left where there is a bridge and a curious stream, will come to a wicket-gate. This is the entrance to the ruins of the Priory of St. Pancras—all that is left of the largest, as it is believed, and most beautiful ecclesiastical building that Sussex has ever known. But the largeness and the beauty have to be imagined—this is no Fountains Abbey, still visible and noble, even though cruelly damaged by the tooth of time. But it was not time, but the hand of man which so reduced to crumbled stone that great Priory of St. Pancras.

The building of this Priory was due to the piety of the first Lord of Lewes after the Conquest, William de Warenne, and his lady Gundrada. It is a tradition that Gundrada was a daughter of the Conqueror. Some historians believe this, and some flatly deny it. Mark Antony Lower said : "Gundrada was the fifth daughter of William the Conqueror by his wife Matilda of Flanders. This statement has been strongly and elaborately contradicted; but there is no reasonable doubt on the subject."

This surely may be admitted when it is realized that the foundation charter of Lewes Priory states Gundrada to have been the daughter of Queen Matilda, and that in the charter bestowing the Manor of Walton in Norfolk on Lewes Priory, King William himself describes Gundrada, wife of William de Warenne, as his daughter.

The great Earl de Warenne so stamped his name and his works upon his castle and town of Lewes that no one to-day can walk there without feeling the weight of him. But in time he wearied of the deeds of war, or maybe felt the burden of some sin pressing upon his conscience, and desired to put himself right with God. In that age and for many later centuries, men who wished to expiate the evil they had done went on pilgrimages, or built a church—sometimes the building of a bridge would suffice. But William de Warenne was a great lord in Sussex, and he intended to build a great church. So he and his wife Gundrada went on a pilgrimage to Rome, but were unable to reach there. But they visited the great Abbey of Cluny in Burgundy and were so impressed with its holiness and discipline that they decided the Priory they would build at Lewes should be a Cluniac foundation.

In the charter of the Priory the Earl de Warenne himself wrote of their pilgrimage : "We turned to the Monastery of Cluny, a great and holy abbey in honour of St. Peter, and there we adored and sought St. Peter. And, because we found the sanctity, the religion, and the charity so great there, and the honour towards us from the good Prior and all the holy convent who received us into their society of fraternity, we began to have a love and devotion towards the Order, and to that house above all other houses which we had seen."

When they returned to Sussex they proceeded to carry out their pious intention, by building on the southward sloping meadows at the foot of the hill on which Lewes stands, in what is now called Southover.

In time this church and monastery was to become one of the most important and richly endowed in the whole realm of England. The first monks and the first Prior, Lanzo—a very holy man of whom it was said that his work "so ennobled Lewes with the grace of monastic reverence that it might be justly declared the peculiar habitation of virtue"—came from Cluny. The Priory, the date of its foundation being 1077, was dedicated to St. Pancras, who ever since has maintained his hold on the Catholic life of Lewes.

8

Having by this pious act made their peace with heaven, in due course the Earl and the Countess came to die. She died in 1085 in child-bed and he followed her three years later. They were both buried in Lewes Priory. There they lay in quietude till the time came that the Priory was in 1537 practically razed to the ground by Henry VIII's myrmidon, Thomas Cromwell. Then, when the ruins had become overgrown and half-forgotten in the course of three more centuries, they were rediscovered when the railway to Lewes was made in 1845. Subsequent excavations, combined with certain letters and documents of Portinari, the Italian who was commissioned by Cromwell to bring down to the dust those noble walls, have given a more complete idea of what that great Cluniac Priory was like before royal greed and impiety destroyed it.

The church was four hundred and twenty feet long and sixty-nine feet wide, and the stately nave had a north and south transept, while the apsidal eastern end was adorned with a crown of seven chapels. Besides the great church, there was a separate chapel attached to the large hall of the Infirmary. There were also the Chapter House, and the Frater, and the Dorter, and the Rere Dorter, and the Warming House; the kitchens and cellars; the cloisters and fish ponds and gardens.

Remembering all this magnificence of building, of ashlar and carved stones—many fragments of which are now preserved in the Barbican House Museum, and many more fragments of which are embedded in existing walls and houses in Lewes, let us now go through that little wicket-gate in Southover which leads to all that remains of Lewes Priory. There in a flat rough meadow will be seen a few tumbled grey stones, a broken bit of spiral stairway ascending to the sky, a portion of old wall draped in ivy that rustles and swings in the wind. This is all that is left of the great Cluniac Priory of St. Pancras. It is strangely pathetic and desolate, the stones in many cases, owing to the staunchness of the mortar, still clinging together in clotted lumps, though tumbled sideways into holes in the earth. One of the old altars, where once shone the candles of the Mass, is still standing. But unless instructed by the excellent guide to the ruins written by Mr Walter H. Godfrey—who has done so much in this and other ways to teach Sussex people to value their heritage—it is not easy to perceive in these confused-looking stones what a splendour of ecclesiastical building was once here.

The fury of destruction which fell upon this Priory of Lewes is almost unknown elsewhere in the many other places which suffered at the Dissolution of the Monasteries. And the smug satisfaction with which it was done adds the final touch of ugliness. Henry VIII bestowed Lewes Priory on Thomas, Lord Cromwell, and he sent down to Sussex the Italian Portinari to superintend and hasten the destruction. Portinari wrote obsequious letters from Lewes to his master, describing the progress of the work. In the first one he says that the church is "in size, length and bigness," much greater than he had expected. "Notwithstanding," he says piously, "with the help of God we make no kind of doubt that all can be pulled down to the ground, even were it twice as much." In a later letter he says triumphantly, "All this, in the name of God, and with a good beginning, is plucked to the ground and was thrown down in two turns which was on Thursday and Friday last."

Portinari brought with him from London carpenters, masons, plumbers and blacksmiths for the demolition, declaring that they were "much better than other men that we find here in the country."

So at least we may be glad to know that it was not Sussex men who pulled down this noble Sussex Priory.

Cromwell had the Prior's lodging converted into a residence for himself—but destiny did not give him much time in which to enjoy the Sussex air, and after his execution in

1540 his estates were forfeit to the Crown. With certain reservations to the King, the land and buildings within the Priory walls, some twenty acres, were leased to a yeoman farmer. During his time and thereafter for numberless years, the ruins, the massive ruins, of the Priory buildings became a quarry for whoever in the region of Lewes would build himself either a mansion or a pigsty, and what was left became clothed with earth and vegetation, and passed out of memory. Then in 1845 the new railway from Brighton to Lewes cut athwart the centre of the ruins.

9

And now comes the strange part of this story in so far as concerns the founders of Lewes Priory, the Earl and Countess de Warenne. They had died within three years of each other and been buried before the high altar, as befitted their benefactions and their rank. But at some time unknown, during the many rebuilding and enlarging operations which took place in the church and conventual buildings during the twelfth and thirteenth centuries, their bones were gathered up and placed in two three-foot leaden caskets and reburied in the Chapter House. There they remained undisturbed through all Portinari's destructive fury, till the picks of the railway navvies discovered them in the middle of the nineteenth century. Over Gundrada's tomb was a beautifully carved marble slab, which was removed at the downfall of the Priory, though the leaden cist was untouched, and cast aside. Later this marble slab was used as a gravestone at another place in Sussex. Years afterwards, when its true history was discovered, it was restored to the bones to which it belonged. Mark Antony Lower described all these vicissitudes when he wrote : "The history, then, of Gundrada's mortal remains runs thus : originally buried, 1085 : re-interred about 1145 : separated from their tombstone, 1537 : tombstone brought back to Southover, 1775 : re-deposit of the bones under the original memorial, 1846."

It is a great many centuries since the death of the Lady Gundrada, yet someone living in this present day is the granddaughter of a man who believed that he had looked upon the countenance of the Conqueror's daughter.

This very strange story came to me in the form of a letter from a correspondent whose permission I had to use it. I have already used it in another book, but it is so interesting that it bears repeating. The mother of the lady who wrote me this letter was born in 1837 and was nearly a hundred years old when she died. "She was a Lewes woman," the letter goes on, "though born in Glynde, and often spoke of the finding of the coffin of the Norman princess. She told us that her father, in some capacity, helped to open the inner case of the coffin, and that the body of the princess could be seen as when interred before falling to dust at contact with the air.

"He carried away two vivid impressions. One was that the face was too long and the nose too big to be considered beautiful, and secondly that the black hair of the princess had grown after death so that it entirely covered the lower part of the body.

"I think that my mother used to say that after reclosing the coffin, the men were ordered to say nothing about the affair, but I have forgotten by whose orders all this was done."

This letter is based on first-hand family tradition, but is somewhat difficult to reconcile with the accepted fact that it was only the bones of Gundrada and her lord which were found in the leaden cists discovered at the making of the railway line. The long black hair may well have been there, but as to the actual countenance of the Norman countess— was it imagination, or was it another lady's coffin mistaken for that of Gundrada?

10

One of the finest brasses that Sussex possesses is that of a Prior of St. Pancras' Priory—of Thomas Nelond. It is probably life-size, as the figure is five feet ten inches in height. The Prior is tonsured and has a grave, sensitive face, with deep-set eyes. He wears the habit of a Benedictine

monk, a cassock and a cowl with hanging sleeves, with a
hood falling like a cape—the long draperies fall with grace
and dignity.

The figure is set in an ornate triple canopy, in the centre
shrine of which is a very charming group of the Virgin and
Holy Child, while on either side are the figures of St.
Pancras, the Patron Saint of Lewes Priory, and St. Thomas
of Canterbury, the Patron Saint of Thomas Nelond.

This noble brass is at Cowfold.

There is extant a vivid account of the death and funeral
of Prior Nelond in 1432, purporting to be written by his
brother Peter Nelond, a goldsmith of London. This was
published by the Cambridge Camden Society in 1846 in
Illustrations of Monumental Brasses. It must be said that in
spite of the standing of the society, much doubt has been cast
on the authenticity of this supposed letter of Peter Nelond's.
But whether genuine or simply a piece of historical fiction
masquerading as something that it is not, it gives an attractive picture of the event it is supposed to describe. Peter
Nelond tells how he journeyed across the county till he
reached "Bristelmstun, a merveylous poore village. And ye
nexte day aboute ye tyme of Complyne, wee cam to ye top of
ye hill yat lyeth over against Lewes. Grete lyghte was yere
from ye windowes of ye Priorye : also ye belles of alle ye
chyrches dide tolle mournfulli." He was welcomed graciously
as the late Prior's brother by the monks. "A very fayre
Abbaye ys hit; and hit lyeth pleasantly among pleasant
meadowes. There dide I see ye tombe of ye Lady Gundrada
de Warrenne, ye which dide of hir proper coste, edifye ye
saide hous : and now lyeth afore ye High Awtor, in ye
myddeste of ye Qwere. Also ye chyrche bin veri large and
grete : and ye cloysteres ryghte delectable."

He goes on to describe how the Prior's body lay in the
Priory Church all that night, while the Penitential Psalms
were chanted, and Matins, and Lauds, and Graduals, till
Prime. Then in the morning the long funeral procession set
out, passing through Lewes and up the hill past St. Anne's
Westout, and along the road under the Downs—that ancient
winding road of which he says, "And so wee went under mer-
vylous highe hills (ye wyche bin of ye contrifolke cleped

downes), and beheld to ye ryghte hande fayre cornfeldes and barley landes." On the right hand going westward on this lovely old road can still be seen fair corn and barley lands. The procession went through Westmeston and Ditchling and Keymer, and about the time of Vespers reached Cowfold. where the Prior, at his own wish, was buried.

There at this day, Nelond's brass may be seen—with, perhaps, a little access of historic imagination because of that letter, whether it be authentic or not.

11

St. Richard, Bishop of Chichester in the thirteenth century, is closely associated with Sussex, though he was not by birth a Sussex man. But he died and was buried in this county, and Mark Antony Lower says, in his *Worthies of Sussex* :

"From the thirteenth to the sixteenth century, few Sussex men failed to invoke him in their daily orisons, and to bequeath in their wills something to his shrine."

His shrine and tomb was in his own cathedral of Chichester, and both before and after his canonization was a centre of pilgrimage.

While he lived in Sussex St. Richard was loved by the poor and somewhat feared by the rich, for he cared nothing for worldly power. Many of the saints seem as enskied and holy as though they had barely set foot in the terrestrial world. But not so St. Richard—he was a man before he was a bishop, and a bishop before he was a saint, though all through his life there runs a great desire for and practice of holiness.

It is not necessary to go into that part of his life which he lived before he was consecrated Bishop of Chichester in 1244 by the Holy Father himself. But when Richard came to Sussex it was as a bishop as poor as a hedge-priest, the King having seized and held all that belonged to the temporalities of the see. Richard bore a mandate from the Pope to King Henry that these should be returned to the new bishop, and Richard took this to the court himself, only to be received

there with scorn. So, possessing nothing but his courageous
heart and his bishop's crozier, Richard went to his see of
Chichester, where he found all faces turned from him
through fear of the King's wrath. All but one, and that was
Simon, the priest of Ferring, who gave his bishop shelter
and food and service in that humble Sussex village. There
those two dwelt together, and Richard walked in the little
garden of the parsonage and showed his country upbringing
by tending the herbs and fruit trees there.

One of the benefactions that Sussex is supposed to owe to
St. Richard is the planting of the forerunners of the famous
fig garden at West Wittering. As it stands it was actually
planted in 1745, but some of the trees are very much older,
and it is claimed that they were planted by St. Richard.

A curious thing about this fig garden, and another one at
Sompting, is that when the figs are ripe, a bird from Italy
called the beccafico is said to come across the sea to eat them,
and visits no other places in England except these two Sussex
villages of West Wittering and Tarring.

But Richard could not contentedly remain a gardener—he
was a shepherd of souls, and if the castles and manor-houses
of his diocese were closed to him, he still could enter the poor
cots and hovels of the fishermen and the peasants. He went
about among his people very much with the same simplicity
as St. Wilfrid had done—among the Downs and in the
valleys where poor rustic hamlets were hidden, and on the
low poverty-stricken seashore. On foot and on horseback the
Bishop visited his flock, and learned from what he saw and
what he heard of the hardness of their lives, of their piety
and their sins.

Before he was consecrated Richard had desired to become
a Dominican friar, but though this was then impossible for
him, during the early part of his life as Bishop of Chichester
he was very close to the existence of a preaching friar in
his poverty and simplicity—no son of St. Dominic could
well have had fewer worldly possessions than this Sussex
bishop.

12

After two years of this life, the King was at last forced to yield up all that belonged to the diocese of Chichester, and Richard at last entered his cathedral city in a fitting manner and was enthroned in the seat of St. Wilfrid. And in the episcopal palace he entertained with due state, though it is recorded that at banquets he seldom ate anything but a little bread soaked in wine : "When there was on his table lamb, or kid, or chicken, he used to say, half in jest and half in earnest, 'If ye could speak how would ye blame our gluttony. We are the cause of your death. Ye innocent ones, what have ye done worthy of death?'"

He was always poor because he gave away anything of which he might be possessed. He practised "holy poverty" as fully as his position would permit, and always preferred to regard himself as priest rather than bishop. In his journeys about his diocese, if he heard of some poor man or woman dead in a parish he was visiting he would take the burial service himself and would himself console the bereaved. When told that he had not the money for some deed of charity, he would command that his palfrey or his silver cup should be sold. When his steward expostulated he said : "Is it just that you and I should eat and drink out of silver vessels while Christ in His poor is perishing with hunger?"

There was a great famine in 1247 and some of St. Richard's early miracles were in helping those who hungered. The corn was nearly gone and beans were being boiled to feed some of the starving people, though there was not nearly enough for the crowds gathered around. The Bishop, passing by, saw this, and lifting up his hand in blessing the scanty supply of beans became sufficient to feed the whole multitude.

On another occasion he was crossing the bridge over the Ouse at Lewes where some men were fishing who had been there all day without catching anything. They asked for his blessing, and when he told them to let down their net again they brought up a good catch of mullet. The same thing happened at Bramber, where a netful of fish followed his benediction, after a day of barren toil.

But Richard could punish, as well as bless; he had the sternness, as well as the gentleness, of the Man of God. The wealthy and powerful who thought to escape the punishment of their sins by offering large sums of money discovered that the Bishop would not permit such an easy way of penance. The town of Lewes beheld the salutary spectacle of a rich knight who had wrongfully imprisoned a priest walking through the streets with the block of wood to which he had chained his captive hanging heavily and humiliatingly round his neck.

There are many more stories of the good Bishop who made himself so beloved by the poor of his diocese and so respected by the powerful.

When his time came to die he was out of Sussex on a preaching mission, and had just consecrated a church at Dover to St. Edmund, to whom he was specially devoted—in his sermon on this occasion he said : "For this I have longed ever since I was consecrated a bishop; this has ever been my most earnest prayer, that before my life's end I might consecrate at least one church to his honour."

It was his last act, and after his death his body was brought back from Kent, right through the whole length of Sussex, to his cathedral at Chichester, where it was buried. After St. Richard was canonized his body was translated to a costly shrine behind the high altar.

At this shrine many miracles were wrought. By prayers in his name the little nephew of the Countess of Arundel, who had been Richard's godchild, was raised from his death-bed. Another child who had been paralytic and crippled for six years was cured at the shrine, as were also a poor washerwoman of Bignor, and another woman of Southwick.

Till the Reformation St. Richard's shrine was the centre of much devotion. The Sussex people had loved the saint who was so friendly to the poor and humble, and that love continued for many generations. But Henry VIII and Cromwell took care to remove the temptation to these "superstitious practices."

13

In Sussex before "Queen Bess's father he come in with his Reformatories," there were some thirty monasteries which, considering the population of the county and the great stretches of uninhabited forest land, showed that Sussex had a just claim to the name of "Selig." There were Dominicans at Arundel, at Chichester, and at Winchelsea; there were Benedictines at Boxgrove (whose sad and lovely ruins may still be seen), Sele and Rusper; Augustinian canons at Eastbourne, Hardham and Michelbourne; Franciscans at Chichester, Winchelsea and Lewes; there were Carmelites at Shoreham and Pynham; Austin Friars at Rye. It is impossible to enter into the history of all these Orders in Sussex—that would need a separate book to itself.

But anyone who visits the village of West Chiltington may behold on the outskirts an enchanting little stone house called The Fryars, which was the abode, it is believed, of a friar of the Dominican Order of Preachers, Friar John Wooderowe —or, as others hold, the house was a cell of St. Pancras' Priory at Lewes.

It is a little stone house, with a Horsham slab roof, that after long neglect has come into good hands and been brought to a homely beauty. Still there is something of religious austerity in its look, in spite of the added shell porch. For long it was believed that a friar was buried under a stone slab beneath the stairs. When the house was restored the stone slab was discovered, but not the friar's bones. But if his bones are missing, his spirit is supposed to haunt the place, which is not surprising—there are many ecclesiastically haunted dwellings in Sussex, and these are not the hauntings that harm.

One of the most notable of these is at St. John's Priory at Poling, which once was in the possession of the Knights Templars. It is now a dignified and charming private house, and the chapel has been divided into two floors, a drawing-room below and bedrooms above. But in spite of these changes the place is still haunted at times by the voices of religious singing plain chant. The sceptics will smile at this story, which is so often connected with old monastic houses, but a well-known archæologist and architect, a man whose statement it was impossible to doubt, and whose brother owned and lived in the Priory, declared that he himself had on many occasions heard that chanting, that unmistakable and beautiful Gregorian plain chant.

Sussex offers, too, in its full glory, in the Catholic church of St. Philip Neri, at Arundel, the Corpus Christi procession. The long stately nave of that church is strewn for this procession from the high altar to the west door with flowers and sprays of leaves, not just scattered haphazard, but laid down in a lovely floral pattern. Over this fragrant carpet the Host, in the golden monstrance, is carried in procession from the gleaming altar to the great west doors, and out across the highway, lined with kneeling crowds, into the gardens of Arundel Castle, where in the courtyard there is an altar set up in the open air for Benediction. The hushed crowds, the singing, the incense, the candles carried in ornate gold and crimson lanterns to guard them from the windy airs, the magnificent vestments, are memorable, and the castle towers, and ancient keep, looking down on the scene, recall that the Howard family gave a martyr to the Church and that at Arundel the Catholic tradition has not been broken.

West Grinstead is another place in Sussex that is closely associated with the Old Religion.

Sussex not only has three saints of her own, but many martyrs, both Catholic and Protestant. The Protestant martyrs are the best known, because for long years Lewes, the county town, was violently anti-Catholic, and raised a memorial to the poor creatures who were burned in Lewes High Street on the hillside that looks down on the town—a pathetically ugly monument. For long enough, too, "No Popery" was an intensely popular cry at the Bonfire Day celebrations in Lewes, and the Pope, as well as Guy Fawkes, was burnt in effigy. Unhappily, neither Catholics nor Protestants can claim to be innocent of bitter and cruel intolerance —intolerance (and greed) destroyed the beautiful Priory of St. Pancras; intolerance burnt the martyrs. But it is not so good to dwell on these things as to remember the known and the unknown lives lived in the love of God since the days when Christianity first came to Sussex with the arrival of St. Wilfrid, when the county which had so long been heathen first became holy and earned the name of "Selig Sussex."

CHAPTER V

THE COUNTY TOWN

1

I HAVE in my possesion a very rare little book, called—to give it the lengthy title that belongs to it—*Baxter's Select Sketches of Brighton, Lewes and their Environs: forming a Series of Engravings on Wood with Descriptions.* This was "Printed and Published by the Proprietor, J. Baxter, 37 High St, Lewes," in the year 1827. It was further embellished with a dedication in the manner of the period : "The following Series of Engravings on Wood is respectfully inscribed to the Admirers of Nature, the Lovers of Antiquity, and the Friends of the Fine Arts, by their obedient servant, J. Baxter."

The interest of illustrations more than a century old is obvious, and the letterpress is equally interesting where it records contemporary things that have now passed away, or been altered beyond recognition.

But Baxter's view of Lewes is still in essentials the same as its aspect to-day—the Keep still dominates the scene from its height, though Baxter's hillock is thick with trees and the Keep ivy-smothered. There are fewer houses and more trees than now, and, of course, no railway.

"The town of Lewes," says Baxter, "is situate on the slope of a hill, and is nearly encircled by an amphitheatre of loftier eminences. The River Ouse, which has two sources, the higher in St. Leonard's Forest and the lower at Telsfield, separates the Borough of Lewes from the Cliffe, and, winding through the levels, falls into the Channel at the harbour of Newhaven. The hills, almost surrounding the town, are of a chalky texture, and distinguished as a portion of the South Downs. Hence the scenery is generally good, and, from the summits of most of the hills, extensive and variegated landscapes may be witnessed."

Of the Keep of the Castle, he says, "Being erected on a

96

Litlington Church
Chichester Cathedral Spire from the north

very high artificial mount, it affords a good picturesque object from what point soever it is viewed. Strong and high walls formerly encompassed the town; they are now only to be traced in a few favourable spots."

The Keep, which is now fortunately in the hands of the Sussex Archæological Society, was then in private possession, and, says Baxter, "admittance may be gained by a trifling *douceur* to the old couple who live in this *eyry*, and who are thus situated by the benevolent proprietor of the domain, T. R. Kemp, Esq., one of the Representatives of the Borough."

This "eyry" of the old couple must have been a cold and draughty abode, judging from what it is to-day, though at some time while the Keep was in his possession, Mr Kemp is credited with having attempted to turn it into a summer-house by the addition of windows in the "Chinese taste." Archæology was certainly in its infancy in those days.

2

A writer of the same period, though of much greater importance than Baxter, gives a very pleasant picture of Lewes and its people in his *Rural Rides*.

"There is a great extent of rich meadows above and below Lewes," Cobbett wrote in 1822. "The town itself is a model of solidity and neatness. The buildings are substantial to the very out-skirts; the pavement good and complete; the shops nice and clean; the people well-dressed; and, though last but not least, the girls remarkably pretty as, indeed, they are in most parts of Sussex : round faces, features small, little hands and wrists, plump arms and bright eyes. The Sussex men, too, are remarkable for their good looks. A Mr Baxter, a stationer at Lewes, showed me a *farmer's account book* which is a very complete thing of the kind. The inns are good at Lewes, the people civil not servile, and the charges really (considering the taxes) far below what one could reasonably expect."

Had Cobbett but called on Mr Baxter a few years later he would, no doubt, have seen the little illustrated book referred to earlier.

Another great Englishman, William Morris, was also pleased with Lewes, and said of it : "You can see Lewes lying like a box of toys under a great amphitheatre of chalk hills . . . on the whole it is set down better than any town I have seen in England."

But much earlier than any of these writers there is a description of Lewes which is worth quoting. This is taken from a *History of Lewes and Brighthelmston*, edited by William Lee in 1795, the author, as Lee says in his fulsome dedication of the book to the Prince of Wales, being "too timid a Parent" to own the work. He claims that the Prince of Wales must feel a peculiar interest in the history of these parts of Sussex, for "That healthful Tract is the favourite Sphere of Your Summer Amusements, and its Inhabitants the admiring Witnesses of your Royal Highness's Liberality, Condescension, Public Spirit and Humanity."

It is pleasant to turn from William Lee's servile bowings before Hanoverian royalty to the anonymous author's description of the Keep at Lewes and the surrounding country :

"One half of the Keep on the western mount, which is the higher, is still standing, and commonly called the Castle. It forms a picturesque object to the distant beholder, as well as an observatory from which some of the most pleasant scenery in nature may be viewed. From the summit of the most perfect of its two remaining towers appear the nether buildings of the town, with its hanging gardens and bustling inhabitants in pleasing miniature. The face of the Downs, diversified by wind-mills, flocks and waving fields of corn, that move so by the skilful hand of Nature; here deeply cragged into chalky cliffs; there gently sinuous; next rising in bold convexity beyond the imitation of art; then a summit, level as a bowling green, all richly clothed with the most lively and fragrant herbage; the serpentine Ouse dividing, in its progress towards the sea, a wide and fertile vale, over-looked by a number of pleasant villages whose church steeples rise above the trees, while here and there a farm-house or neat cottage is seen between them; the shipping at Newhaven brought by perspective deception within a league of the delighted spectator, and a background to complete the piece, with a succession of vessels of all sizes, riding in the English

Channel, form the southern prospect from this spot, which, to be adequately conceived, must be seen, and, if seen, inexpressibly admired. On the north, a rich and varied inland scene invites the eye of taste to roam among all the beauties of the cultivated Weald. Amidst meads and ripening fields may be seen the spreading canvas of the barges moving majestically along, while every road or lane seems an alley, and every farm but a compartment in this extensive landscape."

3

This enchanting scene, so justly if elaborately praised by the retiring author at the end of the eighteenth century, may still be enjoyed and admired from the summit of the Keep, in all essentials as he beheld it, with the exception that sheep no longer pasture on the slopes of the Downs, that the windmills—Lewes once was rich in windmills—have vanished, and that an eruption of new houses has here and there blotched the scene. But the geographical position of Lewes on its steep and narrow hill has fortunately preserved it from devastating changes. The configuration of the surrounding Downs is striking, and the entry into Lewes from the west by the very old road that winds along the foot of the Downs from Westmeston and Plumpton is singularly beautiful. At intervals along this road on the northern side, which twists and turns to fit itself to the thrust and retreat of the chalk hills, are strips and thickets of trees which are the remnants or descendants of the great forests of the primeval Weald. And the changing views of the Weald given by the eastward progress of this road, with the Downs looming all along on the right hand, may be taken as an epitome of essential Sussex. It is a scene of which no Sussex man or woman can tire—in all seasons, in all aspects of weather it is enchanting. On the one hand the immemorial turf of the Downs, in the past cropped by sheep, but uncultivated save on the edges; on the other the stretches of corn and roots, the little farmsteads with their groups of ancillary buildings, the narrow, deeply hedged lanes going northwards, the dark woods here and there spread out in brown or green.

Then as the road draws near to Lewes, after it has passed through that lovely avenue of beeches on the level ground, it swings round and once more runs on an elevated ridge high above the water meadows of the Ouse that lie below Lewes. In winter, when the floods are out, there is a curious magic in the scene—it seems to go back to something very primitive and remote as the evening mists rise and the red sun sinks behind the hill. And beyond the hollow of the hill on which is Lewes is the outline—the strange and notable outline—of Firle Beacon, so definitely a part of the Lewes scene.

When the floods are out it is interesting to see how exactly the little farms and steadings are planted on the rising bits of ground that just—and only just—keep their feet out of the waters. Beautiful old Hamsey Church on its cliff-like peninsula is planted well above danger, and so is Malling Church, guarding its flock of white gravestones that look like sheep; but the railway running on its artificial embankment beside the lazy Ouse has somewhat the look of a toy that is in some danger from the spreading waters.

Beyond Lewes to the southwards are more level meadows through which the Ouse meanders on the way to the sea, and two little green hillocks called the Rhies. It is characteristic country, and the more charming the more known.

4

Lewes has laid a certain Georgian decorousness upon the much older Tudor and Jacobean houses in which the town is rich. The frontages upon the High Street give a general effect of eighteenth-century seemliness and restraint—the graceful, small-paned bow windows, the handsome doorways —spoiled, of course, here and there, by commercial plate-glass and tasteless design. But down a side lane—and many side lanes dart southwards down the steep of the hill from the High Street—may be seen here and there the shoulder of a house whose front looks Georgian, but the shoulder shouts Tudor in vast beam and jettied overhang. Lewes is a town of surprises, and there is no house so unpromising in its face to the street but may conceal charming secrets.

An opened door often reveals a garden whose existence right in the middle of the town seems impossible.

Keere Street is one of the most surprising in Lewes, though its exploration is hardly to be embarked upon except by those of steady hearts and steady heads, for its steepness is almost Alpine. The house at its top westward corner is so timbered and overhung and irregular in roof-line as to look like an illustration to a fairy-tale, and the cobbler who works in one of its dark little shops really should be a goblin whose shoes should display peculiar and unexpected qualities. This is one of the charms of Lewes—its mixture of a placid eighteenth-century atmosphere, overhung by a Norman fortress; with Gothic and Tudor trimmings in side streets and secret corners.

Keere Street itself is a fair example of all this—medieval timber building at the top, odd cottages of all periods either side of the cobbled street; down at the bottom the solid stone magnificence of the Tudor Southover Grange (which actually is not in Keere Street at all) and on the eastern side glimpses across cottage gardens of the grim-looking old town wall of Lewes. This wall can be traced again in the little hidden way called Pipe's Passage, where is also a round cottage which is the remains of the town windmill. From Pipe's Passage there can also be had an enchanting view of the Keep raised high and romantic on its mount.

Lewes Castle is unique in having two artificial mounds—the western one still bearing the rugged remains of the Keep; the eastern one, bare of any building in this day, is known as the Brack Mount, this name, according to the anonymous eighteenth-century historian of Lewes, meaning "Crumbling-mount, from the Saxon verb *brœcan*, to break or moulder."

The entrance to what was Lewes Castle has two gateways, built across what was the moat, and the outer one, the Barbican, is one of the town's most notable possessions. Few artists visiting Lewes have failed to paint or etch it. This gateway was built early in the fourteenth century by the last of the Lords de Warenne. The beautifully knapped and squared flint work of the southern front is a superb example of craftsmanship—and shows also what an indestructible material is flint; stone moulders with time, but knapped flint keeps its hard and icy glitter. The machicolation of this gateway is very decorative. To walk under its echoing archway is to feel the hand of the past laid upon one's shoulder. All about here, in what are called Castle Precincts, there are many pleasant and ancient things, including a delightful bowling-green, one of the oldest in England, where the game has been played for many centuries. This bowling-green was originally the tilt-yard of the Castle.

5

Barbican House, adjoining the Barbican gateway, is a house not only important to the town of Lewes, but to the whole of Sussex, for it is the home and headquarters of the Sussex Archæological Society. It was not acquired until 1908, though the Society was founded in 1846. From 1850 the Society had rented the Castle as a museum, till in 1920, by the generosity of the late Sir Charles Thomas Stanford—to whom Sussex archæology owes so much—it became the property of the Society. By so becoming it is secured of care and preservation, for gone are the amazing ignorant years when such ancient monuments, such historical treasures, were regarded as nothing but a quarry in which any man might delve to build himself a pigsty. In the early seventeenth century the Castle was dismantled, and the citizens of Lewes were allowed to buy walling stone and flints at fourpence a load. Portions of the ruins of both the Castle and St. Pancras' Priory at Southover are built into the walls of many an existing Lewes house.

Barbican House, which is the headquarters of the Sussex Archæological Society, and houses the Society's admirable museum, is a pleasant square-fronted red-brick corner house, facing the High Street and running up a side street to the Barbican gateway. The plainness of its appearance is broken by brick string courses and a parapet. By the chimney at the side, above the second story, is a curious wooden door, which opens into nothing but air, having no apparent reason for its existence. The house was once owned by an eighteenth-century Lewes wool merchant, and this was the door of his wool-loft.

Barbican House is a mixture of periods, partly sixteenth, seventeenth and eighteenth century. In the earlier stages of its existence, when it had three gables instead of this parapet, the old Market Cross of Lewes used to stand almost opposite to it. But though dignified and pleasant to look at, and architecturally interesting, as are most houses that can claim an age of several centuries, it is not for this that Barbican House may lay claim to be the most notable house in Lewes, but because of the treasures of Sussex history it contains.

Too many museums are depressing affairs, filled with the junk and debris of the centuries, ranging over the globe, disconnected and meaningless. This museum at Barbican House is no such matter, its exhibits are all, as it were, strung on a single thread; they tell a connected story, and that story is the history of Sussex. The museum still retains its agreeable air of being a private house, instead of an official building, and the members of the Sussex Archæological Society are often to be seen strolling about the rooms as if they were in their own homes. The general public, those who are not members, have to pay sixpence for this privilege—but it is a sixpence very well spent.

In the first place the exhibits are not overwhelming in number—the archæological inquirer is not crushed by countless cases of worked flints and sherds of pottery. He walks first of all into a nice stone-floored hall from which a charming Wren-like staircase rises with the easy grace of its period. The hall is hung with all sorts of interesting Sussex pictures and maps, including a perfectly gorgeous ancient estate map. From there he goes into what was the ancient kitchen of the house, which has a noble old hearth, and this hearth and kitchen are adorned and hung about with domestic ironwork that would turn a collector's cheek green. There are a superb Sussex iron fire-back, iron cauldrons, pot-hangers, three-legged skillets, rush-light holders, varied and decorative brass candlesticks, a very large bronze mortar, dated 1669, long-handled frying-pans and skimmers, fire-dogs, and also Sussex kitchen pottery ware. All very attractive, even to those who are not archæologically inclined—and perhaps a reminder that the prime study of archæology is the way our ancestors *lived*, not how they were buried, though in the periods of pre-history their graves are the only record they have left us.

There are four other rooms on the ground floor of Barbican House, devoted respectively to the Stone Age, the Bronze Age, the Early Iron Age, and the Medieval Period. On the floor above are the Anglo-Saxon Room, the Roman Room, and two smaller rooms, one finely panelled in oak and displaying some excellent old oak furniture, and the other showing Lambert's interesting water-colours of eighteenth-century aspects of Sussex and Lewes antiquities, many of them now vanished. On the top floor is the useful and valuable library of the Society, this being open only to members. This attic library—a noble attic, with great tie-beams running across the ceiling—is a most pleasant place to work in, and from its windows can be obtained a wide-spreading southward view of the Ouse valley, and intriguing glimpses of the roofs of Lewes, which seen from this height are obviously so much older, so much more irregular and surprising, than would be guessed from the façades of the houses they cover which front the street. A new front was often put on an old house—the roof was less often interfered with, and frequently hidden from ground level view by a parapet such as Barbican House itself possesses.

A day can easily be spent with profit in studying the admirably arranged exhibits in the different period rooms of the museum, which help to bring the past history of this county of Sussex so vividly before the mind. Lewes is rich in having such a museum and Sussex is rich in having such an active and admirable Archæological Society.

6

As the Society was founded in 1846 it is one of the oldest societies of its kind in England. The history of its founding is particularly interesting, as it was largely due to the rediscovery of the ruins of the great Cluniac Priory of St. Pancras at Southover, and the coffins of Gundrada and William de Warenne, first Norman lord of Lewes, when the railway was dug, that the Sussex Archæological Society came into existence.

Why the ruins had sunk into such oblivion that no one took any interest in them, it is difficult, at this distance of time, to explain. Probably they were to a large extent covered with earth and smothered in ivy and brambles, till they had become almost unintelligible. Anyway, when the picks of the railway navvies began to expose the ruins once more to the light of day, considerable antiquarian excitement was caused and the meeting which led to the formation of the Sussex Archæological Society took place in June 1846. This, as it says in a contemporary report of the proceedings, was at the suggestion "of a few gentlemen in the town and neighbour-hood of Lewes, who, on hearing the interest excited by some recent antiquarian discoveries, were anxious to promote a readier acquaintance among persons attached to the same pursuits and to continue their exertions in illustration of the History and Antiquities of Sussex."

So great was the interest aroused that within three weeks the infant Society had obtained nearly a hundred members. The great Sussex landowners and bearers of historic names gave their countenance and support, for the first president was the Duke of Norfolk, and the patron the Duke of Richmond. This kind of support, as well as that of learned antiquaries and historians, has never failed the Society in the hundred years of its existence. The first honorary secretary, writing in the first volume of the Society's *Collections*, said, with the rather pleasing pomposity of his period, "the Society cannot fail of success, after having enlisted in its favour so much of the noble, the learned, the pious and the enterprising zeal of the county of Sussex."

Certainly the learned have given generously of their services to the Society in the generations between its founding and this present day.

The first general meeting took place very suitably in the ruins of Pevensey Castle, on which historic building Mark Antony Lower read a paper. In 1865 the Society held a general meeting at Amberley Castle, and there is a rather amusing contemporary drawing of the event, showing the archæologists gathered on the greensward within the Castle walls. There are at least as many ladies as gentlemen present, giving an almost garden-party air to the scene with their sweeping crinolines, swirling cloaks and floating bonnet ribbons—it appears to have been a breezy day. The gentlemen look much more solemn with their beards, high black stove-pipe hats and frock-coats.

These general meetings in the different Rapes of the county, as well as local meetings, three or four each summer, have continued ever since, save for the horrid interruption of war. There is no better way to become acquainted not only with the look of Sussex, but with its meaning, than these meetings offer, as all know who have attended them. More than this, the Society has been the means of preserving for posterity much of Sussex antiquity that otherwise was doomed to decay. Much has unhappily gone; much more would have disappeared if it had not been for the efforts of the Sussex Archæological Trust, the legal holder of the Society's properties. The Trust is now possessed not only of Lewes Castle, Barbican House, the Anne of Cleves House at Southover, but of Wilmington Priory, the "Long Man" on the Downs adjoining, and the site of the Roman villa at Southwick.

One of the first things the Society did was to rescue from oblivion the grave of one of the earliest of Sussex antiquaries, saving, "from the earth into which it had sunk, the tombstone of this John Rowe, who died at Lewes in 1636."

7

Barbican House is only one of the more notable houses in Lewes. The more wealthy Sussex landowners in past centuries, who would by no means so far disentangle themselves from their native clay or chalk as to reside in London, yet were not averse—or their wives and daughters were insistent —to having a "town-house" for the winter in Lewes. Many of the old substantial residences in High Street and adjoining thoroughfares were such town houses of the local gentry. In numerous cases they are now turned into shops or banks or schools or hotels. What is now Lewes Post Office was once

a select Academy for Young Ladies. Few of these changes
have been to the architectural advantage of the town, though
Lewes still possesses a number of fine old houses which are
little altered.

Defoe, in his *Tour thro' the Whole Island of Great
Britain*, written in the first quarter of the eighteenth century,
spoke of Lewes as a "fine pleasant town, well built, agreeably
situated . . . on the edge of the South Downs, the pleasantest
and most delightful of their kind in the nation." But the
thing that evidently impressed him most deeply was that
"both the town and country adjacent is full of Gentlemen of
good Families and Fortunes."

One of the houses which belonged to a Gentlewoman of
good Family and Fortune—how eminently desirable to the
eighteenth-century mind were those two assets and how
redolent of the sweet snobbery of Jane Austen!—was the
mansion known as Shelleys, which was outside the town walls,
hence the name of the parish, St. Mary Westout, and in its
Tudor days would, no doubt, have been surrounded by extensive lands. It is a dignified and substantial Elizabethan house,
with a porch bearing the date 1577. It was originally an inn,
known as The Vine, and it has a room decorated with a
contemporary wall-painting of vines. In the eighteenth century additions were built on at the back of the Tudor front,
and it became the residence of the Shelley family, whose name
it still bears. The Misses Shelley, who were resident there
at the beginning of the nineteenth century, were notable
spinsters who scorned the married state, and when one
of the sisters actually consented to change her name the
other sisters were disgusted. "It was an unheard-of thing
that a lady of the Shelley family should marry," they
declared.

In his *Recollections of a Sussex Parson*, so full of good
Sussex lore, Edward Ellmann has some pleasant tales to tell
of these ladies. When the census of 1841 was taken, the
collector called at the Shelley mansion and found to his surprise that the ages of the two surviving Miss Shelleys and
also of all their female servants were put down as being
twenty-five. As this did not seem to be in accordance with
facts he requested to be allowed to see the elder Miss

Shelley, and when duly ushered into her plainly unyouthful presence, he politely suggested that there must have been some small mistake made in the age entries. Miss Shelley rose in her wrath and declared indignantly that "never in her life had she met with such impudence as to ask the age of a lady. In that house they were all unmarried females, and she could not think of putting each down as more than twenty-five."

It is like a scene out of *Cranford*, and Miss Shelley is twin sister to Miss Deborah. In these days of "forms" and bureaucracy there is an air of glorious freedom in the little tale.

8

There is another house not far from Shelleys, a little lower down, on the opposite side, close to the quaint little witch-capped house that stands between Rotten Row and St. Anne's Hill, which presents a plain and uncompromising front to the street, but behind is full of Georgian grace, and looks southwards to a most lovely garden, surprising in its size and seclusion in the midst of a crowded little town. But that is Lewes—especially on the southward slope of the hill—the most unexpected and charming gardens, where no garden seems possible, beautiful and ancient things hidden away behind modern lack of charm. Lewes House, on the slope of School Hill, and its neighbour, School Hill House—once called Lorkins—hide behind their solid dignified proportions the most enchanting old-world gardens with stabling and other appurtenances. And down a side-lane near by is another fine old Lewes house, Pelham House, built in 1579. The White Hart Hotel, not far away, was once the town house of the Pelhams, whose name is notable in Sussex history. In St. Michael's Church in the High Street, with its thirteenth-century round tower (one of the famous three in the Ouse Valley) is a noble Tudor monument to Sir Nicholas Pelham and his wife, kneeling stiffly opposite each other, with their six sons and four daughters kneeling equally stiffly beneath. Sir Nicholas died in 1559, and his famous exploit is commemorated on this tomb in the well-known lines :

What time ye French sought to have sackt
Sea-Foord
This Pelham did repell them back aboard.

Pelham House has a particularly fine panelled room, with
beautiful delicate carving over the fireplace, and a series of
caryatid figures round the walls. The panelling is mostly of
pine in a lovely tone of grey-brown. The Elizabethan heart
of the house has an outer and later casing of eighteenth-
century brickwork. The southern windows look out upon
another of these old Lewes gardens, still beautiful, though
the view down towards the railway station and its networks
has completely lost the grace it must have possessed when
Pelham House was built.

It is impossible to describe, or even name, all the historic
homes of Lewes, but one must not be omitted, especially as
it may be inspected for the price of a cup of tea, and is now
the property of the Sussex Archæological Trust, and that is
Bull House—it used to be the Bull Inn—at the top of the
High Street, just where the old West Gate in the town wall
stood. It is of fifteenth and early sixteenth century date, and
has a charming classic chimney-piece in the front room, and
a vast open hearth in the back one, while the great wealth
of timber used in its construction is visible in the upper
stories. There are two curious carved figures of satyrs on the
outside.

9

Southover, which is actually a continuation or extension of
Lewes, down the slope of the hill and continuing to where
St. Pancras' Priory stood, has a very pleasant High Street of
its own, containing a number of varied and interesting old
houses, of all ages and all angles. The most outstanding of
these is the Anne of Cleves House, which belongs to the
Sussex Archæological Trust, and is open to the general public
on the payment of a small fee. It contains a number of instruc-
tive "bygones" of a generally domestic and agricultural
nature, being more a kind of folk museum than the Society's
other one at Barbican House.

Like the Anne of Cleves House at Ditchling, this building was bestowed on that fortunate queen of King Henry's who escaped the headsman's axe, but again like her possession in Ditchling it is doubtful if she ever dwelt therein. This house at Southover is a very fine specimen of its period. The front to the High Street shows every variety of building material, brick and flint, timber, plaster and stone, a long stretch of rosy tiling, a roof partly the original Horsham slabs and partly later tiling—all these different materials are used with the most enchanting skill and grace.

In an account of this house in the *Sussex Archæological Collections* by Mr Walter H. Godfrey (who surely knows more of the ecclesiastical and domestic architecture of Sussex than any living man), he says :

"In Sussex we have a very happy combination of building materials of which our ancestors took full advantage. Our quarries yield serviceable building stone which, unlike that of many other districts, is variable and pleasing in colour. Our chalk Downs provide flints in abundance, our brickfields— Ringmer among them—have been producing for centuries, while Sussex oak held a high reputation in medieval times. There was no lack of material for roof-covering; Horsham slabs, tiles, and of course thatch, were the products of Weald industries."

The porch of the Anne of Cleves House carries the date 1599 in one of the spandrels of the doorway, but Mr Godfrey considers that portions of the house are at least a century older. In its mixture of periods, its mixture of building materials, and the extraordinary variety of beauty of the south, north, east and west elevations, this is a very remarkable and valuable example of medieval and Tudor architecture, one of the treasures of Sussex, which is rich in this type of house. It is a matter of deep satisfaction that it is now the property of the Sussex Archæological Society, owing to the generosity of Mr Frank Verrall.

Inside, part of the hall-place is still open to the roof timbers, in the ancient fashion, and it has many other attractive rooms, including a perfectly glorious attic where whole oak trees may be seen holding the house together.

In earlier days this dwelling had sunk into decay, and was

shunned as being haunted. In fact, so bad was its reputation that those who had to pass it after dark did so at a run.

Among the many interesting things contained in the Anne of Cleves House is a table to which is attached a strange history. After the murder of Thomas à Becket, the murderers on their flight from Canterbury stayed the night at South Malling. They flung down their arms on to a table in the hall while they sat by the fire, talking, as may be supposed, of the dire deed. Becket himself had often eaten at this table holding the blood-stained weapons, and it began shaking, so that its unholy burden fell to the ground. When the arms were replaced it again cast them off, "though," as the chronicler records, "the table was large and massive and firmly fixed, and no sign of movement could be seen when lights were brought."

That is the story, and this same table is now housed in the Anne of Cleves House at Southover. The top of this table is not oak, as might be expected, but a massive slab of grey Sussex marble. Of its solidity there can be no question.

10

Southover was without the ancient walls which once encircled Lewes, and so was Cliffe, into which School Hill runs down, coming to the Ouse and the bridge over it, at the bottom, and then Cliffe High Street divides to right and left, the right hand following the river, which just here provides an odd little bit of canal-like scenery, which quickly swings into the quiet charms of the Ouse Valley and the beauties of Mount Caburn and Beddingham. But before reaching these Downs an unimportant-looking little inn is passed, called the Snowdrop—the name, recalling that innocent flower of early spring, may seem a curious and inappropriate one for an inn. But it is not the flower at all that is intended by that name. There is a little colour print of Baxter's which I found one day in a Lewes antique shop, framed in a wide old bird's-eye maple frame, that gives the true origin of the Snowdrop Inn, for it depicts an avalanche of snow descending on some cottages.

This was in the year 1830, and the account of the storm in and around Lewes, taken from the contemporary description in the *Sussex Weekly Advertiser*, is very interesting in its sidelights on the local life. There had been a tremendous hurricane in the week before Christmas, followed by a steady fall of snow for two days, and this was heaped by the wind into great drifts sometimes twenty feet deep, while other places were swept bare.

"So effectually were the roads choked up on Monday," says the *Weekly Advertiser*, "that the town of Lewes was blockaded from the slightest communication with the surrounding country, except by means of the river. Not a vehicle was seen in the streets during the whole day, most of the shops were shut, and all trade was at a standstill. The Brighton mail coach arrived here and returned on Sunday evening with the greatest difficulty; and it was only by the utmost exertion and perseverance that Mr Leney's coach, which started from Lewes the same evening, could be dragged to Brighton. . . . It was found to be totally impossible to forward the mail from Lewes that night."

It was not possible to clear the roads for traffic even partially till the Friday of that week, and even then six horses were needed for the coaches.

"It was observed," continues this admirable piece of newspaper reporting, "on Monday that the violence of the gale on the previous night had deposited a continuous ridge of snow, from ten to fifteen feet in thickness, along the brow of that abrupt and almost perpendicular height which is based by South Street and the Eastbourne road, where tons upon tons seemed to hang in a delicately turned wreath as lightsome as a feather, but which, in fact, bowed down by its own weight, threatened destruction to everything beneath."

Under this overhanging avalanche of snow was a row of labourers' cottages known as Boulder Row, and efforts were made to induce the inhabitants to move out from their threatened abodes. But in the typical English manner they were very reluctant to do so, some refused altogether, some started to try to save their possessions, with the sad result that when the wall of snow fell most of them were caught. The *Weekly Advertiser* says :

Manor House, West Hoathly
Old Shoreham

"A gentleman who witnessed the fall described it as a scene of the most awful grandeur. The mass appeared to him to strike the houses first at the base, heaving them upwards, and then breaking over them like a gigantic wave to dash them bodily into the void; and when the mist of snow, which then enveloped the spot, cleared off, not a vestige of a habitation was to be seen—there was nothing but an enormous mound of pure white."

The houses were shattered by the snow's weight; many of the inhabitants were injured seriously and eight people, six women and two men, were killed. These were buried in one grave in Malling churchyard, and a tablet commemorates them.

The Snowdrop Inn is named in remembrance of that Christmas Eve tragedy of 1830, and stands on the spot where it happened.

11

In the old days to look down on Lewes from any height would be to see it adorned by the sweeps and towers or "smocks" of many windmills, testifying by their number to the close connection between the corn grown and ground and baked at home—that bread which was in every sense, spiritually and materially, the "staff of life." But the windmills have fallen down, caught fire—these creatures of wind have always been subject to flames—been pulled down as no longer needed, and the Lewes scene suffers from their loss. In the narrow little Pipe's Passage, nearly opposite Bull House, is the base of the old town windmill, converted into an amusing little dwelling-house. Further up the hill, beyond St. Anne's Church, is the Black Horse Inn, which is on what is believed to be the site of the historic windmill of the Battle of Lewes in 1294, when, as Percy's *Reliques of Ancient Poetry* set forth,

> The Kynge of Alemaigne wende do ful wel,
> He saisede the mulne for a castel.

The Downs, with their height, freedom and continually blowing winds, were ideal sites for windmills—though not

I   113

only at Lewes but all over the Downs they are vanished and vanishing. The most notable of all, because of their position on the very crest and crown of the hill, the Clayton windmills, a black tower and a white post mill, known as Jack and Jill, still happily exist and adorn the Sussex scene with their enchanting silhouette, but it is a long while since either of them has been working.

The outline of a windmill is often more striking than that of a church because of its elevated position—but from its very nature and its structure it is infinitely more ephemeral. But even churches disappear and are destroyed. Lewes has not only the tragic loss of the great St. Pancras' Priory to deplore in her historic past, but the actual town is the poorer by the complete disappearance of many a church that once raised a skyward pointing finger. The narrow lanes that run southwards from the High Street, bearing saints' names like St. Martin's Lane and St. Andrew's Lane, commemorate the sites of vanished churches. St. Martin's Church was in being until the fourteenth century, and the ancient overhanging house at the western corner, still existing, dates from the same century. The commonplace name of Station Street was once St. Mary's Lane, so called after the church of St. Mary-in-foro. St. Andrew's Church was joined with that of St. Michael—still standing in the High Street—in 1545. Once Lewes had ten churches within the town wall and four without the wall—of the latter there still exist the beautiful Church of St. Anne, which used to be called Blessed Mary Westout; the Church of St. John the Baptist at Southover, where the dust of Gundrada and William de Warenne now reposes; and the Church of St. Thomas à Becket at Cliffe. But of the many churches within the wall only three now remain of the original ten.

St. Michael's Church, with its ancient round tower, fronting right on to the busy High Street, has tucked away behind it a most unexpected and peaceful churchyard, with a vast weeping willow and old dignified tombstones, and a particularly romantic and charming view of the Castle Keep on its mound. This mound in spring is thick with happy clumps of primroses, growing in complete security from the clutching hand, and in the crevices of old walls gay flags of yellow wallflowers—and wallflowers are so much better growing on walls than in garden beds—flaunt in the breeze, as if imitating the banners that once flew there.

That is Lewes—continually full of surprises, little bits of ancient history, of ancient beauty, continually cropping up in the most unexpected places. It cannot be grasped in one visit, it is worthy of constant study. Its twisting narrow streets, the unexpected bits of town wall and town ditch, the queer little cottages tucked away behind or in the pockets of other houses, the lumps of ashlar and carved stone in old walls, the odd windows and doors blocked up, all add to the fascination of exploration. Guide-books tell of the important and historic things in Lewes—but there are such lots of little, perhaps unimportant, but fascinating things to be found there.

For a final thought of this old county town of Sussex and one of the most solemn contrasts it can offer, stand in a certain spot in the High Street, while the Southdown omnibuses and lorries and other modern vehicles rush by, and the shoppers pursue their necessary quests, and look across to the opposing Down, on the crest of which will be seen the crouched outline of a Long Barrow, which from its solitary height, in the loneliness of an infinitely remote past, looked upon the hill on which Lewes stands when it was empty and bare to the sky. Within eyeshot of each other—that past and this present.

CHAPTER VI
SOME SUSSEX VILLAGES
1

BEFORE all others the natural feature that spells Sussex is, of course, the Downs—to any exile from the county that will be the first vision which comes to the nostalgic inward eye of memory. But Sussex has another treasure of a different nature in her many delightful villages and hamlets, small manor-houses and farmsteads, scattered about the county. It is practically useless to look for these along the coast— any core of decent old building between Brighton and Little-hampton, where the alluvial plain comes down to the sea, is smothered and hidden in modern slums. And to the east-wards there is the shoddy Peacehaven and the progressive Seaford. Most of the Sussex coast, except where it is actual chalk cliff, is shabby and out-at-elbows, littered as if with a giant child's cheap toys. The nobility of Old and New Shore-ham churches amid their squalid surroundings is a perpetual reproach—each gracious fabric, so satisfying and solid in every line, an island of beauty in a sea of commonplace. These churches are large enough and important enough to stand out still from their surroundings, but the old cottages are much more easily smothered. Here and there in a dreary street, perhaps at a corner, may be seen a little nautical cottage, its upper story hung with black-tarred timbers, its casements white-painted, and displaying cheerful red-potted geraniums. It suggests smuggling nights in the time when it stood alone on the shore, and "the Gentlemen" were trotting by with their lace-and-brandy ponies. It is a little sturdy free-hold that has escaped the grasp of the speculative builder. Or it may be a seemly Georgian cottage that stands out amid the general ugliness, with well-proportioned small-paned windows and a charming fanlight like a slice of lemon above the front door. But even as one admires these gracious things, while the buses and the lorries thunder past, one feels that they are doomed to fall very soon beneath the juggernaut of "Progress." Long stretches of seaward Sussex are past praying for.

The not very distinguished song of "Sussex-by-the-Sea" would do better to hymn Sussex-the-Other-Side-of-the-Downs, for inland, on the northern side of the chalk escarpment, there is a considerable treasure of old building that has escaped improvement.

Each English county has its own vernacular style of building, because in the old days each English county built with the material that was to hand—stone in a stone county, timber in forest country, and so on. The principal building materials of the Wealden clay are oak—the oak is a tree of the Weald—and brick; while in the seaward parts of Sussex there is some very fine building in knapped and squared, and also whole, flints. Brighton had, and still has, some charming examples of Regency and earlier flint work—though many a perfect example has been pulled down to be replaced by steel and concrete. And much older knapped flint work is to be seen in various church towers, and in the great Barbican gateway at Lewes.

Owing to the original vast forests of the Weald, Sussex is rich in timber houses of medieval construction, or of timber combined with brick and tile-hanging of the upper story which is typical of much old Sussex building. One of the most magnificent specimens of early brickwork in existence is Herstmonceaux Castle, recently so nobly restored by Mr Walter H. Godfrey, and on a humbler scale the brickwork of Laughton Place is notable. Then for the mixture of brickwork and tile-hanging and timber framing, or timber and plaster and brick, are such houses as Westmeston Place, Wapsbourne, East Mascalls, Brickwall, the two Anne of Cleves Houses at Southover and Ditchling, the remarkable old thatched cottage at Bignor, Peppers at Ashurst, Strawberry Hole Farm, Little Walstead Farm, near Lindfield, and many others. In some of these or similar houses will be found the typical medieval timber construction—usually altered and changed, but sometimes intact—of a house of three bays, two of them making the hall, the third floored to make the solar, with a room beneath. A great number of these houses were floored right across and a brick chimney built to take the place of the central hearth, in late Tudor or early Jacobean times.

It is hardly possible to walk or drive down a solitary curly Sussex lane without coming across some treasure of Sussex architecture, even though it be but an ancient farm labourer's cottage, which in earlier times would have been a small yeoman's house. And to a considerable extent you can tell in what part of Sussex you are by the type of cottage and farmhouse seen.

In the eastern parts of the county the comely Kentish type of building has strayed here and there over the border—the long, low house, its upper story hung with whitewashed weather-boarding. On the coast this weather-boarding is often tarred black. In the coast towns, too, will be seen the flint-built houses, sometimes the flints set in even kidney-shaped rows in wide mortar courses, sometimes knapped and squared and set close with little mortar showing.

Then in central Sussex the most typical Sussex house of all takes possession, built of warm orange-rosy bricks baked from the clay of the Weald, hung with weather-tiles of an enchanting and different shade of red, with a brown tile roof —the whole tone of colouring being that of a very russet and outdoor peach. Sometimes the roof will be the most perfect one of all, slabs of Horsham stone, on which lichens will gather and house-leeks be at home. But if that is the case it will be a house or cottage of considerable age, for extremely massive roof timbers are needed to bear the weight of Horsham stone "heeling." Occasionally a minute old cottage will be seen still standing up to the burden of its Horsham roof, and in this case Sussex humour will almost certainly have christened it "Slab Castle."

Still further west the roofs of the cottages will be largely thatch—the delightful village of Amberley is almost completely thatched, with straw thatch, not reed, for reed is not a native Sussex material.

2

Amberley is almost too popular and well-known. People who have never been there are familiar with it, because it has been so often painted—pictures of Amberley in all lights and aspects have hung on the walls of Burlington House and of Bond Street galleries. But even if perhaps over-painted, Amberley retains a sturdy and simple charm. As E. V. Lucas said, "It is sheer Sussex—chalky soil, whitewashed cottages, huge wagons." Also cows—I have always found when I have been there that the principal inhabitants of the village (apart from artists) are cows, ambling peacefully between the cottages, udders swinging, tails swishing, brown eyes gazing at nothing in particular, attended by remarkably small boys kicking up the white dust. The boys are so small that they seem inadequate to the control of cows; still nothing happens—indeed it is impossible to think of anything really happening in Amberley. It is that rare treasure in these days —a really sleepy old village.

In that delightful book of his, *A Sussex Peep Show*, Walter Wilkinson says this about Amberley :

". . . there it lay beneath us as simple as ever, with the smithy and heaps of old iron still in the centre of the village, with children in pinafores playing in the village street, and men in their shirt-sleeves tidying up the sweet-smelling flowers in the riotous gardens. But above all we could see the cricket field, and when a small man came out of the pavilion, ran up the club flag, removed the tennis nets, and rolled the pitch, we came down the hill to see the game as played in the county that fostered its beginnings. The square, level field, surrounded by trees, with a church tower and cottage roofs showing through the boughs, was the classic setting for the white-flannelled players."

A very beautiful thatched cottage in the village, with a high wall hiding the garden, is where that admirable painter of Sussex scenes, Edward Stott, lived. In his pictures he showed, in the excellent words of E. V. Lucas, "how the clear skin of a Sussex boy takes the light, and how the South-down sheep drink at hill ponds beneath a violet sky, and that there is nothing more beautiful under the stars than a whitewashed cottage just when the lamp is lit."

Amberley Wild Brooks—what a delicious name !—all flooded into a great sheet of water in wet winters, add further mysteries and charms to the place in the artist's eye. But the villagers, not unnaturally, perceive certain disadvantages in all this soaking water—though the village itself stands high enough out of it. The classic Amberley story is that when the local inhabitant is asked in the summer where he lives he answers proudly "Amberley, where would you?" But the same question in winter brings forth the mournful response, "Amberley, God knows!"

Other Sussex villagers have been known to declare that the dwellers in Amberley grow web-footed.

A stately touch of history is added to the rural peace of the village by the high ancient walls of what is known as Amberley Castle—the fortress palace of the Bishops of Chichester in the past. Happily wars and sieges never came to Amberley Castle, only the pomps and beneficences of the Church. And beyond the great walls, which now are but a shell, enclosing in one corner a pleasing little later manor-house, there is the level land of Amberley Wild Brooks— that name which is like a poem in itself.

So many of the Sussex names are lovely, or, what is just as pleasing, odd. Amberley itself like Adversane, spells romance and might have come from the pages of the *Morte d'Arthur*; Piddinghoe promises well, as do Rodmell, Ripe, and Rusper, Udimore, Peasmarsh, Duddleswell and Yapton. Rumbolswyke is a place one surely ought to see, and Appledram is hard to resist, as are Pippingford and Chuckhatch, while Wiston and Ringmer have a gentle charm.

The emphasis in Sussex place-names is almost invariably on the last syllable—particularly when the last syllable is "ham" it is pronounced separately and firmly apart from what goes before. Bosham is the standard example, and anyone who pronounces it Bosh-am, instead of Boz-ham, reveals himself not a native. This vernacular speech goes back to the Saxon origin of so many of the names when the village was the "ham" of the person whose name it bears—not a "sham," which means nothing. Hilaire Belloc bewails the modernized pronunciation of Horsham in that poor fashion, instead of in the old authentic manner of Horse-ham. Even in Horsham at this day, he says, the equine animal is not a horsh.

3

Under the northern escarpment of the Downs are some very old and, happily, out-of-the-way and therefore little-spoilt villages—hardly more than hamlets many of them. Fulking is one of these. It is set so close under the Downs that the great curves of the hill brood over the cottages like a hen over chicks. To look southwards is to tilt the head and look up at those indescribable coloured slopes of rough turf —they are not green, and they are not brown—before the sky is seen. Fulking is notable with water. At the foot of the steep little village street, which slopes sharply downward to a hollow curve, there is one of the most glorious springs in Sussex, leaping out of the chalk with a shout. It gushes and sparkles ceaselessly day and night, with an aspect of strength and generosity that is so inspiring it is hard to believe that in earlier times a shrine was not erected here to the Goddess of Water.

In the days when there were abundant sheep upon these Downs—all sadly vanished now—this spring used to be dammed in the hollow of the lane and a sheepwash made in the bend. The inn just above is called the Shepherd and Dog.

On the steep of the same bank as the inn—that is, actually on the very slope of the Down—is an ancient dwelling bearing the somewhat unusual name of Septima Cottage. It has all the elements of a proper fairy-tale witch's cottage, dark, and beamed with low crouching timbers waiting for the unwary head, tiny windows, a great wide smoky hearth in which a black cat with gleaming eyes should sit in the shadows. It is quite enchanting, and its garden is breath-taking, not just because it has all that a proper cottage garden should have, gnarled old apple-trees and graceful cherry-trees tossing petals in the wind, and borders full of cottage flowers all crushed together and fighting for their lives and thoroughly happy, and roses that actually are a hearty red and smell as sweet as honey—but breath-taking because of the way the great shoulder of the Down seems to lean over it, to lift it up and hold it.

In this cottage lived for many years an old Sussex woman,

and it was from her that it took its name of Septima—she was Ann Septima Cuttress, and became Mrs Benjamin Baldey. She lived in this cottage for eighty years, from the time she was six years old—as a girl, a wife and a widow (her husband lived to be eighty-five). She did not, as she would have wished, die there, because after her husband's death, when she had been living completely by herself for some years, attending her garden and housework, some of her relatives insisted that she should come and live with them. This she was very reluctant to do, and would not leave until she had been able to gather in the autumn produce of her garden, which she had tended so long with her own hands. She had fifteen children, and all the joys and sorrows of life came to her in this little cottage under the Downs, where she lived, rooted and wholesome as a lavender bush, for eighty years out of the eighty-six allocated to her. Such a life is worthy of remembrance, and in the old quiet days, in the old quiet villages, Sussex produced many lives like that of Ann Septima Cuttress. May the cottage be spared the too common fate of many Sussex cottages—that of falling into the hands of some moneyed "foreigner," furbished up with all modern conveniences and the old honoured name changed—without a moment's thought or qualm—to something more showy.

4

This little perched-up Septima Cottage at Fulking recalls another one even more clutched into the side of a hill at Pulborough. This is high above the road, clinging almost like a swallow's nest to the sandstone rock on which it perches. It is a fifteenth-century cottage, and its deep cellars, which are actually hewn out of the sandrock, are believed to have been storage places for smugglers' spoils. The interior of the cottage, both from its position and its ancient structure, is curiously fascinating, with doors and windows in quite unexpected places, and the outlooks from the windows full of surprises. Like many old houses, it reveals its bony structure in the great oaken timbers which visibly support and weld it together, so that it has the air of vitality and growth and reality which reinforced concrete so lamentably lacks.

The timber skeleton of a typical old Sussex farmhouse or cottage is an almost perfect example of the natural use of natural materials. Upon the low foundation wall of brick or stone or flint a massive oak sill was placed. Into this upright posts were tenoned—in early building usually set close, in later times wider spaced. There were two reasons for this : the closer set uprights were stronger against attack, and as times grew safer the timber was also growing scarcer, as the forests dwindled, and was used more thriftily. The corner posts of ancient houses were often whole tree trunks, usually root end at the top, for the broader base served to support the upper story, and it was found that when the sap could run out by this reversal the timber had a much longer life. On this simple principle the whole oaken cage, with its diagonal "dragon beam" and its rafters for the roof, was constructed. In the old days they talked of "rearing" a house. There then remained the filling of the spaces between the timbers, which was very commonly done by springing wooden laths between the uprights and plastering them on both sides —"wattle-and-daub." Sometimes in early examples the filling was like sheep-hurdles are made to-day—a very ancient craft with the plaster laid on. In some of the prettiest old houses the filling between the timbers is brick-nogging, either plain or herringbone brickwork. Sometimes this is the original filling, sometimes it has been added later, because the old wattle-and-daub has shrunk and let in the rain.

Sussex is rich in such timber-framed houses, because Sussex was once a county of great forests, and it was the natural material to the hand of the village craftsman-builder, who did the whole job, from the planning—no need to send to London for an architect; such people were never seen in villages—to cutting down and seasoning the timber. And the final result, as if it were a law of nature, was comeliness and beauty, a building that *belonged*. It had grown out of the soil, both literally and spiritually. Let us not forget what we owe to the old country builder—that simple and anonymous man.

5

There will probably be as many opinions as people if the old question is asked as to which is the most beautiful of the Sussex villages. "Each to his own," as Kipling says, but few who have seen it will deny that Burpham is an enchanted village. It must be enchanted, for apparently it has not changed for centuries—it might still be living in the seventeenth century, even, in some respect, in an earlier century.

There are two reasons for this. One is that it is a village which leads nowhere—you cannot go through it to get somewhere else. If you go there by mistake you have to turn back again. Beyond Burpham there is nothing but the bare Downs and a "Lepers' Way." That is one reason for the secrecy of Burpham. The other is that it is built on a sort of Downland cliff, the cottages all more or less have an air of hanging on by their thatched eyebrows, there is practically no room even to insert another bee-skep into Burpham. The thought of honey is a natural one in this village, for it had for vicar that delightful Sussex author, the Reverend Ticknor Edwardes, who wrote (besides many charming Sussex tales) that classic *The Lore of the Honey-Bee* and *The Bee-Master of Warriloo*. The second of these bee-books is now rather difficult to obtain, and so a quotation from it will be welcome.

"His were all old-fashioned hives of straw," writes Ticknor Edwardes, "hackled and potsherded just as they must have been any time since Saxon Alfred burned the cakes. Each bee-colony had its separate three-legged stool, and each leg stood in an earthen pan of water, impassable moat for ants and 'wood-li's,' and such small honey-thieves. Why the hives were dotted about in such admired but inconvenient disorder was a puzzle at first until you learned more of ancient bee-traditions. Whenever a swarm settled—up in the pink-rosetted apple-boughs, under the eaves of the old thatched cottages, or deep in the twigs of the hawthorn hedge—there, on the nearest open ground beneath, was its inalienable pre-determined home. When, as sometimes happened, the swarm went straight away out of sight over the meadows, or sailed off like a pirouetting grey cloud over the roof of wood, the old bee-keeper never sought to reclaim it for the garden.

" ' 'Tis gone to the shires for change o' air,' he would say, shielding his bleak blue eyes with his hand, as he gazed after it. ' 'Twould be agen natur' to hike 'em back here along. An' nought but ill-luck an' worry wi'out end.' "

The village of Burpham on a summer morning does suggest all the sweetness and simplicity of honey. The cottages are small and cosy and thatched, climbing on each other's shoulders. The gardens are just a bee's paradise. But this paradise has a guardian in a fierce St. George who points his spear, outside the village inn, at the unwanted stranger who may think it would be nice to have a week-end cottage here. Burpham has no empty cottages—the happy inhabitants no doubt live in them till they are one hundred and four, and then their great-grandchildren immediately take possession.

Simple as the village is, Burpham has a very remarkable church—square and solid and plain amid all the domestic grace of thatch and casement windows and cottage steps and doorways. Inside, the church has much to offer in dignity and peace. The massive arches are built of alternating blocks of chalk and sandstone, giving a most unusual and pleasing effect. The beautiful springing roof of the little chancel with its ribbed groining must be admired, and still more the south transept arch with its chevron moulding unlike anything else in Sussex, of so lovely a design—thought by some to be symbolic of the Crown of Thorns—and so marvellous an example of the stonemason's skill, almost as though stone were a malleable material and had been plaited instead of carved. The craftsman who carved so elaborately and so delicately that transept arch carved it for the love of God, not for the praise of a small village congregation.

The north wall of the church is late Saxon, with a small "wind's-eye" window visible in it. The font is beautiful, of early fifteenth-century date, and of the same century are some rigid, stiff-backed oaken benches.

Altogether a church full of old religious beauty. And Burpham has another remarkable thing in a curious earthwork of Saxon or Danish origin—the archæologists are not

quite agreed as to which—from the heights of which enchanting views may be had of the village and the surrounding
country. But the best view of all is from the edge of the bluff
on which Burpham is built, dropping sheer down to the River
Arun—here all tangled up with reeds and rose-bay willow
herb, it is not the navigable part of the Arun—and beyond
that the towers of Arundel Castle, looking, if the river mists
are rising, like a vignette to a fairy-tale.

6

Not so far away from Burpham is a village called Felpham
which must not be overlooked—not so much because of any
special charms, but because in a cottage there, which happily
still exists, William Blake once lived for three years, and
saw angels in the Sussex air. "Sussex is certainly a happy
place," Blake said, "and Felpham in particular is the sweetest
spot on earth."

Blake's biographer, Gilchrist, describes the cottage in
which he dwelt :

"It is still standing on the southern or seaward side of the
village. It is really a cottage; a long, shallow, white-faced
house, one room deep, containing but six in all—small and
cosy. Its lattice windows look to the front, at back the
thatched roof comes sweeping down almost to the ground.
A thatched wooden verandah, which runs the whole length
of the house, forming a covered way paved with red brick,
shelters the lower rooms from the southern sun. In front lies
the strip of garden enclosed by a low flint wall. Beyond, corn-
fields stretch down to the sea, which is only a few furlongs
distant."

At Felpham Blake discovered more wonders than have
ever before or since been found in a Sussex village :

Away to sweet Felpham, for Heaven is there;
The Ladder of Angels descends through the air;
On the turret its spiral does softly descend,
Through the village then winds, at my cot it does
    end.

You stand in the village and look up to Heaven;
The precious stones glitter on flight seventy-seven;
And my brother is there, and my friends and thine
Descend and ascend with the bread and the wine.

The bread of sweet thoughts and the wine of
    delight
Feed the village of Felpham by day and by night,
And at his own door the bless'd hermit does stand
Dispensing unceasing to all the wide land.

Also in a letter to Flaxman Blake described how delighted
he was with this Sussex village so close to the sea.

"Felpham is a sweet place for study, because it is more
spiritual than London. Heaven opens here on all sides its
golden gates; the windows are not obstructed by vapours;
voices of celestial inhabitants are more distinctly heard, their
forms more distinctly seen; and my cottage is also a shadow
of their homes."

It was while at this cottage that Blake saw the fairy's
funeral, the "procession of creatures, of the size and colour
of green and grey grasshoppers bearing a body laid out on
a rose-leaf, which they buried with songs and then disappeared."

But it was hardly to be expected that the stolid Sussex
natives would altogether understand this visionary man.
There was a little trouble of one kind and another, and it is
only fair to admit that Blake wrote, besides the lovely Felpham verses, these lines also :

> The Sussex men are noted fools,
> And weak in their brain-pan.

Not good poetry, and not, let us hope, entirely true.

7

To Amberley, in spite of its being rather dangerously
popular, and to Burpham, may be added a third charming
and secluded Sussex village which has not suffered the spolia-
tion that has unhappily overtaken many other villages—

which in situation and structure were equally delightful. I am not suggesting that these three villages are the only unspoiled ones in Sussex—that would be a fantastically gloomy view; there are scores of others, and even those that have suffered heavily on the outskirts from the foul hand of the commercial builder manage in many cases to preserve their hearts largely unchanged. But Amberley, Burpham and West Chiltington may be taken as typical of what Sussex villages in ancient days were like. Amberley has an acknowledged beauty, with the fascinating quality of the Wild Brooks, haunt of wild fowl and wild flowers, to mark it out. Burpham is distinguished by a complete seclusion, a notable church, and a mysterious earthwork; while West Chiltington has also a very fine church, with unusual features, and an enchanting little folk-museum. This is but a humble and domestic affair, nevertheless it presents a survey of old Sussex life which is worth a journey to see, even if West Chiltington was not in itself so unspoiled.

The objects in this tiny cheerful museum are mostly domestic and agricultural, though there are also some local worked flints. But it has more the feeling of a farmhouse kitchen than that associated with museums. The seventeenth-century housewife returned here would find her long oven-peel with which she put in and took out her batches of bread from the brick-oven. She would find the pan in which she melted the tallow for her candles, and the mould in which they were shaped, as well as the candlesticks to which she was accustomed, and the iron rush-light holders and the tinder-box, and also her spinning-wheel.

Her husband would find his flail and his smock, very beautifully worked, which kept him warm and dry, also his ox-yoke, or, if he were a shepherd, his crook and his sheep-bells.

But the finest example of needlework in this museum is not the smocking, good though it is, but a patchwork quilt which was made by a little West Chiltington girl only thirteen years old, in 1816. This quilt has inlays of patchwork in the most delightful delicate colourings on white calico. The taste and skill shown in the design and making could not be bettered, and all the charming bits of print were

bought in halfpennyworths at the village shop. Such prints could not be bought now at any shop—a curious result of "progress." It is satisfactory, at any rate, that West Chiltington has the wisdom to cherish this quite enchanting piece of handiwork produced in the village nearly a century and a half ago.

Also exhibited in this museum is a doctor's bill of over a hundred years old in which two of the items are "Journey and bleeding, 2/-; Hypnotic potion, 1/-". It would be interesting to know what went into the hypnotic potion!

Another Sussex domestic museum, on a larger scale than this one at West Chiltington, as it occupies a whole dwelling, is the one in the lovely old Priest's House at West Hoathly, which belongs to the Sussex Archæological Society.

Instead of a green, West Chiltington has a charming little square, set about with old cottages and the fine village church. The church has some remarkably massive arches, very interesting frescoes, and a curiously long and wide leper's squint, almost big enough for the poor leper to crawl along, instead of humbly looking. There are also a large village pond, a smithy, two inns, and the shell of the windmill. Here in this Sussex village was everything needed to support and adorn a wholesome life. The people of West Chiltington— and of many another Sussex village in the old days—had no need to be looking out of the window, as Cobbett scornfully said, for other people to bring them their food and drink. Or for London contractors to build their cottages for them. On the outskirts of this village is one of the most perfect examples of the Sussex cottage I have ever beheld—completely perfect in proportions, materials and colouring, with a truly noble roof of Horsham stone. It was stately in its perfect rightness, yet truly a cottage, though not a small one. And as if to crown its beauty, in the garden was what surely must be the most superb walnut tree in the whole county of Sussex. A great and nobly grown tree is a glorious sight, and one of the things that no amount of money can provide where it has not grown. Time alone will do that, and time cannot be purchased.

Hartfield

A larger and more sophisticated village than West Chiltington is Lindfield, which instead of being remote is dangerously accessible. But in spite of this, Lindfield has managed to preserve the long street of enchanting old houses of which it principally consists, in a remarkably unspoiled condition. Lindfield climbs up a long hill and at the bottom of the hill is a most decorative pond in which swans sail calmly, and in which the adjoining houses and little sloping gardens seem to gaze at their own charms. The houses at this end of the village have a pleasant eighteenth-century air, but as one climbs the hill the dwellings seem to get older and older, till round about the church cluster the most marvellous Tudor houses and cottages, almost too good to be true in their solid and decorative beauty. Beyond the church is Old Place, one of the finest timbered houses not only in Sussex, but in England, and, as if one such house was not enough, there are also Pax Hill, Buxshalls and East Mascalls, which years ago was a hollow timbered ruin, with the roof fallen in, all smothered in destructive ivy—tragically beautiful and desolate. But it is now restored to its ancient grace and dignity. This house and many others at Lindfield belong to the time of what Camden justly called "the great bravery of building which marvellously beautified the realm."

Pax Hill is not a timber-framed house, like East Mascalls, but belongs to the type and period of other Sussex mansions such as Danny, Wiston (under Chanctonbury Ring), Parham, Streat Place and Glynde—of opera fame.

Remembering these and other stately Sussex houses the saying of a Sussex man in 1542 comes to mind. "I had rather not to buyld a mansion or a house," said Andrew Boorde, "than to buylde one without a good prospect in it, to it, and from it. For yf the eye be not satysfyed the mynde cannot be contented, the heart cannot be pleased."

But in the aspect of their houses the Tudors had other views than ours—they thought the south unhealthy and a breeder of disease, and that is why so many of their buildings face north; they considered both the north and the east winds "clean."

The old cottages of Lindfield are in their own way as gracious and charming as the more important mansions— and the roof-lines of the village, whether straw-thatched, tiled or "heeled" with superb slabs of Horsham stone, are admirable. And the insides of these old cottages are as enchanting as the outsides would lead one to expect. One house at least has the original tapestry of soot, gone hard and stone-like, left upon the ancient rafters from the old open hearth in the hall, in the days before chimneys.

Lindfield should be remembered for something more than the beauty of its old houses and its spacious green or common, for there, in the eighteenth century, a Quaker, William Allen, conceived the curious, and, as it was thought, almost impious notion, that the children of the poor should be taught reading and writing and useful handicrafts. He built decent cottages for labourers, and let them at a rent suited to their poverty. He encouraged allotments, and believed that able-bodied men were better on the land than in the poorhouse. People who realize how the landless labourer, ruined by the Enclosures, was treated at this time, will also realize how extremely unusual were this Quaker's ideas of justice and charity to the poor, and feel glad to think that he practised them in Sussex.

9

As the mind circles round Sussex one realizes how many delightful villages there are—so many of these villages have their roots in the Heptarchy—and how impossible it is to describe them all, even those that one knows well. And tucked away in corners, hardly on the map at all, are little hamlets and secret farmsteads that in some marvellous way seem completely outside this desperate century. But to find such places it is well to keep to the northern side of the Downs— there are very few on the seaward side. Yet once upon a time Brighthelmstone was a small, poor fishing village, and the chalk cliffs to the east of it were bare and clean, with here and there a little cluster of cottages not altogether innocent of smuggling. Almost within the space of a life-time Rottingdean was such a place, and I have talked with a now dead inhabitant who remembered when the only water supply of the village was carted round from house to house on the back of a donkey. In the old days Rottingdean was thick with smugglers, and the vicar, Dr Hooker, was hand in glove with them. When Rottingdean, like all the Sussex coast, was hourly expecting Napoleon's invasion, the chief of the local smugglers at Rottingdean, who respected the fighting spirit of his parson, came to him and said that he wished to put him at the head of fifty men "who feared neither God nor devil" to repel the French if they landed. No wonder the French dare not face such opponents!

The old centre of Rottingdean, the Green with the old houses round it, and the little grey Saxon church—with the old indigenous Sussex names on the gravestones, the Mock-fords and the Moppets, the Dudeneys and the Snudders—still exists; but all round, spreading, smothering, is a new, ugly, graceless town, enough to discourage anyone attempting to penetrate to the heart of the old village.

In the later years of the nineteenth century and the early ones of the twentieth, Rottingdean was the home of Sir Edward Burne-Jones, who lived in the long low white house facing the Green which was made by throwing Prospect House and Aubrey Cottage into one and was later called North End House. He dwelt there from 1880 till his death in 1898. His ashes and those of his wife lie in a niche in the wall of Rottingdean Church, which is adorned by some of his stained glass windows. The inscription over their ashes is *Lux perpetua luceat*.

In her delightful *Memorials of Edward Burne-Jones* his wife tells how she discovered Rottingdean and the house they were to live in :

"It was a perfect autumn afternoon when I walked across the Downs and entered the village from the north; no new houses then straggled out to meet one, but the little place lay peacefully within its grey garden walls, the sails of the windmill were turning slowly in the sun, and the miller's black timber cottage was still there. The road I followed led me straight to the door of a house that stood empty on the village green, and we bought it at once."

Burne-Jones always loved Rottingdean, and from there he wrote "Two black oxen drawing a cart have just passed. . . . I don't want much in this world—I like black oxen drawing carts."

Near to North End House, at The Elms, an unpretending house behind a high garden wall, Rudyard Kipling lived for some years when he was at the height of his fame. But in spite of his garden wall he could not secure the privacy he desired—the persistent char-a-banc loads that came out on the switchback cliff road from Brighton to peep and peer at his house drove him from Rottingdean. He fled further east to Burwash, to the stately stone house called Batemans where he wrote those perfect Sussex books, *Puck of Pook's Hill* and *Rewards and Fairies*. The setting of these stories is the Burwash country, where the Kentish oast-houses are beginning to creep into the Sussex scene.

10

In these eastern parts of Sussex there are many old and simple villages which partake of the gentle austerity of the eastward Downs. The rich cosiness of thatch is seldom found here—there is something about thatch that suggests deep sunken lanes and abundant wild flowers—but the roofs are mostly tiled in soft browns and reds, or if slated, as some of them are, the slate is mellowed with that orange lichen which comes near the sea. The walls of houses and barns are often flint-built, sometimes with brick quoins and window settings, or are plain brindled brick. The cottages are humble, the church is grey—the whole scene is modest, with happily no claim to being a beauty-spot, but possessed of a quiet and increasing charm as it is known or lived in, and typical of many hamlets in East Sussex which from the Weald look up at the Downs so bare that a little clump of wind-blown trees like that of Black Cap is a landmark.

Rodmell beyond Lewes is one of these villages, and so is Kingston near by, and little Iford—so retiring as to have little save its church to show, where the effects of interior light, owing to crossing arches, are so mysterious. All these villages are in the gentle Ouse Valley, a region as mild in itself as the poetry of Cowper, yet stabbed here and there into sharp beauty by magic angles and aspects of the Downs —the marvellous double curve of the profile of Firle Beacon, the majestic promontory of Caburn, and all the little liftings and swellings of the ground which have no names.

Rodmell has two very beautiful cottage houses in it which have been skilfully restored and enlarged in recent years by the same hand, and which from their flint-walled gardens have views that may be considered essential Sussex—typical of all that this part of Sussex stands for in its peace, its rural simplicity, its unchangingness. The rest of the village consists of very humble houses and cottages, an inn with a most curious slanting window, and a very hidden-away little church in a rough field full of cow-pats, that yet abounds in interest. It is a church that has the proper village smell of eld and oil lamps, without which no village church is perfect. The font here is of Sussex winkle-stone, very solid and simple, and so old that it was hewn out of the native marble before the Normans came to the Sussex shore. Snowdrops grow abundantly and tall in the little churchyard, and under a mill-stone, instead of a tombstone, lies the last miller of Rodmell.

Rodmell is set in a kind of circlet of the Downs. Kingston is so close under the northward steep that the Downs are right in the village back gardens. Kingston really consists of nothing but a tiny street of cottages, all quite charming in that irregular, innocent way that the village builder of the past achieved without effort. There is an absurd little shop; a fine and large church, which has one of those curious gates, swinging on a central post, known as tapsell gates. Also it has a charming small manor-house, into the walls of which are built some pieces of carved stone that were filched long ago from the ruins of Lewes Priory. The garden of Kingston Manor slopes right up to the foot of the Down behind it, is enclosed in high grey flint walls, and has in it all the old country flowers and trees that are needed to complete its charm. It is surprising to discover in even the simplest Sussex villages how many are the tended and charming gardens and delightful houses and cottages tucked away behind walls, and hidden in remote and unfrequented lanes.

11

Sussex also possesses many famous and stately gardens which are "shown" to garden-lovers for various good and charitable causes, and among these is the garden at Gravetye which belonged to that notable gardener, William Robinson, he who, with Gertrude Jekyll, did so much to rescue English gardening from the stiff and ugly formality of Victorian "bedding out." His book, *The English Flower Garden*, has been for many years a classic, and when he died he left his Sussex garden at Gravetye, on which he had lavished his knowledge and skill, to the nation.

But if he left it and the freedom to view it to the English people, it is a remarkably difficult place to find. Even when you are in the right neighbourhood it hides away as if it wanted to escape all notice. Well I remember the search for it, and the long rough forest track up which the car reluctantly crawled, only to end up in a farmyard where there was nobody even to question, the only living things being a sheep-dog and a turkey-cock. It seemed the end of everywhere, but as it appeared easier to go on than to go back, and we had been told we were on the right road, persistence was at last rewarded and we came to the gates of Gravetye Manor, a large gabled Tudor stone house surrounded by the wonderful gardens. The house is on a kind of ridge and it, like the gardens, looks down sloping fields across to another ridge, crowned with forest. There is a lake from which the Medway rises—that river which soon deserts Sussex to become Kentish. The gardens are wonderful, as is to be expected, considering the fifty years of care and skill devoted to them, but the outlook is restricted and in a curious manner rather gloomy—in Sussex there always seems something wrong if one cannot see the Downs, even as a line of ghostly beauty on the farthest horizon.

Another Sussex garden comes to mind more enchantingly than Gravetye, and that is the garden of Field Place, near

Horsham, where Shelley was born. This garden possesses that combination of stateliness and freedom, the mansion and the cottage, as it were, commingling, which represents the English garden at its best. And the house it surrounds and adorns, with its well-proportioned dignity, and its roof of Horsham stone slabs, is equally satisfying.

The flowers bloom richly and happily in the gardens, the water shines and moves there, the trees cast their gracious shade, but the spirit of Shelley was never at home in this pleasant mansion of his father, though over the chimneypiece in the room in which he was born is this inscription :

> Shrine of the dawning speech and thought
>   Of Shelley sacred be
> To all who know where Time has brought
>   Gifts to Eternity.

12

Shelley was not one of the spirits born to happiness in this world, but this parish of Warnham of his birth had another little country boy, born about the same time, who made of his humbler existence a much happier thing. His name was Michael Turner, and he was a small farmer's son, and grew up to be the parish clerk and sexton, as well as leader of the choir. He played the fiddle, and played it so well that he was in great demand at the village dances and also at the big houses. He sounds just like one of the joyful old rural characters from *Under the Greenwood Tree*. He was so beloved in Warnham that when he got too old to work his village undertook to support him. He died with his fiddle in his hand, and it is to-day preserved in the vestry of the church. On his gravestone are cut these simple friendly verses :

> His duty done, beneath this stone
>   Old Michael lies at rest;
> His rustic rig, his song, his jig,
>   Were ever of the best.

With nodding head the choir he led,
That none should start too soon,
The second, too, he sang full true,
His viol played the tune.

And when at last his age had passed
One hundred less eleven,
With faithful cling to fiddle string
He sang himself to Heaven.

In the old days Sussex country people tended to long and contented lives, as many a record and many a memory of still surviving gaffers and gammers show. But these old people are rapidly disappearing, and the human links with the past which they represent are being snapped with a sadly increasing speed.

13

One of the sanest and sweetest men who ever lived, Gilbert White, though Hampshire is the county that claims him, has also happy associations with Sussex, particularly with the village of Ringmer, beyond Lewes, where he used to stay with his aunt, whose enchanting name was Rebecca Snooke. The house in which she lived (she had married a son of the Vicar of Ringmer) is still in existence, and is called Delves House. It is just the kind of simple pleasant English country home that makes a proper setting for Gilbert White—the same type of people lived in Delves House, Ringmer, that lived at The Wakes, Selborne. They are the people who inhabited half the rectories and vicarages of southern England at that time, and are to be met in the pages of Jane Austen, and, half a century later, in those of Trollope.

Delves House, under the name of Northdelve, is mentioned as far back as 1340, in the Ringmer Court Rolls, but the present abode is roughly of the period of Queen Anne, and has a well-proportioned façade of rosy brick, and a charming white-painted pillared porch. The gardens have all the proper trimmings of yew-hedges, mulberry trees, medlars and quinces. And there lived the celebrated tortoise, Timothy, whose portrait is painted on a signpost leading to Ringmer Church.

This tortoise is part of Sussex history and cannot be ignored. It lived at Delves House with Mrs Rebecca Snooke for a great number of years, and Gilbert White, as was to be expected, was much interested in its habits when visiting his aunt. "No part of its behaviour," he wrote, "ever struck me more than the extreme timidity it always expresses with regard to rain; for though it has a shell that would secure it against the wheel of a loaded cart, yet does it discover as much solicitude about rain as a lady dressed in all her best attire, shuffling away on the first sprinklings and nursing its head up in a corner." He was also, he says, "much taken with its sagacity in discerning those that do it kind offices," for as soon as his aunt, who had fed it for more than thirty years, appeared it hobbled towards her "with awkward alacrity; but remains inattentive to strangers."

One cannot help feeling that even the slowest tortoise might know its feeder after thirty years.

In April 1780, Gilbert White wrote from Selborne that this "Sussex tortoise" had come to live with him, after being carried "eighty miles in post-chaises. The rattle and hurry of the journey so perfectly roused it that when I turned it out on a border it walked twice down to the bottom of my garden."

Gilbert White rode frequently from Selborne to Ringmer to stay with his aunt, and it was of these journeys he wrote in the well-known letter from Ringmer of 9 December 1773 :

"Though I have now travelled the Sussex Downs upwards of thirty years, yet I still investigate that chain of majestic mountains with fresh admiration year by year; and I think I see new beauties every time I traverse it. This range, which runs from Chichester eastward as far as East Bourn, is almost sixty miles in length, and is called the South Downs, properly speaking, only round Lewes. As you pass along you command a noble view of the wild, or Weald, on one hand, and the broad Downs and sea on the other. . . . For my part I think there is somewhat peculiarly sweet and amusing in the shapely-figured aspect of chalk hills."

Gilbert White has been smiled at for his description of

the Downs, but those who know them best realize that "majestic" is a word that fits them in many of their aspects. And it must be remembered, too, the manner in which he saw them, not rushing at excessive speed on a hard highway in the modern manner, but riding along them year after year on his quiet-paced horse—under those conditions both the "majesty" and the "sweetness" of the Downs had time to soak into his receptive spirit.

In another letter he says "the prospects and rides round Lewes are most lovely." And then we have this nice little Sussex picture : "As a gentleman and myself were walking on the 4th of last November round the sea-banks at New-haven, near the mouth of the Lewes river, in pursuit of natural knowledge, we were surprised to see three house-martins gliding very swiftly by us."

It is pleasant to think of Gilbert White pursuing "natural knowledge" on the coast at Newhaven.

14

Ringmer has other claims to remembrance apart from its happy associations with Gilbert White and his tortoise, for here was born Gulielma Springett, who married that great Quaker, William Penn, and lived with him at Warming-hurst. The bust of her father, Sir William Springett, is in Ringmer Church, and the inscription says : "Here lyeth the Body of Sr William Springett, Knt. He had issue by Mary his wife one Soune John Springett and one Daughter Gulielma Maria Posthuma Springett. He being a Collonell at ye Taking in of Arundel Castle in Sussex : there Con-tracted a sickness where-of he Died being 23 yeares of age." His wife went to him at Arundel Castle when he was dying, and her account of the journey shows both her undaunted and devoted spirit, and the terrible state of the roads. Her love for her young husband was so strong that she journeyed all the way from London to Arundel, though she was near the birth of her second child, the Gulielma Posthuma who was to become Penn's wife. When her husband summoned her, feeling that he was near his end, she said in the narrative she wrote—full of that vividness which seventeenth-century ladies seemed to command with their pens—"The coachmen were so sensible of all the difficulties and the badness of the way between London and Arundel, at that time of the year, that in all the neighbouring streets they refused to come with me. . . . It was a very tedious journey; we were benighted, and in the dark overthrown into a hedge. When we got out we found there was on the other side hardly room to get along, for fear of falling down a very steep precipice, where we would have been all broken to pieces."

They had various other unpleasant adventures on the way, but at last reached Arundel. "When we came to Arundel," said Lady Springett, "we saw a most dismal sight—the town depopulated—the windows all broken from the firing of the great guns—the soldiers making use of the shops and lower rooms for stables."

Her dying husband could hardly believe she had surmounted the dangers of the journey to Arundel, and she gives a pathetic account of his joy at seeing her and embracing her. But his joy was brief. He died very soon after his brave lady's arrival. His body was taken back to Ringmer for burial, and a handsome monument erected there by his wife "in testimony of her dear affection for him."

With this valiant Sussex lady and the siege of Arundel may be linked another lady and another siege of a much earlier time. This lady is Lady Joan Pelham (a name that is part of Sussex history), who wrote to her husband at the end of the fourteenth century when she was besieged in Pevensey Castle during his absence fighting elsewhere. It is not only a brave and beautiful letter, but it has the further interest of being one of the earliest of English letters in existence :

"My dear Lord—I recommend me to your high Lordship, with heart and body and all my poor might. And with all this I thank you as my dear Lord, dearest and best beloved of all earthly lords. I say for me, and thank you, my dear Lord, with all this that I said before of your comfortable letter that you sent me from Pontefract, that came to me on Mary Magdalene's day : for by my troth I was never so glad as when I heard by your letter that ye were strong enough with the grace of God for to keep you from the malice of your enemies. And, dear Lord, if it like to your high Lordship that as soon as ye might that I might hear of your gracious speed, which God Almighty continue and increase. And, my dear Lord, if it like you to know my fare, I am here laid by in mannr of a siege with the county of Sussex, Surrey and a great parcel of Kent, so that I may not out nor no victuals get me, but with much hard. Wherefore, my dear, if it like you by the advice of your wise counsel for to set remedy for the salvation of your Castle and withstand the malice of the shires aforesaid. And also that ye be fully informed of the great malice-workers in these shires which have so despitefully wrought to you, and to your Castle, to your men and to your tenants; for this country have they wasted for a great while.

"Farewell, my dear Lord; the Holy Trinity keep you from your enemies, and soon send me good tidings of you.

"Written at Pevensey, in the Castle, on St. Jacob's day last past,

"By your own poor
"J. Pelham.

"To my true Lord."

Sussex has reason to be proud of those two brave ladies, Lady Pelham and Lady Springett.

15

Returning from Pevensey to the Ouse Valley, we find there those three remarkable round church towers of late twelfth or early thirteenth century date, all appearing much as if built by the same hand. One is in Lewes High Street. The other two are outside Lewes, though not far away, at the two small hamlets of Southease and Piddinghoe. Southease is a tiny hamlet, tucked away and apparently forgotten, close to the main highway that leads from Lewes to Newhaven. The church, half-hidden by trees, slipping down a little slope, and with one of the Sussex "fool's cap" spires, has its roots in the far past—very small and simple and old. Inside it has some faded frescoes, very faint, showing scenes from the life of our Lord, which represent Him, somewhat unusually, with yellow hair and a black nimbus. The church is rather like an ancient whitewashed barn, with its open timber roof. Even the chancel arch is of oak, instead of stone, the arch itself being filled in with oak beams and lath and plaster, very primitive and rough and irregular. It is a curiously humble and lovely little edifice.

Southease itself is but a cottage or two, a farm and barn, a few pigs and hens rootling about. The whole thing might have come out of the Luttrell Psalter, instead of being on the very edge of the road to Newhaven, where the punctual Southdown buses pass and return. That is one of the odd things about Sussex—the proximity of the primitive and the modern.

Piddinghoe, a little further on this same road and a little nearer to the dreary outskirts of Newhaven, is also curiously remote and aloof. The church has the third of these thirteenth-century circular flint towers, and is enchantingly set on a little hill, round which curl the sluggish waters of the broadening Ouse, not far from their union with the sea.

Piddinghoe is also nothing but a handful of farms and cottages and what was once a kiln, with a pleasing little house attached.

At no great distance away, on the inland side of the Downs, is the old Saxon village of Wilmington. The village itself is very simple and pleasant, not much more than an agricultural hamlet—but it is notable for three things, a most magnificent though partly ruined barn, Wilmington Priory, and the "Long Man" on the Downs beyond the Priory, who, as Kipling said, "looks naked towards the shires."

Wilmington Priory, which happily is now the property of the Sussex Archæological Trust, upon which it was bestowed by the Duke of Devonshire, is a most appealing place. It has all the attractions of antiquity and ecclesiastical dignity, combined with homely agricultural use, for the monastic remains are all mixed up with a farmhouse, and the great barn is much vaster than the church. Even in its early days, Mr Godfrey says in his *Guide to Wilmington Priory*, "In all probability it approximated much more nearly to a grange or manor-house than a monastery."

In the eighteenth century S. H. Grimm made a very attractive drawing, showing the wall and empty windows of the fourteenth-century hall. The Priory is a fascinating place in which to wander, and in the roofed and still inhabited parts there are some wonderful things to be seen, great rooms with great rafters and tie-beams and interesting stonework, much of which dates from the thirteenth and fourteenth centuries.

And on the Downs beyond the Priory, on Windover Hill, is one of the strangest things in Sussex—the "Long Man" cut in outline in the chalk, when, why and by whom nobody really knows. He is a mystery, like his brother the Giant of Cerne, who rudely threatens with his club the little Dorset village of Cerne Abbas. Our Sussex giant is in a milder mood than the Dorset one, and holds in each hand a staff, which has led to the idea that he represents Balder opening the doors of dawn. In an early drawing of the figure the two staffs are represented as the short-bladed scythe and rake of Saxon times, which suggests that in periodic "scourings" of the chalk these additions to the staffs may have gradually been overlooked and the turf allowed to grow over them. No idea as to the origin of the Sussex and the Dorset giants could be less likely than the suggestion which has been made that these figures were cut in the chalk by the Benedictine monks whose monasteries lie at the foot of the Downs on which they stride. Anyone who looks at these great naked figures, especially the Dorset one, will realize how extremely unlikely it is that monks should have cut them. Indeed, there is some evidence that the monks of Wilmington made an attempt to obliterate the great figure, though fortunately, in the interests of archæology, they did not succeed. It is surely writ in the chalk itself that both these figures belong to a long-past and primitive age, before Christianity came to England. We may imagine that on the autumn westerly gales the Dorset Giant sends uncouth messages from the "dark backward and abysm of Time" to his brother in Sussex.

The "Long Man" of Wilmington is indeed long, being 240 feet high—the greatest chalk figure in England. The Giant of Cerne is only 180 feet in length, though in appearance he is so much fiercer and more uncouth.

Alfriston is a beautiful village, with a fine and finely set cruciform church which is often called the "Cathedral of the Downs." But though Alfriston has many charms and a famous richly beamed and carved and decorated inn, it is one of the too-popular, too-well known villages of Sussex, in danger that its very beauty and accessibility will be its destruction. One of the treasures of Alfriston is the ancient Priest's House, which has been already described, and it has also the mere stump of a market cross—very different from the famous one at Chichester. Alfriston is admirably set among the Downs, and in all directions round about there are delightful walks, and many lovely little hamlets and villages like Alciston and Lullington and Litlington.

But having looked at so many of the smaller villages it must not be forgotten that Sussex also has jewels of a somewhat larger size, small market towns which have a greater spaciousness of building, like Petworth—"proud Petworth" —and Steyning and Arundel.

Petworth itself is not particularly proud, though it would have some excuse for being so, with its delightful little streets and domestic buildings. It is Petworth House that has such an air of arrogance, with its rows and rows of windows on the monotonous façade. The great towering walls and spiked gateways that guard Petworth House from any contact with the common people have an air, in these days, not only arrogant, but absurd—the helmeted stone coat-of-arms, ludicrously pompous, on the gate-posts speak of eighteenth-century intolerance, and recall monumental effigies of the same period where bewigged landed proprietors are received in Heaven by effusive and servile angels.

But the little town of Petworth itself is charming. And not so very different from what it was when Cobbett wrote of it :

"Petworth is a nice market town, but solid and clean. The great abundance of stone in the land hereabouts has caused a corresponding liberality in paving and wall building, so that everything of the building kind has an air of great strength and produces the agreeable idea of durability. Lord Egre-

mont's house is close to the town, and with its outbuildings and garden walls, and other erections, is, perhaps, nearly as big as the town; though the town is not a very small one."

Stone walls and stone paving still give to Petworth its comfortable air of solidarity, and though the general aspect is that of a little eighteenth-century town in the seemly proportions of numbers of the house fronts, yet many of the irregular roof lines and jutting angles, combined with the narrowness of some of the streets, like Lombard Street and Middle Street, suggest a much older Tudor Petworth. The little Market Square has a stiff dignity that is rather charming, though it is to be regretted that the open arches of the Market Hall have been filled in.

17

Petworth is dominated by Petworth House, and Arundel is even more overshadowed by Arundel Castle. It is a half-enchanted, half-asleep feudal town, set on a marvellous steep hill, obviously intended by nature to be crowned by a romantic castle. And to add to the romantic appearance of the site a modern miracle has happened there—the modern Gothic Church of St. Philip Neri, built by the late Duke of Norfolk, the fifteenth duke, is so admirably and delicately poised on the side of the steep hill, is so genuinely Gothic in feeling, that instead of being a blot on the perfection of the little town it is an enchantment. There is an old saying, "There are many beautiful places in the world, but there is only one Arundel," so it is a piece of singular good fortune that the Duke's new Catholic church has not spoiled, as it so easily might have done, the Duke's town, for the period at which it was built was a bad one architecturally. I lived for many weeks in full sight of that church, beheld it in sunshine and in moonlight, and found that it grew upon the mind as if it were some fabric of ancient beauty, and had sprung up in Gothic Ages of Faith, instead of in the utilitarian nineteenth century.

The Castle itself is a curious mixture of the old—the Keep was there when Queen Matilda fled to Arundel—and the comparatively modern, for large parts of it have been rebuilt and restored in quite recent periods. But in spite of this, the effect of the whole is undoubtedly impressive, and its position and the way it dominates the surrounding country-side is superb. It should be approached up the excessively steep High Street; it should be seen from the tree-shaded walk that runs roughly parallel with the river; it should be looked at from the water-meadows below the bridge; from the end of Maltravers Street; and from the old coaching-inn yard of the Norfolk Hotel. In fact there are innumerable points from which to observe it, as it were circling round it. The most romantic of all is from the edge of the bluff on which the adjoining village of Burpham stands. Then, to complete the impression, from the heart of the Castle itself, from the ancient Keep, the surrounding country should be surveyed on all sides. It is a fine and varied view to each point of the compass—much history is in it and much of the beauty of Sussex. Arundel, indeed, needs to be something exceptional in the way of a town, for the road into it is so enchanting—up the superb steep of Bury Hill, with Houghton Bridge and the chalk pits below, and on the left-hand side the dark woods of Arundel Park folded like wings. The road into Arundel actually runs some way through the woods, and in spring the radiant young green of the beeches shot with sunlight, and in the autumn the tawny bronzes of the dying verdure, are equally astonishing. At all the seasons the beech is a lovely tree, even in late summer its foliage never takes on the dull heaviness of many other trees—light seems imprisoned in those delicately ribbed leaves.

There is something of the quality of fairy-tale about Arundel, in spite of its model post office, its Mayor, and its remarkably gloomy and threatening police station.

It once had a great house in Tarrant Street bearing the romantic name of Nineveh, which was built so long ago as some time between 1415 and 1422, and was a treasure of riches. But Nineveh has completely vanished away.

Hollar's drawing of Arundel shows this house, on the banks of the Arun. It stood alone, and had trees about it, a fine mansion, enriched with much superb carved oak inside, and a very remarkable staircase. This house eventually sank

down to being used as labourers' tenements and part of the
beautiful carved work was wrenched from the walls and
burnt as firewood; the elaborately carved balusters of the
staircase were also nearly all destroyed. And then the house
itself was pulled down, and in its place was built the gloomy
Nonconformist chapel which still exists in Tarrant Street,
and whose only interest is that George MacDonald, who
wrote that delicious story for children and grown-ups, *At the
Back of the North Wind*, was for a time minister there. He
ought to have written a story about Nineveh. That a house
so unusually early in date and so rich in detail was allowed
to sink into a slum, and then completely disappear, is a
matter both for regret and reproach.

Those who know and love the town of Arundel will agree
with what Dr G. W. Eustace, historian of *Arundel: Borough
and Castle*, who has also been its Mayor, says at the end of
his book :

"Arundel, under all skies, but especially in the first morning light when the mists in the valley are beginning to lift,
presents a striking picture; its intermingled roofs of tile and
slate rising tier above tier; its stately Castle perfectly balanced
by the noble church of St. Philip Neri; the whole backed by
the rapidly ascending wooded slopes behind, and, at its foot,
the winding Arun flowing gently down the valley to the sea."

18

Steyning is the town of Chanctonbury—it is dominated by
that noble tree-covered Down, as Arundel is by its Castle.
It is the background to Steyning's day, as it is the mystery
of Steyning's night, thrusting its darkness against the moonlit
sky and the stars. There are many reputable and learned
people who consider it unwise to walk round Chanctonbury
Ring at night-time—curious things are apt to happen. But in
the day-time in Steyning, at the end of little streets, from odd
tucked-away windows, over garden walls, you perceive with
ever fresh delight that Ring—it is impossible to grow tired
of it, or fail to remember gratefully that eighteenth-century
Goring who in his youth planted those trees and painfully

watered them, and in his old age saw that his work was good. Perhaps no action of one man has had such a wide benedictive effect upon the landscape of Sussex as his.

In such a scene it is pleasant to recall Blackmore's meditative words in the opening of his Sussex novel, *Alice Lorraine* :

"Westward of that old town of Steyning and near Washington and Wiston, the lover of an English landscape may find much to dwell upon. The best way to enjoy it is to follow the path along the meadows, underneath the inland rampart of the Sussex hills. Here is pasture rich enough for the daintiest sheep to dream upon; tones of varied green in stripes (by order of the farmer), trees as for a portrait grouped, with the folding hills behind, and light and shadow making love in play to one another."

Steyning is one of the most pleasant and friendly little towns in Sussex—it combines the Middle Ages with the eighteenth century in a completely charming and incongruous fashion. Nothing quarrels with anything else—Gothic rubs shoulders amiably with Regency—because nothing was planned, but all grew together naturally and unconsciously, because builders of medieval times, of Tudor, and of the seventeenth and eighteenth centuries, all had the art of building harmoniously with what was already in existence—an art we have so conspicuously lost.

In the High Street, which curves and dips up and down in a pleasing manner, and in Church Street, there is a charming medley of buildings—Georgian inns and banks, full of the flavour of the period; dignified and simple Carolean houses; Tudor ones with jettied overhanging stories; cottages of no architectural period, as they come straight out of a fairy-tale; and the noble Brotherhood Hall, one of the most satisfying buildings in Sussex. The post office is, or was—I hope it has not been altered—pure *Cranford*, and no woman unadorned with a crinoline should be allowed to enter it. In Church Street is the cottage, deeply and steeply thatched and ancient, that is called Saxon Cottage, and beside it is another with a very beautiful roof of Horsham stone. Around the corner is Chantrey Green, very small and secluded and Georgian in appearance, though many of these apparently

Georgian dwellings are actually Tudor, and have an impressive interior timber construction, having been refronted and windowed in the fashion of the day in the eighteenth century. It is part of the fascination of ancient houses that one never knows what may be hidden away inside them.

The streets of Steyning still look as though the mail-coach and a smart curricle or two would come dashing along at any moment.

The church stands a little aside from the town. It is very fine and solid, with beautiful brickwork in the walls and the massive tower, and when one opens the marvellous door of oak and ironwork, and goes down the steps in the nave, it is to be conscious of a kind of shock at the massiveness of the interior—the solemn Norman weight of the great arches. This is not the church the humble St. Cuthman built, though it is dedicated to him.

Steyning has a market, and once Steyning was a port, difficult as it is to realize that on looking at the well-cultivated country all round about it now. Steyning certainly deserves to share the praise that Cobbett gave to Horsham when he wrote in his *Rural Rides* : "This is a very nice, solid, country town. Very clean, as all the towns in Sussex are. The Sussex women are very nice in their dress and in their houses."

19

One more village remains to be described out of this chosen handful—chosen not because they are supposed to be representative or typical, or the most beautiful of the Sussex villages, but simply because they happen to be best known to the writer, and it is always better to speak of what one knows. The facts about any place can be acquired from any reliable guide-book—the atmosphere of a place can only be realized from personal knowledge.

Ditchling is a village set almost in the centre of Sussex—it is almost in line with Chailey Common whose white and toy-like windmill and pointed trees are generally considered to mark the middle of Sussex. There are people who hold it the best village in Sussex, not because it is the most beautiful, or the most unspoiled, for unfortunately its popularity has resulted in some undesirable buildings on its edges. But it is superbly set in regard to the Downs on a little hill of sand-rock, at the perfect distance away to survey the chalk range as a whole from Black Cap to Chanctonbury and beyond. The string of little old villages close under the Downs such as Fulking and Edburton and Clayton are much too close to see the Downs as anything but an overshadowing presence. But Ditchling is just far enough away to gain a wide-spreading impression of their lovely sweeping line, and yet so near that a twenty minutes' walk brings any inhabitant to the foot of the hill.

The central point of the little eminence on which Ditchling is built is crowned by a very beautiful and very Sussex-looking church. If St. Margaret's Church was snatched up by a giant hand and set down in Warwickshire or Somerset—county of stately Perpendicular towers—it would cry "Sussex" so loudly that it would have to be put back again without any delay. It is built of flint—the most Sussex of all building materials, some of the work knapped and fine, some coarser and of whole flints. It has a low tower with a pointed cap covered with oak shingles. There is an idea, from the strength of the masonry of the supporting arches, that the central tower—it is a cruciform church—was intended to be considerably higher than it actually is, but few Ditchling people would desire it raised by even a foot—the nave and chancel, the north and south aisles, with the low central tower, give a motherly and brooding look to the church, which a higher tower would spoil.

Inside the church has suffered somewhat from nineteenth-century "restoration"—how badly was William Morris's "Anti-Scrape" needed in those pompous years. The northern wall of the nave was rebuilt, for no known reason, destroying Saxon work, and some very bad stained glass windows put in. But the northern wall of the chancel has retained its ancient windows, very widely splayed, as the actual window openings are unusually narrow, and these windows, and the east window, have interesting corbel heads of chalk, supposed to be those of kings and queens, though nobody knows, apparently, which kings and queens.

In this wall is a beautiful little thirteenth-century door, now blocked up. The church also possesses a fine shapely thirteenth-century oak chest.

In the churchyard, which from its elevation yields most delightful views both of the red roofs of the village and of the Downs, there are, among the more permanent and usual stone and marble tombstones, one or two of those rapidly decaying long low wooden grave-boards which recall old wood-engravings illustrating Gray's "Elegy in a Country Churchyard"—that most essentially English of all English poems. One of these grave-boards is to the memory of George Howell, who was born at West Hoathly on 6 June 1754, and who died at Ditchling on 7 May 1855, aged, so the inscription proudly states, 100 years and 336 days. What the span of such a life had covered—when he was born the French Revolution and the Napoleonic Wars were in the future, the name of Nelson was unknown to English history, and Trafalgar and Waterloo unfought. Railways did not exist, and not one of Dickens' novels was written. When he died the last of the Hanoverian Georges was dead and Queen Victoria was seated on that throne which she occupied for so long. And it is tolerably safe to say that through all those events George Howell probably spent the whole of his long life within the confines of Sussex—a visit to Brighthelmstone being possibly the furthest extent of his travels between the secluded and charming village of his birth, and Ditchling, where he died, and where his bones have rested for nearly another hundred years.

Just below the churchyard on the south side is a noble Tudor building known as Anne of Cleves' House, or Wing's Place, as it was sometimes called in the past. This house is the pride of the village, and even to-day the cause of some rather mixed historical ideas. A former vicar of the parish, of the mid-nineteenth century, records in the *Sussex Archæological Collections* : "Of this house, one person declared to me that it was built by Alfred, and when I told him that to be so 'it must be more than a thousand years old,' he seemed to see the fallacy of his own statements. Another asserted that Gundrada built it for stabling, and that Mr Poole, whose monument is in the north transept of the church, was

master of her hounds and was its first inhabitant—without
for a moment considering that in that case he must have
lived to a greater age than even Ditchling people ever attain
unto, viz., 500 years."

The only truth in these misshapen stories is that Ditchling
belonged to William de Warenne, and was not too far away
for Countess Gundrada to ride over from Lewes and inspect
it, if she felt so inclined.

The Anne of Cleves House is only a portion of the fine
dwelling that was once here, the part to the eastward having
completely vanished. It was bestowed upon the "Flanders
mare" by Henry VIII for her wise complacency in accepting
the part of his "sister," instead of the dangerous position
of his queen. In consequence she kept her head, as well as
the manor of Ditchling, and others at Southover, Preston,
and other places. The people of Ditchling like to consider
that Anne of Cleves lived in this pleasant house of hers in
the village, with its garden dropping down the slope of the
hill and gazing across the fields to the Downs which make
the southward horizon. But there does not seem to be any
real evidence that she ever actually lived here. She had many
other manors to visit and choose from, and she did not live
to be very old.

West Street, the short street facing the church, in which
is Anne of Cleves' House, ends at its eastern corner in
another Tudor house—a house which saw the coming and
the dispersal of the Spanish Armada, and was there during
the whole lifetime of Shakespeare. Between the two ancient
dwellings are a few shops, which though presenting a more
or less modern aspect to the street (save for one charming
Georgian bow-fronted shop-window, happily not yet "improved" away) are actually much older than they look, and
may easily be in their foundations as old as anything in the
village—for round the thirteenth-century church and the hill
on which it stands would obviously be the earliest building.
These shops have deep cellars—the premises of one shop
boast a ghost !—and in one of them was an enormous ancient
well, now filled in, almost as alarming in its circumference as
the vast kitchen well at Bodiam Castle, which still brims
with dark and fearsome-looking water.

Ditchling still has a surprising number of wells in existence, if not actually in use. They may be seen in cottage gardens, sometimes with the well-head and bucket, sometimes covered in with a heavy slab of stone, or completely built over. There are a variety of village stories of the ground giving way without warning, and people tumbling into deep holes which were old forgotten wells. One of the reasons for Ditchling's original existence was that it had good water, was one of those places, as Belloc says, "where the pure water having dripped through the chalk of the high hills gushes out in fountains to feed that line of steadings and of human homes." Northwards of Ditchling, on the Common which bears its name, though separated by a couple of miles from the village, and round about, the water is bad —the water cannot be drunk unboiled, save by the oldest inhabitant to whom it has become, by use and wont, a "vintage brew." In many a group of farmsteads and cottages only one dwelling will have a well that is usable and which does not dry at a very moderate drought.

Ditchling has a village pond, just by Court Farm—a place of some importance in the early medieval history of the village—fed by a spring from Lodge Hill. This sudden, abruptly steep, little hill is by the romantic-minded regarded as the burial-place of Dicul, the founder of the village of Dicul's people. Some day the spade of the archæologist may discover if there is any truth in this legend—the hill has never been dug. But the crest and top of Lodge Hill is a superb viewpoint from which to overlook the village, and not only the village, but a very considerable portion of the county of Sussex. The height of the little hill is not great, yet it is so placed that it commands a wonderful stretch of the Downs, from Black Cap in the east near Lewes to Wolstonbury and Chanctonbury Ring, Duncton Down and Rackham Hill, and misty and mysterious hills reaching almost to Chichester. Then to the north-west Hindhead and the Hog's Back, and to the north St. Leonard's Forest, Ashdown Forest, and Crowborough Beacon. In the east are Rotherfield, Mayfield, Heathfield, Dallington and Brightling Needle. Even the woods of Battle on the edge of the county may sometimes be discerned. The beauty of this varied encircling view, beheld from a height not much greater than the chimney-pots of Ditchling, is indescribable. And from this fortunate spot the beauty of the old village is not marred by the later additions which prowl about the outskirts. The centre of Ditchling is still rich in ancient and characteristic Sussex building. At a bend of East End Lane there is a group of old houses, with irregular and varied roof-lines that it would be difficult to better in all Sussex. And hidden away behind the forge—Ditchling is fortunate in still possessing that proper appurtenance of a proper village, a blacksmith's smithy, and not so long ago had also a wheelwright—is a timber-framed and interesting old cottage with a noble roof-line, while opposite, across the road, is another, which has an immense "cat-slide" roof and backs on to the beautiful Star Field that runs up to Lodge Hill, in which the celebrated Ditchling Gooseberry and Copper Kettle Fair has been held since 1822. Much older fairs than this had Ditchling, but they have vanished.

Scattered about the village are other ancient houses and cottages, sometimes refronted or otherwise altered, but in essentials sturdy and enduring. Ditchling is typical of many Sussex villages—assaulted by modern ways, touched by modern haste and ugliness, but yet resistant and valiant at heart, because of a long past.

20

Sussex has not only an array of ancient villages, but several castles of great historic interest. Two of them—Bodiam and Herstmonceux—have a particular appeal, as they are both extremely unusual and extremely beautiful.

About Bodiam there is some dream-like quality that is hard to explain, for its walls and its drum-towers are solid enough, but at certain times and in certain lights it appears as though it might float away, or sink into that lilied moat which surrounds and embraces and enhances its magic.

It is a castle without a history, built too late for "war's alarms"—apart from that episode in English history known

as the Civil War—its hollow interior, its roofless apart-
ments, are not due to the ravages of cannon, but to time,
decay, neglect and ivy. It is no longer neglected. Lord Curzon of Kedleston saved it, restored it, and finally presented
it to the nation.

One of the reasons—if magic needs, or will endure, a
reason—for the peculiar fairy quality of Bodiam, is that it
seems to swim upon a lake (and this lake is full of white and
yellow water-lilies) instead of being simply surrounded by a
moat. Another reason is the arresting contrast between the
almost perfect and undamaged exterior and the ruined desolation of the interior—it is a skeleton of a castle, a skull
from which the life has fled. And this romantic castle, unlike
most of its kind, is not enthroned upon a hill, boldly defying
all comers, but so ensconced and hidden away that it is not
seen till one is close upon it, and then bursts upon the eye
with such a romantic and inevitable loveliness that one can
but stand still and say, "It can't be true!" Forgetting its
Perpendicular date it seems to typify all the castles of
romance—Morgan le Fay must have dwelt there, or the
Lady of Shalott have taken her fatal glance upon the outer
world from its battlements that stand reflected in the moat
below. It is a place that makes all the fairy-tales true. And
it is more than this, for as Lord Curzon said in the noble
monograph he wrote about Bodiam Castle, it is "although a
partial ruin the most perfect and splendid extant example of
its style."

The decay to which it had sunk in the eighteenth century
is depicted in a drawing in Grose's *Antiquities* of 1784. "This
view," he says, "shows the inside of this venerable structure,
whose mouldering towers and rugged walls, beautifully
mantled with ivy, afford at once a most picturesque subject
for the pencil, and a solemn and pleasing theme to the antiquarian and pensive philosopher."

There are eighteenth-century water-colours by S. H.
Grimm showing how devastatingly Bodiam Castle was
"mantled with ivy."

Lord Thurlow, at about the same date, wrote a characteristic poem "On Beholding Bodiam Castle," in which he
said :

... thou hast had thy prime,
And thy full vigour, and the eating harms
Of age have robb'd thee of thy warlike charms,
And placed thee here, an image in my rhyme;
The owl now haunts thee, and oblivion's plant,
The creeping ivy, has o'er-veil'd thy towers;
And Rother, looking up with eye askant,
Recalling to his mind thy brighter hours,
Laments the time, when, fair and eloquent,
Beauty first laugh'd from out thy joyous bowers.

The first viewing of Bodiam Castle across the moat gives the shock of beauty; the first sight of the interior after entering the great gateway gives the shock of surprise. The exterior, with its massive grey walls—the average thickness of which is seven feet—all cleared of ivy, immensely strong and apparently as perfect as when first built, gives no indication that the interior of the castle is a complete ruin, roofless, floorless, the courtyard grassed and empty, the floor of the chapel and of the great hall a green lawn. On the walls the openings of many fireplaces cling, blackened and cold.

Lord Curzon wrote of Bodiam :

"It is remarkable, among all contemporary buildings, for the number and extent of its internal comforts. Ten spiral stone stairs, apart from wooden staircases, led to the various chambers in the upper storeys. In the wall faces are as many as thirty-three fireplaces."

At the date of Bodiam's building wall fireplaces were most unusual—the much later Tudor Harrison complained of the new fashion, and declared that such softness and luxury as chimneys, instead of the central fire, with the smoke escaping through a hole in the roof, was making our "oaken men" into "men of straw."

Till Lord Curzon took in hand the repair of Bodiam Castle, which he did with great thoroughness and antiquarian feeling, everyone had been puzzled that the castle, which boasted comforts in advance of its time, appeared to have no well, but the well was eventually discovered, completely buried under fallen masonry, in the tower nearest the kitchen —a vast well, eight feet across going down nearly four feet

below the bottom of the moat, where it is fed by a still flowing spring, so now that it is cleaned and cleared of rubbish
it brims with dark water.

Bodiam Castle, restored perfectly to what time has left of
it, now stands in strength and beauty to face the time to come.
All Sussex people will rejoice that it stands on the right—
and Sussex—side of the Rother. It is but by a narrow margin
that Bodiam is not in Kent.

21

Herstmonceux Castle is moated, like Bodiam—in every
other respect it is completely different, except in the fact that
it also is beautiful, but in a later, more domestic, more comfortable manner. It is a castle built of brick—and therefore
right outside the castle tradition—but it is brickwork of a
quality and colour quite astonishing. Like Bodiam, for long
all this lovely brickwork was smothered in great swags of
clutching and destroying ivy. Prints of a century or so ago
show every architectural grace hidden by this poisonous
plant. In past years people seemed to think the principal value
of historic buildings was that they made a prop for ivy—
ivy-mantled ruins were regarded as a most helpful aid to
"pensiveness."

The builder of Herstmonceux Castle was Sir Roger de
Fiennes, who fought at Agincourt, and later became
Treasurer to Henry VI. He pulled down an older mansion
which stood on the spot, and in the year 1440 began building his great and noble brick castle—the bricks were Flemish,
and probably the bricklayers were also Flemish, for brick
buildings at that time were little known in England. This
castle of Sir Roger de Fiennes was ambitious in character
and new in plan, for it was designed as a stately domestic
residence, and yet had many of the old elements of defence
—it had battlemented walls, machicolated towers, a draw-
bridge, portcullis and moat. The entrance gateway, with its
massive flanking towers, is a noble piece of work, and the
workmanship, and the warm peach-red of the bricks make a
lovely picture in the Sussex landscape. And all this beauty

was smothered under a cloak of ivy for years, till the castle gateway looked like a crouching old crone.

But in recent times Herstmonceux Castle has been restored to all, and probably more than, its ancient beauty, under the skilful hands of Mr Walter Godfrey. The plan of the castle is that of a great square, with a tower at each corner, two towers flanking the main gateway, and eleven other towers set at intervals along the walls. All this brick-work is of fifteenth-century date, as are the staircase hall and the circular staircase at the main gate, one wall of the chapel, and a little of the interior walling which looks on to the green-grassed courts. All the rest is modern, with the exception of a little dating from the seventeenth century. And all this modern work shows that we can build as beauti-fully, when historic knowledge and a proper reverence for the past are in charge, as ever building was done in England.

A woman's greed and jealousy was the reason that this great castle was so fallen to ruin that nothing remained but a shell, the interior all removed and the place thus rendered uninhabitable. Herstmonceux Castle, through deaths, both natural and violent, came into the possession of the Hares —a Canon Hare of Winchester being its first owner of that name. As his second wife Canon Hare married Henrietta Henckel, who, in traditional stepmotherly fashion, jealous that her predecessor's children, instead of her own, would inherit the castle, persuaded her ageing husband to let her dismantle the interior of the castle and with the materials build a mansion for her own children. Poetic justice was, however, satisfied, for after the house was built it was dis-covered that it had been erected on entailed ground. But the damage wrought by the jealous lady was tragic, for not only did she pull down the interior of the castle, but she discarded and dispersed all its priceless collections of ancient furniture and pictures, which she considered old-fashioned.

In earlier days, Horace Walpole visited Herstmonceux and described it with a certain acidity :

"One side [of the castle] has been sashed, and a drawing and a dining-room and two or three rooms wainscotted by the Earl of Sussex, who married a natural daughter of Charles II. Their arms, with delightful carvings by Gibbons, particularly two pheasants, hang over the chimneys. Over the great drawing-room chimney is the coat-armour of the great Lennard, Lord Dacre, with all his alliances. Mr Chute was transported and called cousin with ten thousand quarterings. The chapel is mean and small; the Virgin, and seven long, lean saints, ill done, remain in the windows; there have been four more, which seem to have been removed for light; and we actually found St. Catherine and another gentlewoman with a church in her hand, exiled into the buttery."

Herstmonceux has both tragic and curious records. One of its owners, the young Lord Dacre, who received Anne of Cleves when she arrived in England in 1540, and who was a "right towardlie gentleman," was executed on Tower Hill for accidentally killing a gamekeeper, but more truly, as Camden said, because of his "great estates which greedy courtiers gaped after, causing them to hasten his destruction."

Then a later heiress of the castle, Grace Naylor, is said to have been starved to death in the room known as the Lady's Bower—a somewhat incomprehensible story, for it is difficult to understand why the governess should have had such uncontrolled power over the only child and heiress.

On the opposite side of the castle there is what is called the Drummer's Hall, where a giant drummer, nine feet high, was said to walk the battlements beating his drum. In Augustus Hare's book on Sussex he gives this version of the legend : "It is said that a Lord Dacre, who was supposed to be dead, long lived here in concealment, and beat a mysterious drum to frighten away the suitors of his widow when they appeared."

One lady dismantled the interior of Herstmonceux; another, the wife of Francis Hare Naylor who inherited the ruined castle, caused it finally to be sold. She was beautiful, but somewhat eccentric, and every day, dressed entirely in white, riding a white ass, with a white doe running by her side, went to drink the waters of a mineral spring in the park. One day the white doe was killed by some dogs, and after that Mrs Hare Naylor refused to live any longer at Herstmonceux Castle, and her husband sold it in the year 1807.

These are but scraps from the long history of Herstmonceux Castle, now restored from ruin and neglect to ancient beauty and dignity, one of the architectural jewels of Sussex.

Sussex is rich in this kind of treasure, though not many are on the scale of Herstmonceux—but such names as Swanborough Manor; the strange, fascinating, half-decayed Old Place, Pulborough; lovely little Charleston Manor, with its great barn and ancient dovecot; and Leigh Manor, near Cuckfield, fully and exquisitely furnished and with gardens designed by Gertrude Jekyll, which is now the property of the Sussex Archæological Trust, owing to the gracious generosity of Lady Chance, come to mind.

And to end up the tale of castles and manor-houses and other impressive places, there is at Northiam a most absurd little house, perhaps the smallest two-story dwelling in England, with a tiled roof pulled down like a cap, and one doll's chimney.

Mill Pond, Cocking
Looking towards Berwick from Wilmington

Chapter VII

THREE SUSSEX COAST TOWNS

1

FEW people credit Brighton with any past older than that Regency one which has been so often written about, so often depicted in old prints, and remains enshrined in the exotic architecture, the onion-shaped pinnacles, of the Royal Pavilion. Those who poke about the narrow Lanes in the quest of antique bargains may catch a hint of the old fishing village of Brighthelmstone here and there, but modern Brighton is so big, the great King's Road is so dazzling in the sunshine of which the town makes so profitable a boast—"Watch the pebbles on the beach," wrote Richard Jefferies, "the foam runs up and wets them, almost before it can slip back the sunshine has dried them again, so they are alternately wetted and dried. Bitter sea and glowing light, bright clear air, dry as dry—that describes the place"—so startling in its rather brazen mixture of Regency dignity, Victorian dullness and modernist steel and concrete, that any coherent impression is rather difficult to achieve.

Brighton can be beautiful, even in these days, at certain times, and one of my clear childish memories is walking along the heights of Kemp Town towards an autumn sunset, the two piers, the Palace Pier and the West Pier, swimming on a pewter-coloured sea, the round globes of the tall electric standards floating like pearls amid the fading pinks and greys of the sky.

Among the most noticeable things at Brighton are the Royal Pavilion and the Dome, and even those who disapprove of the architectural absurdities of these buildings— Sydney Smith's remark that the Pavilion looked as if the Dome of St. Paul's had come down to Brighton and pupped, continues to raise a smile—and their complete unfitness to a Sussex seaside resort, would regret their disappearance, for

M   161

Wiston Lake near Steyning
The High Street, Ditchling

they have become part of Brighton's memories of Regency revels.

But a later and much more beautiful thing has disappeared completely—slain in a night by the sea it so definitely adorned—the old Chain Pier. Few piers are beautiful, but the Chain Pier was unquestionably so—it had the rare quality of elegance, as the old prints show, and the swing and dip of the great chains on which it was slung added an attractive grace to the somewhat barren sea-front.

2

This pier was begun in October 1822, and opened just over a year later on 25 November 1823. The foundations of the four pairs of iron towers which carried the suspension chains were oak piles driven into the rock under the sea, and the landward ends of the chains were carried over fifty feet into the cliff where it begins to swell upwards to the heights of Kemp Town.

One of the things that made the Chain Pier an object of beauty was the simplicity of its lines, and the way the sway of the suspension chains between the iron towers responded to the noble scimitar-like curve of the Kemp Town cliffs. Many an old coloured print, which a few years ago could be picked up for a small sum in the little crowded shops of The Lanes, showed the grace of those curves, enhanced by the plain and seemly architecture of the rows of houses fronting the sea at the east end of Brighton.

The Chain Pier was designed by a naval officer, Captain Samuel Brown, who was in active service in the Navy in the days before and after Trafalgar. He missed that ever-memorable battle, but he was with Sir Richard Strachan in the action off Ferrol. In his later years he was knighted by Queen Victoria, who visited his pier, as earlier had the "Sailor King" and his Queen Caroline.

In spite of this, the coveted presence of royalty was not obtained for the official opening of the pier, though all that Brighthelmstone could offer in the way of beauty and fashion was present. There was a ball—on the floor of the ball-room

the Chain Pier was depicted in chalk—followed by a supper.
These festivities were attended, says the local contemporary
chronicler, by many ladies, "elegantly attired, and including
some of the loveliest women in creation."

So, to the sound of revelry by night, the Chain Pier was
opened to the higher circles of Brighton society—it is amusing to record that the payment of twopence, which was
required in order to pass the turnstiles, was considered sufficient to keep out the lower orders. "You *must* allow the
Chain Pier to be a great luxury," said Sydney Smith to Lady
Holland.

But the sea had something to say on the matter, from the
earliest days of the pier's existence. When it was just a year
old a tremendous storm arose, which was afterwards called
the "Birthday Storm." Huge waves obliterated the pier, even
submerging the tall cast-iron towers, and tearing away large
lumps of cliff. But the Chain Pier stood up valiantly to this
daunting christening, losing nothing except a few minor trimmings. Then in 1833 and 1836 two further gales, amounting
to hurricanes, smote the pier. On both these occasions the
structure suffered extensive and serious damage—in the first
case the damage was believed to be due to lightning more
than waves, a great flash being seen to descend out of black
clouds, running along the metal of the suspension chains and
bursting into a blaze, twisting and destroying the second and
third bridges. Brighton rose up with subscriptions to repair
the cherished pier, but three years later a tremendous November gale—all these storms were in the autumn—smote the
Chain Pier again, and, as before, the bridge between the
second and third iron towers was shattered. The excitement
of the people watching on shore was greatly increased because
two rash men had gone to the end of the pier in the height of
the storm. They had the utmost difficulty in getting back and
had to crawl on their hands and knees and several times were
nearly blown into the sea; they had only just crossed the criti-
cal bridge when it was smashed completely behind them.

Queen Victoria visited the Chain Pier, and no visitors to
Brighton during her reign could avoid taking away with them
when they returned home a picture of the Chain Pier framed
in bright electric blue or crimson plush.

The end of the old Chain Pier came with dramatic sudden-
ness during a December storm in 1896. The watchman had
just lit the lantern at the head of the pier when the terrific
gale then raging smote it, and, according to eyewitnesses, the
whole structure disappeared under the battering of wind and
waves in a few moments. The *Brighton Herald*, describing
the disaster the next day, said, "The actual work of destruction was the matter of but a few seconds; but, so far as there
was any difference of time, the light at the pierhead was the
last to disappear."

Nothing was left except the two suspension towers nearest
to the shore, which were smitten sideways in a drunken
manner. When the people of Brighton woke up the next
morning that was all that was left of the Chain Pier which
had arisen in the reign of the Georges and continued until
the final years of Queen Victoria.

3

One of the places familiar to all visitors and residents at
Brighton is Pool Valley, that curious little dip or hollow close
to the King's Road and the sea, which runs by a narrow lane
into East Street. Originally it was actually a pool, and from
there, which was its mouth, ran along a valley back to
Patcham—that now completely urbanized village which once
had a forge and a blacksmith and a working windmill—
whence rose a stream that flowed down the broad valley
which is now Withdeane and Preston Park (where there is
a fine Saxon church) to the Brighton Levels, and so to Pool
Valley and the sea. This was the Wellsbourne, and from a
corruption of that name came Whalesbone, which is the
name of the Hundred in which Brighton is situated. In
Domesday Book the name is Welesmere, and in the time of
Edward I it became Wellesbourne. Till quite recent times
this river ran in the winter, thus being a winterbourne. In his
History of Brighthelmstone, published nearly a hundred
years ago, John Erredge said of this river : "Within the last
thirty years it burst out with so large a current as to inundate
the Level to the north of the town, and even the greater part

of the Stein. In the spring of 1806 it laid the north of the town under water."

Were this stream still running in the sunshine down the long valley from Patcham to the sea, it would add much to the attractions of Brighton and its environs, peculiarly lacking in water, apart from that which is salt. But with the curious lack of imagination that so often afflicts corporations and such official bodies in their dealings with water, it has been forced underground and into pipes.

The original Brighthelmstone, the poor fishing village, is long buried under the sea. Both that completely vanished Brighton and a much later one have suffered heavily at times from storms. The earliest Brighton settlements were under the cliffs. Forty acres of this was robbed by the sea between 1260 and 1340. In 1665 considerably more of Brighthelmstone disappeared, though in 1703 there were still as many as one hundred and thirteen tenements under the cliff, but two years later a tremendous storm finally wiped out the fishermen's ancient village. Lyell said that "the sea has merely resumed its position at the base of the cliffs, the site of the old town having been a beach which had for ages been abandoned by the ocean."

That old Brighthelmstone was built on the alluvial flats laid down by the lost river which used to flow from Patcham to Pool Valley. A further glimpse into the remote geologic past of our present sophisticated Brighton is given by Gideon Mantell when he wrote : "The level plain called the Steyne, at Brighton, is entirely formed of elephant bed, which extends up to the valley of Preston and Patcham. In the latter place bones and teeth of elephants have been found."

It is strange to think of prehistoric reptiles and mammals wandering on that Steyne which was later to be the scene of the flippant society of the Regency, of revels at the Royal Pavilion, and hysterical dippings in the salt sea. That sea can still rise in storms, as it showed when it destroyed the Chain Pier in a single night. Modern Brighton is so civilized and smooth that there is a kind of fearful joy in seeing the ocean rise up from his flat bed and hurl great angry handfuls of shingle in the faces of all the staring houses on the King's Road.

4

Regency Brighton has almost obliterated the earlier history of Brighthelmstone. It is quite difficult to imagine the easy-going sprawling place as a small walled town with four gates—East Gate, Portall, or Porter's Gate, Middle Gate and West Gate. Brighthelmstone in Tudor times had cause to defend herself, for she had neighbours across the sea, "Dunkirkers," who did not love her, and thought it no small prank to slip across from the French coast in the dead of night and set a torch to a few Brighton roofs and a sword at a few Brighton throats. Rye and Winchelsea, further to the eastwards, also had many of these experiences.

There is a curious old map of Brighthelmstone which gives some idea of what the place was like—so simple and sparse and bare, so completely different from a pleasure town. There is very little of this ancient town left in these days—it has been smothered and overwhelmed and hidden by great hotels and blocks of concrete flats. But the old heart still beats, even if faintly, in certain corners. One of the oldest bits of Brighton is only just off broad and sunny East Street, in a little square known as Brighton Place, where the carriers' carts used to gather on their arrival and setting out on their slow journeys about Sussex. It is still the point of arrival and departure for the carriers, even though they drive motor-vans now, instead of tilt carts and quiet clopping horses. And beyond Brighton Place is The Knab—believed to be the oldest inhabited spot in the town. The Knab, with its brief barbaric name, and St. Nicholas' Church on the hill, are the most ancient things Brighton has to show. Brighthelmstone in its early days lay between East Street and West Street, with the sea as the southern boundary, and North Street defining the northern edge with the old church of St. Nicholas on the rising steep of the Down behind. Within those narrow confines lay The Lanes and The Knab and all the oldest parts of the town. There is a different atmosphere in the little tangle of streets in this centre of old Brighthelmstone—even when the houses are not particularly old, the lines and the amazing narrowness of these streets display their ancient origin.

St. Bartholomew's is part of this old town, and once there was a priory or chantry here, and a Mockbeggar's Close, which some antiquarians think may have been connected with the Franciscan Friars. In the late eighteenth century some digging was being done about here, and the labourers unearthed a lot of human skulls and bones. This disconcerted them and they refused to go on digging any more in what was obviously a graveyard. But—as is told in an ancient history of Brighton, without a quiver of either humour or compassion—a clergyman was fetched to these labourers who "applauded their veneration for the supposed remains of *Christians*, but assured them that all who had ever been interred there were *rank papists*. Their first prejudice being thus laid by a stronger, the men resumed their work, and turned over the rest of the bones with the apathy of gravediggers."

The inconsistency of blind prejudice is shown by the same author in the same book when he reproves some eighteenth-century churchwardens of St. Nicholas' Church for vandalism :

"The font of this church," he says, "was much admired for the sculpture which adorned it ; but in the year 1743 it was nearly effaced by the churchwardens who had their names cut on it, and thereby have rendered a curious piece of ecclesiastical as well as local antiquity, a monument of their own false taste, vanity and ignorance."

He has apparently overlooked the fact that the carved font, as well as the fourteenth-century church, was the work of papistical hands.

5

St. Nicholas' Church, set on such a steeply rising Down as to be in the old days a seamark to mariners, is linked to one of the most remarkable inhabitants of Brighton—Phœbe Hessel. She is buried in the churchyard, after a life of almost incredible adventure. She was born in 1713, not in Sussex, but at Stepney, and when only fifteen years old fell in love with a soldier whose regiment was under orders for the West Indies. Phœbe promptly followed him, enlisting in another regiment that was also ordered to the West Indies. She served in this regiment for five years without her sex being discovered. From there she and her regiment returned to Europe, where in 1743 she fought in the battle of Fontenoy and received a bayonet wound in the arm. She was also at the siege of Gibraltar, and from there came her first link with Sussex, remote though it was, for General Elliot was made Lord Heathfield, after the Sussex village where he bought a park in which he erected the Gibraltar Tower.

Phœbe Hessel eventually confessed that she was a woman, got her discharge from the army and married her soldier, who had been wounded, and received a Chelsea pension. They lived together for many years, and when he died Phœbe married a fisherman named Hessel and apparently took up her abode at Brighthelmstone. Here her second husband died, leaving her in such poverty that some of the people of Brighton bought her a donkey, with which she travelled about to the nearby villages selling fish. But the fish business was not sufficiently profitable to save her from coming to the workhouse, but she was discharged in 1806, being allowed "a pair of stockings and one change on leaving the poorhouse."

Beginning to feel her age, the indomitable old woman used to seat herself at the bottom of the Marine Parade, near Old Steine Street, with a basket of apples, bull's eyes, and gingerbread for sale. She was warmly clothed against the Brighton gales in a brown stuff dress, a black cloth cloak with a hood, a black poke bonnet over a mob cap, a white apron, and a pair of heavy man's boots. She became one of the recognized features of Brighthelmstone, and when there were festivities to celebrate the fall of Napoleon in 1814, Phœbe Hessel, then aged ninety-nine, as the oldest inhabitant, sat beside the Vicar of Brighton, and was given several presents of money. She also took part in the celebrations for the Coronation of George IV, being then one hundred and seven years old and completely blind. A portrait of her was sold in the streets on which was inscribed: "An Industrious Woman living at Brighton, with very slender means of support, which she can only earn by selling the contents of her basket, for whose assistance this etching is sold."

She died in December 1821, being one hundred and eight years old, having lived through nearly the whole of the eighteenth century and two decades of the nineteenth. Certainly she may be regarded as one of Brighton's most notable inhabitants.

6

Brighton's connection with the escape of Charles II has been greatly over-written—indeed, it might almost be imagined from some books that Brighton had only existed during the reigns of Charles II and George IV. The Captain Tattersall who aided that royal escape was a citizen of Brighthelmstone and gained not only a considerable reward in cash but a quite undeserved reputation as a hero and a patriot in consequence. On his tombstone are the swelling words :

> Within this marble monument doth lye
> Approved faith, honour and loyalty.
> In this cold clay he hath now ta'en his station
> That once preserved the Church, the Crown and
>   Nation.

Having found the saving of his Sovereign such a profitable transaction, Captain Tattersall, come to power, proceeded to persecute certain of his fellow citizens of Brighton with whose forms of religious belief he did not agree. It is not a pretty story. But Brighton owes him one good memory, for it was he who built the original Old Ship Inn at the corner of what is now Ship Street, but was then called Hempshares Street, as it was on that land the Brighton fishermen grew the hemp for making their nets. Tattersall had used the ship in which he conveyed King Charles to safety and exile as a show ship, and by so doing he made another nice little nest-egg out of loyalty. Eventually a beam from the stern was built into the Old Ship Hotel, where it remained till the beginning of this century. It is now in the Brighton Museum.

Another street in this region of Brighton, Black Lion Street, commemorates a martyr. In the sixteenth century a

man called Deryk Carver came to Brighthelmstone from
Flanders and built a brewery on land adjoining the ground
where the fishermen grew their hemp. Over his brewery he
put the Black Lion of Flanders, and from that Lion—still
standing in the air with tail outspread, not, it is to be feared,
the original Lion, but his successor—the street is named. It is
a condition of the lease of the brewery that the Lion must be
preserved. Below this Black Lion is an old flint wall, one of
the oldest in Brighton, and on the wall is an inscription which
tells a sad tale of the man who originally built this brewery
and named this street :

Deryk Carver
First Protestant Martyr
Burned at Lewes, July 22, 1555,
Lived at this Brewery.

7

The Brighton fishermen, in the old days, had many ancient
and curious customs. One of them was skipping in the Fish
Market on Good Friday—the fishermen turned a long rope
and people ran in and out to skip. It was called Long Rope
Day, and the rope was said to be symbolic of the rope with
which Judas Iscariot hanged himself. This custom may possibly date back to the thirteenth century, when almost all the
Brighton then existing belonged to the Priory of St. Bartholomew. The Priory has long vanished, the name still exists.

The skipping on the Hove barrow, also on Good Friday,
will be remembered. The buns baked on Good Friday were
believed to keep the fishermen from death by drowning when
they took them to sea.

The beginning of the mackerel season was marked by
Bending-in Day, which was the relic of a service of blessing
on the boats—Benediction. When the boats reached the fishing grounds and let out the nets for the first time each season
the fishermen took off their caps and bowed their heads while
the captain said aloud, "There they goes then. God Almighty
send us a blessing, it is to be hoped."

Small barrels were attached to the nets to keep them afloat

170

and show their position, and the fishermen had a verse for this :

> Watch, Barrel, watch !
> Mackerel for to catch;
> White may they be
> Like blossom on a tree.
> God sends thousands,
> One, two, three;
> Some by their heads, some by their tails,
> God sends thousands and never fails.

Those who go down to the sea in ships, even if they are only Brighthelmstone fishermen, have a sense of the eternities.

8

Sussex-by-the-Sea contains few greater contrasts than those between modern Brighton, medieval Rye, and that Sleeping Beauty of the past, Winchelsea.

It is not from the railway, or even from the grim old Land Gate, that Rye should be approached for the first time. The ideal manner of arrival is unfortunately rather impracticable —but it is across the marshes from the south that Rye should be first beheld, rising above the green and water-threaded levels in her most true and pregnant aspect—for this little Cinque Port ever turned her face seawards, whence the enemy came. Red-roofed, the town clusters and climbs to the great red-roofed church—almost cathedral-like in its size and beauty—which crowns the very summit of Rye rock. There is a sense of completeness about Rye. The Ancient Town is small, but sufficient to itself, as though still shut in from too much contact with the modern world by the invisible presence of the walls which have long since fallen.

But if the walls have fallen—those walls which Richard Lion-Heart first authorized and considered "the greatest safeguard which could be made in these parts for the security of our kingdom"—and if only one of Rye's five gates remains a still older relic of the feudal past is standing in all its rude

Norman strength. No one who has seen Ypres Tower can forget it, set squarely upon the angle of the cliff, the Keep of the ancient castle of William de Ypres, Earl of Kent, and long ago the last retreat of the people of Rye on the numerous occasions when the French sacked the town. Ypres Tower—simplified into Wipers by the Sussex tongue—was built some time in the twelfth century, and, with the exception of Dover Castle, is the oldest fortification now existing in any of the Cinque Ports. Grim and blind stands old Wipers in a corner of the Gun Garden, unsoftened by all the centuries that have passed over its head. Though small, it has to the full that quality of awful aloofness which some old buildings possess. Its narrow windows no longer look outwards, as do the windows of inhabited houses; instead, they are turned inward, gazing into "the dark backward and abysm of Time," blind to all the present.

Yet, in spite of grey and solemn Ypres Tower—which can be seen from new aspects if one descends the long flight of stone steps that wander leisurely down by the Tower to the marsh below the rock of Rye—in spite of the dark-faced old Grammar School in the High Street, more like a prison than anything else, the prevailing note of Rye is a warm gaiety and cheerfulness. The windows of the houses shine, the doorsteps are whitened, the brass knockers gleam like gold. Most of the houses in the Square round the church, in Watchbell Street, and many in Mermaid Street, are small—some of them quite tiny, like the quaint little pointed Store House (which is a private dwelling) set in its toy garden in enchanting Watchbell Street. And in the days before the shortages of war, one and all, big and little, they were all as fresh and gay as spotless paint could make them. Indeed, if Rye had a fault it was a slight tendency to be too picturesque. The steep pitch of Mermaid Street, the cobbles and the tumbling irregular roof-lines, a little suggested an operatic setting, and one almost expected a casement to be flung open and an elaborate soprano lady to lean out and pour forth a profuse flood of song with a far from unpremeditated art.

That street takes its name from the Mermaid Inn, a beautiful old timbered and tiled building, rich in dark oak and carved stone chimneypieces. As far as can be traced there

172

has always been a Mermaid Inn at Rye, and when it is remembered that John Fletcher, the Elizabethan dramatist, was born in Rye in 1576, it seems to bring the whole place into quite close connection with Shakespeare and the more famous Mermaid Inn of Broad Street. But the finest house in Mermaid Street is not the Mermaid Inn—which shows a comparatively modern frontage to the street and keeps its best treasures of oak and plaster and ancient diamond-paned windows at the back—but the Old Hospital, as it is called, which once belonged to the well-known Rye family of Jeake. It is an almost perfect specimen of a timbered building, with a jettied first story, with three pointed, overhanging gables, steep tiled roof, and charming leaded windows whose diamond panes bulge in and out with age, and catch the light at all angles. There are many other enchanting, crooked cottages and houses in Mermaid Street, many of them wreathed in coloured vines and creepers, and the whole effect, as one looks up and down the steep street, at the time-softened red walls, at the vista of climbing roofs, sharp-angled and ruddy against the sky, is so absolutely as it should be that it seems a mistake ever to build houses on the level.

So medieval is the aspect of Mermaid Street that at night one almost expects to meet the constable going his rounds as he did in 1575, according to the town records of Rye, "to see lanthorns and candle hung out by such as are of ability to maintain the same."

At the top of Mermaid Street, round the corner into West Street, Henry James once lived in Lamb House—a dwelling of great dignity and retirement. It only presents a shoulder to the gaze of the passer-by, turning its fine front to a high-walled garden. Rye must be proud to feel that so great and subtle a writer chose to spend his latter days within her vanished walls. How he understood the special kind of country hereabouts he shows in a few words when he speaks of "the wide, ambiguous flat that stretches eastward from Winchelsea hill . . . little lonely farms, red and grey; little mouse-coloured churches; little villages that seem made only for long shadows and summer afternoons."

Coventry Patmore, who also knew these eastward parts of Sussex, said of Rye : "The glory of the town is in its command of so many great views of the marsh which stretches for miles on every side of it. The beauty of these views is beyond all description, and has never been expressed even in painting. What strikes me as being most characteristic and least noticed in these views is the effect of the sunshine . . ."

9

Watchbell Street is one of the oldest in Rye. It overhangs Watchbell Cliff, and took its name from the fact that a bell hung at the west end, which was rung in times of danger to summon the stout hearts of Rye to the defence of their valiant little town. But now Watchbell Street, in spite of its name, seems to have folded its hands and gone to sleep, while the moss creeps over the cobbles. At the end of the street is a little platform where one can sit and see the sun sink behind Winchelsea, and the mists come up over the marshes. But there is an even better place from which to study the wide-spreading marshland—a favourite resort of the town under the very shadow of Wipers Tower, called the Battery, or Gun-Garden. From here one looks down the edge of the cliff to a line of black-tarred boat-buildings below. Years ago ship-building flourished at Rye—Sussex oak, the best in the kingdom, as all good Sussex people know, being close at hand. The Rock Channel Shipyard had a reputation among fishermen. On the level marsh, half-way to the line of sea lying like a narrow blue ribbon upon the horizon, is grey old Camber Castle, built by Henry VIII. It is difficult to reach owing to the number of rhines or dykes, but once attained is an interesting, if slighty eerie, place—the flat solitude, the crumbling walls, the sound of the wind, the wandering sheep, the sense of the crawling sea so near.

On the extreme right from the Gun-Garden is a glimpse of the secretive wooded steep of Winchelsea, and on the other hand

> The doubling Rother crawls
> To find the fickle tide.

Rye's age-old tragedy is the desertion of the sea. Once the

waves came to its very walls, and ships rode at anchor where now flocks graze. The sea has not been kind : the first Rye was drowned and destroyed in a tremendous storm, by reason of "the olde rages of the See." The Rye that now sits so proudly on its rock is the successor to that doomed forerunner. But the treacherous ocean that could no longer submerge Rye, then deserted and crept away to the horizon. But the people of Rye had stout hearts—they needed them in the days when this indomitable little port was making history—so they continued to hammer away at the building of ships. If the sea will not come to them, they will go to the sea, as they do by painfully sailing and tacking down the muddy winding reaches of the river.

The Rother, being tidal, changes its aspect continually, as all such rivers do—at the ebb it is low and flat in colour, but at the flow comes up gay and blue from the sea. There is a certain fascination in wandering about the Strand Quay and the Town Salts; in walking on narrow dykes raised above the muddy flats, and looking at ancient stakes stuck upright in the mud, which perhaps represent all that is left of the many desperate schemes for creating a harbour and bringing back the sea to Rye. One of their attempted harbours was called the Wish, but it was a wish that never reached fruition.

10

In order to appreciate the full charm of Rye it is necessary to get outside it and survey the little town as a whole from the marsh level, where the crouching grey keep and outer walls of Camber Castle lie lonely and bare. At the time Camber was built it stood upon a sand-spit, something like Chesil Beach, which stretched from Winchelsea to east of Rye; but within fifty years of its building the castle, which originally had stood upon the sea-edge, was stranded some distance from high-water mark, while the shallows behind were steadily filling up with alluvial soil brought down by the Brede, the Rother, and Tillingham Brook. So long ago was it that the sea deserted Rye, and by so doing turned a very fighting little port into the resort of authors and artists. But as one looks at the sheep quietly cropping the Pett Level, at the exquisite pale shimmer of the marsh grass against a blue sky, with Rye standing up redly behind, there seem to be compensations even for the regretted departure of the sea.

The pathway leading back to Rye from Camber Castle runs by little rhines and water-cuttings filled with purple flowering reeds, whose sharp, sword-like leaves whisper against each other—a sound in harmony with the silence, the low voice of the distant sea, the rare cry of a seabird, and the curious suspended feeling of the past that hangs over the sun-washed marshes stretching up to the rock of Rye.

There is an extraordinary clarity of air here in fine weather. The town stands out with the fineness of an etching. But when the mists come up from the sea there are times when Rye seems to float in air like a town in a mirage. Turner painted a picture of Rye, with a foreground of flooded marsh, which shows this kind of unearthly effect. When the mists turn the marshland to a semblance of the unstable sea, Rye once more looks the ancient port that left her mark deep on our history. In those days, as in these once again, we were the "shut island of the north," and Rye —with Winchelsea and the Five Ports—one of our guarded and assaulted gateways. Sack and reprisal, reprisal and sack, was the order in the fierce early days of Rye's history. The town was taken, and retaken, by the French, who spared none. Soon after the death of Richard III they again ravaged Rye with sword and fire. "They, within five hours," said the historian Stow, "brought it wholly into ashes, with the church that then was there, of a wonderful beauty, conveying away four of the richest of the towne and slaying sixty-six, left not above eight in the towne."

And not only war, but plague, and fire, swept often through the narrow streets of Rye. But as one of Rye's historians wrote, the town "had an incredible hold upon life and its beloved rock." An indomitable temper, and a readiness to believe that to-morrow would be better than to-day, were necessities of life in a Cinque Port. It was that temper which cheerfully rebuilt Rye from its frequent ashes, and raised up the great church that now so beautifully crowns the rock, and deserves not less than in Jeake's time his praise as

Bodiam Castle, near Hastings
Mermaid Street, Rye

being "the goodliest edifice of the kind in Kent and Sussex, the cathedrals excepted." It is of a warmth and richness of colour unusual in churches, for the far-spreading roof is red-tiled like the humblest Rye cottage, while the grey stone walls in autumn are also red with a mantle of crimson creeper. The massive dignity of the whole building can be best appreciated from outside Rye, for the houses in the enclosing square nestle up as though some power of comfort and protection resided in the church, and so rob it of the space its size requires.

The northern side of the church-tower is adorned by an old and curious clock—supposed to be the oldest going in England—which tradition claims as the gift of Queen Elizabeth to the town that she christened "Rye Royal" on one of her long-past progresses. The clock is remarkable by reason of its two gilt "quarter-boys," who strike the quarters with a thin clear note upon two bells, and between them is a kind of shield bearing the solemn words : "For our time is a very shadow that passeth away." Just inside the great doorway below is a long gilt pendulum that swings slowly from side to side above the heads of all who enter, measuring the minutes as they pass in Rye.

Queen Elizabeth must have had a liking for the "Ancient Towne." The year after the Armada she presented it with "six brass guns beautifully ornamented with the arms of Spain, which stood on the spot called the Green."

11

Rye ships and Rye men took part in the defeat of the Armada. But that battle practically marks the end of Rye's fighting history as a member of the great confederation of the Cinque Ports. Thenceforward the defence of the kingdom fell more and more to the Royal Navy as it is constituted to-day, and the valiant cogs, crayers, snakes, and cockboats of the Cinque Ports that had represented the might of England on the seas, passed out of sight and memory.

But instead of recalling the melancholy years in which the sea receded steadily, it is preferable to look backwards to the

Winchelsea, the Strand Gate
Buckmans Corner, Billinghurst

vital times long before the keels of the Armada vessels were laid down, long before Camber Castle was built—the years when the second Winchelsea was newly set upon its hill by King Edward I. Those were the great days of the sister ports of "Rie" and "Wincenesee." Who that has read it can forget Froissart's engaging account of the Battle of L'Espagnols-sur-Mer, fought off Winchelsea in 1350, when England first defeated Spain upon the sea. It is too long to quote, except for a few sentences. The Spaniards, says the chronicler of this "gentle and joyous" battle, "thought and held themselves strong enough to fight upon the sea the King of England and his power; and, in this mind, came they swimming before the wind." Edward III stood upon the deck of his ship "dressed in a black jake of velvet, and wore upon his head a cap of black beaver, which well became him." He had put a guard on "the top-castle of his ship," and suddenly this guard cried out. : "Ho ! I see one come a-sailing; and I think it is a ship of Spain." Asked if he saw more ships he answered : "Yes, I see one, and then two, and then three, and then four," and finally cried, when he saw the great fleet : "I see so many, if God aids me, that I cannot number them."

These being the sort of odds that England has always accepted upon the sea, the two fleets closed and the battle began—a fierce and desperate engagement, where ship grappled with ship, and "the king's ship was so astonied that its seams opened and leaked." "In the end," says Froissart, "the day fell to the English and the Spaniards there lost fourteen ships. The rest passed on and saved themselves. When they had all gone, and the said king had no one with whom to fight, they sounded with their trumpets the retreat, so they went their way towards England, and took land at Rye and at Wincenesee, a little after the day was done."

The poor queen had watched the battle from afar : "She had had great anguish of heart that day through," says Froissart, "for fear of those Spaniards; for, at that place of the shores of England, there are mountains from which they had seen the strife, for it had been a clear day and a day of fine weather."

But now, where the ships of England and Spain fought in the curve of Winchelsea Bay, the quiet sheep crop the rich marsh grasses, and the cloud shadows shift and play across the levels to the sea. But still Rye, that "port of stranded pride," remains to illuminate history. None who have felt the spell of the place can leave it without at heart repeating the words that end its old Customal—"God save Englonde and the Towne of Rye."

12

Winchelsea and Rye were sister ports in the old days, who shared fortunes and gazed at each other across the sea and marshes. But since their original fighting and sailing days they have gone on different ways. Rye has increased her activities and bustled about, and grown—not thereby adding to her beauty. Winchelsea has gone to sleep, and as a consequence kept hers to a remarkable degree untouched and unspoilt by the "progress" which has ruined so many of the Sussex coast towns. Some people would call Winchelsea dead, instead of asleep. If dead, then she is embalmed in a peace that not even war's alarms can fundamentally destroy The atmosphere of Winchelsea descends at once upon the spirit of the susceptible traveller as he enters the Strand Gate, climbing up the steep approach that leads to it slowly, on his feet, so that he may savour the entry into this embalmed portion of the past of Sussex and of England—there is no other place quite like it in the county or the kingdom. Entered within the shade of the noble gateway it is well to turn and look at Rye—from here seen at its most enchanting—and then face round and gaze straight up the serenity of the High Street, so curiously unlike the cheerful bustle of most village High Streets. This is the kind of High Street that might be in the background of some medieval painting of the Virgin and Child.

It was King Edward I who planned New Winchelsea after the first Winchelsea had been swallowed up by the sea. Hollinshed gives a vivid account of this event in the year 1250, which reads as if he had accomplished some juggling with time and been there in person :

"On the first day of October, the moon, upon her change, appearing exceeding red and swelled, began to show tokens of the great tempest of wind that followed, which was so huge and mighty, both by land and sea, that the like had not been lightly known and seldom or rather never heard of by men then alive. The sea forced contrary to his natural course, flowed twice without ebbing, yielding such a roaring that the same was heard (not without great wonder) a far distance from the shore. Moreover, the same sea appeared in the dark of the night to burn as it had been on fire, and the waves to strive and fight together after a marvellous sort, so that the mariners could not devise how to save their ships where they lay at anchor, by no cunning or shift which they could devise. . . . At Winchelsea, besides other hurt that was done in bridges, mills, breaks and banks, there were 300 houses and some churches drowned with the high rising of the water course."

After this disaster the King planned a new Winchelsea on a higher and safer site—"which was at that tyme a ground wher conies partely did resort," said Leland, in his *Itinerary*. The town was designed in dignified squares and rectangles, "quarters," as they were called, which began with the first quarter in the north-east and ended with the thirty-ninth quarter in the southern side. This plan produced straight, quiet streets running parallel and across, which to this day make the pattern of Winchelsea and give lovely vistas athwart the sun.

These squares are lined with simple satisfying old houses, set amid green sward and fine old trees. Of the largest of these squares—that in which the church is set—Coventry Patmore, who once lived in Winchelsea, said, "I am never tired of contemplating the humble and touching dignity of this square from the window of a little house which I am so fortunate as to possess in it. The great half-ruined ivy-covered church—an exceedingly fine and peculiar specimen of thirteenth and fourteenth-century architecture—immensely predominates over any other building; but it is a predominance of gentleness and sweetness and 'the melancholy graces of decay,' and seems in strange harmony with the bright and dreamy marsh which stretches in endless peace at its feet."

The great church of St. Thomas is noble and impressive, though but a fragment of the church that had been intended, had not the Black Death intervened. Even as it is, this church seems much too great for the needs of this small village of Winchelsea—for in spite of its lordly name and history, that is all Winchelsea is. It is dedicated to that most popular medieval saint, Thomas à Becket.

At the edge of the square is a tree under which John Wesley preached his last open-air sermon, on the 7th of October 1790. Only a short distance away is a stately house called the Friars Minors, who were in Old Winchelsea soon after the Order was established in England in the first quarter of the thirteenth century. About 1277 the Grey Friars were transferred to New Winchelsea, and now, in the grounds of this house, the roofless choir of their ancient chapel is all that remains to tell of them—a beautiful and peaceful ruin, in a lovely setting of trees and grass.

The New Winchelsea of King Edward I was about five years in building and the inhabitants of Old Winchelsea thankfully took up their abode on the hill—the sea completely destroyed the old town just as the new one was completed.

13

Winchelsea still has three old inns—the New Inn, facing the church, and at the corner of a lovely little row of houses; the Salutation Inn, and the Castle Inn. A rich supply for so small a place; but once there was a fourth called the Three Kings, and antiquarian opinion is uncertain as to whether the name means the Three Kings of the Epiphany or the three Kings of England, Edward I, Edward II and Edward III, to whom Winchelsea owed so much.

Add to these three remaining inns the three remaining gates, the Strand Gate, the Pipewell or Land Gate, leading to Rye by Udimore, and the New Gate leading to Pett and Fairlight. Through this gate the French came when they attacked the town in 1380, entering before sunrise—tradition holds that the New Gate was opened to them by treachery. High by the side of the Strand Gate is a charming cottage in which, once upon a time, Ellen Terry lived. Whatever inclined her to leave such an enchanted spot for Kent, fascinating as is her house at Tenterden, is a thing no Sussex person can understand.

Besides three gates and three inns, Winchelsea has also three remaining wells still flowing—those of Pipewell, St. Katharine's and St. Leonard's wells.

The Court House of Winchelsea is an ancient, solemn, and solid building, with much the feeling of a church about it. There are two silver maces and a seal. The mayoral seal of Winchelsea is amusing—a shield upon which three very fine lions are romping, the hind parts of the lions developing into castellated ships, and surrounded by three flying griffins. There can be little doubt as to the challenge of this seal to the enemies of England.

A feature of Winchelsea that is not realized by the casual visitor is the remarkable series of vaulted cellars, often with fine carved corbels, to be found under many of the ancient houses. Mr Salzman says that Winchelsea "probably contains more such cellars than any place in England."

So Winchelsea has not only many visible beauties, but hidden ones as well. And over it all, more markedly, perhaps, than in any village in Sussex, broods the sense of the past, the feeling almost as if time had stopped. Even the weather in Winchelsea seems to have an atmosphere of its own, a serene autumnal quality, as though yellow leaves were slowly dropping in a windless air. No doubt the residents of Winchelsea can tell of violent storms, of snow and rain, but my experience when there has always been of the same kind of still and silent weather. That is the essential atmosphere of Winchelsea—it is in keeping with the ghosts which, I am told, haunt so many of the Winchelsea gardens—full of a quiet, withdrawn beauty, standing aside from this our troubled day. But Winchelsea's past, it must be remembered, was remarkably different from its present "stillicide"—to use Hardy's strange haunting word. The story of Winchelsea in the Middle Ages was active and gay, as complete to itself as a brilliantly coloured page in an illuminated missal or Book of Hours—but the red and the gold were often those of blood and fire. Winchelsea was grim, as well as gay—as was to be said of a much later and much less gay England. So bowered in trees, so deserted by the sea, as Winchelsea is now, it is difficult to realize how New Winchelsea, as she was called then, shouted defiance to her foe across the Channel, thrusting out to the ports of France like a shaken spear. It was for this very reason that the French raids on the hill port were so fierce. There were many raids, and some of the worst took place in the years 1357, 1377 and 1418. In the raid of 1357 Winchelsea was burnt and plundered to such an extent that many houses and a mill were completely destroyed and a greater number left destitute of anything of value. The people were so ruthlessly massacred that to this day there is a lane in Winchelsea called Dead Man's Lane, where the victims were buried.

There was an Abbot of Battle who displayed a most war-like courage and took over the defence of Winchelsea when the French had burned Rye. Triumphant with that success, they sent to the Abbot and demanded that he redeem Winchelsea, if he would not have it sacked like Rye. The Abbot replied in valiant words that he needed not to redeem the thing which was not lost. The French attacked, but were beaten back and so, on that occasion, Winchelsea was saved. Fuller said of him : "I behold this Abbot the saver not only of Sussex but of England." This was the view taken by the Commons when in 1384 they petitioned the king that steps might be taken for the defence of the often-attacked Rye and Winchelsea, "because if these towns were taken, which God forbid, the whole country would be destroyed."

After the French attack of 1418, combined with the inning of the marshes and the retreat of the sea, Winchelsea ceased to be a fighting port. It sank into unimportance and from that to decay, as some two centuries later John Evelyn, the Diarist, was to describe. "There are to be seen," he wrote, having walked over from Rye to look at Winchelsea, "vast caves and vaults, walls and towers, ruins of monasteries, and of a sumptuous church, in which are some handsome monuments, especially of the Templars, buried just in the manner of those in the Temple in London. This place being now all in rubbish, and a few despicable hovels and cottages only standing, hath yet a mayor."

14

In the Middle Ages the little towns and villages of England were self-contained and complete in a manner that seems to exemplify a natural and proper way of living. In the case of Winchelsea we have a singularly clear picture, with the names and occupations of the inhabitants. On the warlike side there were the gatekeepers, the pikemen, the trumpeter, and the cross-bowmen. Then there were ten bakers, with three bakeries between them; six butchers, with a slaughter-house that by law was without the walls, and conveniently near to the dwelling of the tanners; five cooks; four cobblers; one cordwainer; several coopers; two carpenters; two water-carriers; two cutlers; a candle-maker; two barber-surgeons; two shipwrights; two house-builders; several masons, cart-makers, ships' caulkers and reapers. There was a tiler or thatcher; a stone-cutter; two tailors; two grocers; several pewterers, as well as fishermen and chapmen. On the more decorative side of life there were six goldsmiths, jewellers and embroiderers in gold and silver, who lived near the church. With the husbandmen who tilled the soil, and the priests and friars who taught the way to heaven, here was a complete and self-contained community. The surrounding marsh, with its growth of rushes and reeds, supplied a livelihood to many of the poorer inhabitants in the making of woven mats, baskets, fishing creels and basket traps, as well as being used for thatching, strewing the floors and making the wicks of candles and rushlights.

Winchelsea had also an official soothsayer or fortune-teller, the caster of horoscopes and nativities.

The names of many ladies who, by reason of spinsterhood or widowhood, were property-owners in their own right, have come down to us. Among these is the gracious name of Petronilla—there is still a Petronilla's Platt in Winchelsea—Johanna, Julianna, Goda, Cronnok, Salerna, and a Lucy who was "called Douce." There was also a lady owning the charming Christian and surname of Juliana Nightyngale. Gervase, borne by the distinguished Alard family, was a very popular Christian name for men. There are also two men whose names sound almost too good to be true—Bartholomew Bone and John Squathard.

These particulars come from a return made in the year 1292. The number of householders in that return is seven hundred and thirty.

It adds to the vividness of Winchelsea history that we not only know the names and occupations of so many of the medieval inhabitants, but also the names of many of their fields and "platts"—a word much used in this corner of Sussex. These names have a lovely air of gaiety, as though they had come straight from the blithe pages of Chaucer—Hop Garden, Pear-Tree Marsh, King's Green, Tinker's Garden, Cherry Garden, Coney Field, Ballad Singer's Platt, Little Monday's Market. In those days you could walk to a well in Pook Lane called Vale Well, and "so east by a little lane, lying between Crooked Acre and Bell Morrice." It sounds exactly like a page out of a fairy-tale.

Wells, needless to say, were very important. Rye was badly supplied with fresh water, but Winchelsea was richly endowed with six open wells—Pipe Well, St. Katharine's Well, Strand Well, Friar's Well, New Well, and Vale Well, or St. Leonard's Well. St. Leonard was a special Winchelsea saint, much besought in the palmy days of the port. It is still said that anyone who drinks of the water of St. Leonard's Well will never wander from Winchelsea without desiring to return. That is a natural enough desire when it is remembered that one of the quarters of the town bore the name of Paradise—though some of us might be quite content to dwell there, as did William and Richard, "sons of Tristram," in the reign of Edward I, who "held on the hill" one acre, "with a house built upon it, value 5s."

One Winchelsea family, bearing the very vernacular name of Cogger, lived there in 1292, and this same family of Cogger lived in Winchelsea for six hundred years without a break; the last of the Coggers dying there in 1892. What a superbly rooted record!

The great, the historic name in Winchelsea is that of
Alard. An Alard was the first Englishman to bear the title
of admiral, and the Alards were in Sussex before the Conqueror came. The Alard tombs in Winchelsea Church—
delicate, elaborate, and rich in their carved stonework—are
deservedly famous.

Rye Church is homely and vernacular. Winchelsea is but
the portion of a superb building, noble in plan, lovely in
detail. The impressiveness of this massive fragment is oddly
mitigated by the very homely-looking little tower, with its
small dormer windows, giving something of the innocent and
homely effect of a dovecot. This contrast is characteristic of
many Sussex churches—the fine fabric crowned by a little
fool's cap of a spire, cosy, or slightly comic in its look. Those
great and stately Perpendicular towers of Somerset and other
English counties have no place in Sussex.

In recent years Winchelsea Church has been given new
windows—or rather, new stained glass to fill the ancient
windows. Three of these windows represent Earth, Air and
Sea. It is good to have brought back some of the medieval
richness and colour that was destroyed at the Reformation
and by Puritan hammer and whitewash. But these new windows are not of the incomparable colours of the ancient
windows—do not even attempt it, as does the jewelled darkness of that other modern window to the Benson family in
Rye Church. One inclines to the feeling that these Winchelsea
windows are too indefinite and restless in design for their
medium—in the case of the Air and Water windows following so closely on aerial and fluid idea as to depart altogether
from the long tradition of ecclesiastical stained glass. But the
effect of their colour is undoubtedly beautiful, even a little
breath-taking, after the white light to which one was accustomed in the church, and completely removes from it the
reproach which had been brought against it, of being too cold.
The colours, while enriching the interior, do not unduly dim
the light. In due time those new windows will be absorbed
into the fabric and atmosphere of the church built and dedi-

cated so long ago to St. Thomas of Canterbury, the "hooly blisful martyr."

New Winchelsea—now so old—has seen many changes and vicissitudes. Once in the very forefront of England, so that Edward IV said of Winchelsea that it was "the key, refuge and guard of these parts against the tempestuousness of the sea and the insults of our enemies."

Then when both the sea and the enemies had done the worst they could, a slow decay, till, in 1790, Wesley, who preached there, wrote in his *Journal* :

"I went over to that poor skeleton of Ancient Winchelsea. It is beautifully situated on the top of a steep hill, and was regularly built in broad streets, crossing each other and encompassing a very large square, in the midst of which was a large church, now in ruins. I stood under a large tree on the side of it and called to most of the inhabitants of the town 'The kingdom of heaven is at hand,' repent, and believe the gospel. It seemed as if all that heard were, at the present, almost persuaded to be Christians."

The walls that once encompassed Winchelsea are fallen and decayed, but the little town has long recovered from its desolation and given up all pretension to be a port. It has become a place of seemly and pleasant order. The wide square wherein is set the church is surrounded by houses and cottages which are charming in mellow brick, or white and yellow washed walls, with shining windows and graceful porches. Down every side street can be found treasures of domestic architecture, from the blandly dignified Georgian to the crooked fairy-tale cottage.

One of the important houses of Winchelsea is the Grey Friars, and Durrant Cooper's *History* of the town gives two engravings of this place taken at different dates. That of 1843 shows the castellated flat-roofed mansion existing at the present time. But the picture dated 1819 gives in its place a charming long, low house, with a wide-spreading tiled roof, below which is a two-story white house with round-headed windows below, and small, heavily mullioned ones above, with fruit-trees or creepers trained elegantly between the windows. The chapel of the Friars is, in the earlier engraving, much less ruinous and overgrown.

One of the things I specially remember about the Grey Friars is the luxuriant and astonishing way in which *Bignonia radicans*, with rosy-red trumpets, grew on the walls there.

The memory of all the changes wrought in past centuries lends a curious charm to the enchanting prospect unfolded before the eyes of those who stand within the Strand Gate. On a clear day the sea is a narrow band of blue beyond the water-threaded levels. And a little to the left, two miles or so away across the marshes, Rye may justly be considered one of the chief treasures of Winchelsea, for wherever the green wooded steep drops away in that direction Rye may be seen, complete and perfect, like a vignette enclosed in a frame of air, standing up crowned with its church, across the wide stretch of Pett Level, where the sun works exquisitely with fleeting clouds and sudden radiance on windy days. Winchelsea offers no such picture to Rye, but hides herself in leafy trees when looked at from the marshes and tells her secrets to the rooks which for so long have thronged and nested and cawed hoarsely there.

To the casual visitor to-day Winchelsea appears no more than a simple village sleeping in the sun. But it has known a marvellous pageant of history on the very edge and forefront of the English coast. "Little London"—as Queen Elizabeth, maybe half-smiling at the pomposity of its mayor and jurats, called it when she visited there—has many memories.

CHAPTER VIII

SOME SUSSEX WORTHIES

1

MARK ANTONY LOWER—who himself deserves to be called a Sussex worthy—wrote a bulky book, published in 1865, called *The Worthies of Sussex*, which has the somewhat alarming sub-title of "Biographical Sketches of the most Eminent Natives or Inhabitants of the County, from the Earliest Period to the Present Day."

It is a vast quarto volume, staggering in its actual weight on the knee, and equally staggering in the industry it displays. It not only contains the biographies of people of real eminence and importance like St. Wilfrid, St. Richard of Chichester, Gundrada, daughter of William the Conqueror and wife of the Lord of Lewes, and of the oldest Sussex families like the Ashburnhams, the Gorings, the Pelhams, the Shelleys, the Gages, the Barttelots, and the Courthopes, whose history is part of the history of the county, but the biographies of many people, mostly Doctors of Divinity, who, if eminent in 1865 are certainly forgotten in this present century. Lower was a little indiscriminate in the people he gathered into his great volume, as well as a little greedy in the way he claimed a man as a Sussex worthy if he had resided in the county for a few years, though he may have been born in Kent and died in Suffolk.

But local patriotism and pride is so excellent a thing, and so properly rooted in the soil and productive of fair fruits, that no Sussex person will have more than a smile for Mark Antony Lower's wide net—and if any man of Kent or Kentish man is annoyed by a little friendly poaching let him go and do likewise.

So, inspired by Lower's example, though perhaps choosing a little more discretely, an outline of the history of some interesting Sussex people is here set forth.

2

The first on the list, John Rowe, has a just claim to our remembrance, for he has been called the "Father of Sussex Archæology," and the value of his work remains to this day. When the Sussex Archæological Society was founded in 1846, this fact was recognized, for almost the first bit of work the Society undertook was to rescue "from the earth into which it had sunk the tombstone of this John Rowe, who died at Lewes in 1636." The memory of his name and labours, at the time of the restoration of his tombstone, had slipped into almost complete oblivion.

An even more effective honouring of John Rowe was the publication of his principal work by the Sussex Record Society in the year 1928, edited by Walter H. Godfrey, F.S.A., under the title of *The Book of John Rowe*.

Rowe's father came from Tonbridge in Kent, and his mother from East Grinstead in Sussex. John Rowe lived a considerable portion of his life at Lewes, where he had received his legal training, and from 1597 to 1622 he was steward to Lord Bergavenny. He lived for many years in a house near the West Gate at Lewes which was called St. Anne's House, and is now destroyed. He reached the age of seventy-eight, and is buried in the churchyard of St. Anne's, in the parish wherein he had lived. He loved the town of Lewes, on which he conferred many benefits, notably the gift of the Town Brooks. He also saved the strange inscribed stones of the Anchorite in the church of St. John-sub-Castro —as a later Sussex antiquary was to save them again from ignorant destroyers in the nineteenth century. Rowe justly describes himself as being among "such as were lovers and favourers of Antiquities."

Sussex owes much to such "lovers and favourers."

Rowe's feeling—his grave and dedicated feeling—on these matters is shown in this statement :

"I have therefore in this 62 year of mine age undertaken to the uttermost of my skill and understanding for the benefit of posterity to set down in writing all the Customs of the aforesaid Manors; whicht I hope to perform and finish with that care, faithfulness and truth as becometh a Christian in the awful fear of that great God that seeth all secrets, and searcheth the heart and intentions of man, whose aid for direction in this business I heartily implore."

The book in which he gathered together all his knowledge and experience of the customs of the Sussex manors with which he was connected—"The whole of Rowe's book," says Mr Godfrey, "is impregnated with the principle that custom is the touchstone of all proper usage"—is written out with delicate care in his own hand. He was evidently a man who was particular as to detail, and to this was added a lawyer's training, and his own strong personal feeling for justice. All of which was to be greatly to the advantage of later antiquaries and historians of Sussex.

In his anonymous History of Lewes and Brighthelmstone, already quoted from, Paul Dunvan, the author, gives a story of Rowe which illustrates his disposition :

"In the year 1600 he held the first Manor Court at Portslade for Richard Snelling, Gent, one of those grasping landlords who seem to think that their tenants, like the trees around them, only vegetate for their convenience and profit. Within this manor there were stinted fines and heriots, which the lord wanted to make arbitrable, and customs favourable to the homage, which he laboured to defeat. Mr Rowe, anxious for an equitable adjustment of the respective claims and rights of lord and tenant, offered to undertake the toilsome revision of all the manorial documents, and the compilation of a fair and explicit customal from them for the future regulation of that manor-court. But the lord, aware of Mr Rowe's motive and intention, refused to let him have those documents; and our virtuous steward has, under the Court-rolls of the 24th of September in the same year, left the following memorandum of that circumstance, and expressions of gentle censure against the petty tyrant of Portslade : 'Here I purposed to have inserted all the tenants, both free and customary, with their several lands, rents and tenures, as they hold of this manor, according to the ancient court-rolls, rentals, surveys and terriers; but Mr Snelling would not have them entered, not willing, as I suppose, that any should know his tenants' terms like himself.'"

Rowe's life was full and honourable, and his children and grandchildren spread to all parts of Sussex. An extract from his will gives us some personal impression of him—a pleasant and kindly impression. It is dated the first day of December 1637, and he says : "Considering my mortalitie, and the uncertainty of death's somons, I do, therefore, in the time of my best health and perfect memorie, make and declare this my last Will and Testament in form following :

"First, I give and bequeath to my loving wife, Susan Rowe, two silver Tankards, parcell guilt; a Silver Bason and Ewer; a Silver Caudle Cup; and all her Jewells, Rings and ready money in her keeping whatsoever, and also one Bedstead, with Curtains and Valence, one paire of Pillows, pillow cotes, bed and bolster of downe or feathers, with two pairs of Sheetes, Coverlettes, Blankets; and all other necessaries thereunto belonging; the beste of each sorte she can or may be pleased to choose."

This is very personal and pleasant, but there are more important things to bequeath in the will than pillow cotes and bolsters—there are messuages in the parishes of St. Peter and St. Mary Westout, Lewes, and these are bestowed on his wife. The will is short, for as Rowe says, "As for Lands, I have none to dispose of, the same being settled long since upon my Wife and Children."

He concludes : "Thus having set in order my worldly affairs, I commend my Soule to myne only Saviour Christ Jesus."

It is a just and generous will, and so may we conclude John Rowe, that admirable citizen of Lewes, and first Sussex antiquary, to have been.

3

Sir William Burrell, to whom Sussex owes much for his antiquarian ardour, so fortunately backed by his great wealth, was not a Sussex man either by birth or residence—his claim to rank as a Sussex worthy is due to the vast collection of Sussex material, notes and pictures, which he gathered in the course of years, at great expense of time and labour and money, for his contemplated history of Sussex.

Knepp Castle, West Grinstead

Burrell, who was born in 1733, at an early age developed his taste for antiquarian pursuits and was elected a Fellow both of the Society of Antiquarians and of the Royal Society when he was only twenty-three years old. At the age of forty he married a young lady (a good deal younger than himself) who was not only a great heiress, but possessed of beauty and intellectual gifts which made her a fitting companion for her scholarly husband. It was this marriage which bestowed a title on William Burrell, as his father-in-law having no son, the baronetcy descended to his son-in-law on Sir Charles Raymond's death. By this death Burrell became not only a baronet, but a Sussex landowner, for a half-portion in Knepp Castle at Shipley became his wife's property, and Burrell himself purchased the remaining portion—which is how the name of Burrell became linked with that of Knepp Castle. He and his wife did not live there, but at the Deepdene in Surrey, where he owned an estate. Why he did not live in Sussex, when he possessed the Knepp estate there, and was so passionately interested in the county, is difficult to understand. But if he did not live there he travelled extensively about the county—in spite of the difficulties of locomotion—in pursuit of material for the history of Sussex that he planned to write. But, unhappily, he was attacked by paralysis, which, though it did not kill him, brought an end to his journeyings, his study of Sussex parish records, and his hopes of writing a monumental history of the county.

We can envisage the work as it would have been, quarto or folio, bound in gold-tooled calf, with masses of dark rich engravings in which the ink would stand up in deep ridges under the finger; full of erudition, a quarry for succeeding students of Sussex.

It must have been a very heavy blow to Sir William Burrell to have to relinquish this work, for not only had he accumulated many volumes filled with his notes, but a fine collection of pictures made at his direction by those admirable artists Grimm and Lambert for the purpose of illustrating the projected undertaking. Realizing that he would never be able to use all this material, he left it in his will, dated 9 December 1790, to the British Museum: "I bequeath my fifteen folio volumes of manuscript, and my eight large folio volumes of drawings executed by Grimm and Lambert, relating to the County of Sussex, to the Trustees of the British Museum for the time being, upon condition that my family and descendants may have free access at all reasonable and proper hours to read and inspect them."

As will be understood, the lapse of time since that will was made has added enormously to the already great intrinsic value of those records and drawings—which actually are much more in number than Sir William Burrell stated in his will. In this large collection the six Rapes of Hastings, Pevensey, Lewes, Bramber, Arundel and Chichester have each their share of attention. The eight folio volumes of drawings are each devoted to one of the Rapes, with one volume of mixed drawings concerning Lewes, Bramber, Arundel and Chichester. And there are volumes of mixed archæological information. They have been a treasure to Sussex antiquarians ever since.

Another of Burrell's services to Sussex was that he restored the original tombstone, which he had discovered at Isfield, to the Lady Gundrada's bones at Southover.

It is fitting that this learned friend of Sussex should be buried in Sussex soil at West Grinstead. A portrait of him in his young days shows him with powdered peruke, tied with a broad black ribbon, a lace stock; an alert, serious face, with a good forehead, and clear, thoughtful eyes.

4

Grouped with John Rowe and Sir William Burrell, though of a considerably later date, must be the names of two other important Sussex antiquarians and archæologists, John Durrant Cooper and Mark Antony Lower, both Fellows of the Royal Society. These two names, so familiar and honoured by the members of the Sussex Archæological Society, for which they did so much, are not as familiar as they should be to the majority of Sussex people, for the foundations they laid, as is the nature of foundations, are apt to be overlooked. But there can be no question as to the value of their work, and its permanence. They both are true Sussex worthies.

They were close contemporaries. Cooper was born in 1812, Lower was born in 1813. They were not only contemporaries but friends, as was natural, considering the similarity of their tastes, and the fact that they were both Sussex men. Cooper was born in the parish of St. Michael at Lewes —perhaps that unusual thirteenth-century tower of his parish church impressed his youthful mind to an early antiquarian bent—and Lower was born in what he called "the obscure agricultural village of Chiddingly in the Weald of Sussex."

Cooper was educated at the Grammar School of Lewes, and his interest in antiquarian pursuits began young. As it says in the memoir of him and of Lower in the 27th volume of the *Sussex Archæological Society's Collections*, "History —history in its topographical and archæological phases— was the study in which he delighted, and he was not out of his teens ere the history and antiquities of his native town and county engaged his constant and serious attention, and as time rolled on he made himself familiar with those of most of the Sussex families of any local importance."

By the time he was twenty-two he had done some useful historical research in connection with the Parliamentary history of Sussex. He also anticipated the valuable work of the Reverend W. D. Parish on the Sussex dialect by publishing in 1836 a *Glossary of the Provincialisms in the County of Sussex*. As a very young man he did much to save the local parish registers from the disastrous state of neglect into which they had fallen, being not only neglected, but in many cases deliberately and wantonly destroyed. When the Duke of Norfolk appointed Cooper Steward of the Leet Court of the Borough of Lewes, he valued the historic nature of the post, which brought him more honour than emolument.

For years William Durrant Cooper was editor of the *Collections* of the county Archæological Society and himself contributed many valuable papers to the different volumes, on a great number of subjects bearing on the history and topography of Sussex. For these services the Society presented him with a silver tray, engraved with Sussex oak leaves and acorns, the arms of Sussex, and those of the Cooper family.

Apart from all these labours, Cooper's most important work was his *History of Winchelsea*, published in 1850, and for long the standard work on the subject.

Though so much of his work was in connection with his native county, that did not represent the whole range of his interests. He was connected with the Camden Society, the Percy Society, and the Shakespeare Society. Both the Kent and Surrey Archæological Societies benefited from his wide knowledge. The Society of Antiquarians welcomed his participation in their labours for a large portion of his life. His enthusiasm for the subjects that held his heart—he remained a bachelor, so his only children were those of his pen— remained so long as his life lasted.

5

Born in Sussex, like his friend Cooper, Mark Antony Lower was never happy save when within his natal county. It was said of him that only the most pressing necessity would induce him to sleep even a night away from it. He married twice, in both cases very happily, and both his wives were Sussex women with good Sussex names, the first wife being Mercy Holman, and the second Sarah Scrase.

Lower wrote the beginning of an autobiography—a mere scrap—but it has a charming little passage about his early life which must be quoted. His father was a country schoolmaster, and the family was musical.

"I recollect," said Lower, "that I was a tolerable proficient on the flute, and a sketcher, before I was seven years old. The singing of sacred music was also one of the family accomplishments and recreations, and we frequently sang hymns set to music by my father himself. Those summer evenings that we spent in the garden, with our family, assisted by some musical neighbours and a few of the pupils, are a thing not easily 'disremembered.' A crowd of rustic neighbours behind the garden wall formed a well-pleased audience, and there we remained until the dews of nightfall warned us to retire to family prayers and to our peaceful couches—each and all as tranquil and happy, and as unmindful of to-morrow's trials, as ever the household of the Vicar of Wakefield could be."

This little scene from the "obscure agricultural village of Chiddingly" is a very pleasant one, and shows how the deep roots grew that always held Mark Antony Lower so close to Sussex soil.

His father had been a village schoolmaster, and so he became, setting up in a very small way at Cade Street, in the parish of Heathfield, and then at Alfriston. While he taught the village children, he also taught himself. It was said that he studied Latin while he ate his dinner. While he was at Alfriston he was engaged in founding a Mechanics' Institute there, with the aid of that very remarkable Sussex shepherd, John Dudeney, whose story will be told later on.

It was in a farmhouse between his birthplace at Chiddingly and his school at Alfriston that Lower met the Sussex girl who became his wife in 1838.

There is a delightfully simple and rural air about the early life of this eminent Sussex historian. His country school-teaching flourished sufficiently for him to remove into Lewes, where, after some years' residence, he then settled himself, with happy appropriateness, in St. Anne's House, which had been the abode of that earlier Sussex antiquary, John Rowe. There Lower lived for thirteen or fourteen years. The house is now vanished, as well as the two historians, but we may imagine them, under that ancient roof, in the Sussex county town, having some satisfactory spiritual communion with each other.

In St. Anne's House, Lower wrote many of the books and articles and learned papers which have permanently linked his name with that of the county he knew so well and loved so much. He had a great deal to do with the founding of the Sussex Archæological Society, and when the first open meeting of the infant Society was held in the appropriate setting of Pevensey Castle on 9 July 1846, the first paper read there was by Mark Antony Lower on those ancient ruins. This was later published as a booklet called *Chronicles of Pevensey*. During his lifetime the *Collections* of the Society contained a wide and varied range of his papers on old Sussex families, parochial records, Sussex churches, Bodiam Castle, water-

mills and windmills, Sussex ruins, and innumerable other
aspects of the same theme of Sussex history and topography.
He not only wrote but often illustrated these papers himself.
For many years he was editor, as well as constant contri-
butor, to the *Collections*. He was not only an antiquary—a
somewhat dusty-sounding name—but a lover of local character and humour, as well as of the old Sussex villages, which
he described as "clusters of lovely habitations, some thatched,
some tiled, some abutting the street, some standing angularly
towards it, all built of flint or boulder. A barn, a stable, a
circular pigeon-house centuries old, with all its denizens
(direct descendants of the old manorial pigeons which lived
here in the days of the Plantagenets), and an antique gable or
two, peer out among the tall elms."

Mark Antony Lower was without doubt one of the
Worthies of Sussex, and deserved the honourable title more
than many of those he enshrined in his own volume.

6

Most people who are interested in the history and quality
of Sussex have taken delight in Parish's *Dictionary of the
Sussex Dialect*. It is more than a dictionary, it is a good reading book because of the examples illustrating the dialect
words which Parish so aptly adds. The quality of his illustration is shown in his note to "adone," meaning leave off.
"I am told on good authority," he says, "that when a Sussex
damsel says 'Oh! do adone,' she means you to go on; but
when she says 'Adone do,' you must leave off immediately."

Here are a few more jewels from Parish's casket.
"Ellynge" is a good word for solitary—"'Tis a terrible
ellynge lonesome old house." "Hem" means very, and very
effective it is in Parish's example : "Hem crusty old chap our
shepherd is, surelye! I says to him yesterday, I says, ' 'Tis
hem bad weather, shepherd,' I says. 'Ah,' says he, ' 'tis better
than no weather at all'; and hem-a-bit would he say any
more." One of the richest of Parish's illustrations is to the
word "spannell," which means to leave dirty footprints on
the floor as a muddy dog does. "I goes into the kitchen and

I says to my mistress, I says ('twas of a Sadderday), 'The old sow's hem ornary,' I says. 'Well,' says she, 'there ain't no call for you to come spannelling about my clean kitchen any more for that,' she says; so I goes out and didn't say nacun, for you can't never make no sense of womenfolks of a Saddaday."

"Ornary" means the old sow was feeling poorly.

The compiler and collector of these treasures of dialect words and phrases was the vicar of Selmeston and Alciston in Sussex, the Reverend William Douglas Parish. For forty-one years, from 1863 to 1904, he worked contentedly as a country parson, on close and friendly terms with all classes of his parishioners. He visited them and talked with them at all times and occasions, really knowing how they lived and worked, and, as the saintly George Herbert admonished the parish priest to do, seeing them when they were "wallowing in the midst of their affairs." It was because of this diurnal intimacy that Parish knew so well the turn of their speech and thought. This intimacy is plain on every page of the *Dialect Dictionary*.

A portrait of the Reverend W. D. Parish shows him more like a typical old-fashioned country squire than a parson— clean-shaved mouth, and chin adorned with side-whiskers, square hat, front-buttoning waistcoat decked with looped watch-chain; the whole man square and broad, with more than a touch of the historic John Bull in the dogged face and set of the shoulders. By no possibility could he be anything but an Englishman, and a rural one at that. A man that any shepherd and ploughman and hedger and ditcher and that-cher, any old flint-breaking roadman, every cottage woman and farm-wife with whom he talked, would recognize as of their own breed, though fully conscious of his superior station and education. He was the gentleman that the Church of England aims to establish in every parish, but he was a man before he was a clergyman.

And from his quiet but full life as Victorian country parson, in villages that had changed but little since the eighteenth century, Parish gathered the material for the slim but valuable *Dictionary* which was published in 1875.

"Every page of this dictionary," wrote the author, "will

show how distinctly the British, Roman, Saxon, and Norman elements are to be traced in words in everyday use among our labouring people, who retain among them many of the oldest forms of old words which although they have long ago become obsolete among their superiors in education are nevertheless still worthy of our respect and affection. Like the old coins which he so often turns up with his plough, the words of the Sussex labourer bear a clear stamp of days long past and gone and tell a story of their own."

Another debt that Sussex people owe to Parish is the arduous work he did for them in transcribing the Sussex section of Domesday Book into modern English. This was published by the Sussex Archæological Society, with the original script on one page, facing Parish's English version, with his notes and explanations. A most valuable and illuminating volume it is for the many who are not learned enough to grapple with the crabbed original.

7

Having given a brief account of these Sussex antiquaries and historians, it is necessary to go back a little for a glimpse of one or two people who helped to make Sussex history, and have in one way or another stamped themselves upon the records of the county.

The name of Mascall belongs to East Sussex, and there is at Plumpton a beautiful old house, still inhabited, which was his home. He lived in the reigns of Henry VIII and his three children, Edward, Mary and Elizabeth. Actual dates of Mascall's birth and death are not available—the only definite dates being those of the publication of his books.

He is interesting, and in his way seems close to us because he represents the type so peculiarly English, that of the country gentleman who finds in his rural estate, large or small, his chief interest in life; who stays at home, and farms and improves the breed of agricultural animals; who reads his *Field* and his *Country Life* by the log fire after a hard day's hunting or shooting, and occasionally writes a letter to the editors of these journals, and gets considerable satisfaction from seeing his letter in print.

Leonard Mascall, having no such weeklies open to him, was forced into the larger ways of authorship, and wrote a number of books on country matters—almost the first of that long and enchanting family of English rural books—which is the principal reason that his name is now remembered.

But according to Fuller he has also another claim. Fuller says of him that he not only "much delighted in gardening—man's original vocation"—but that he was the first "who brought over to England from beyond the seas carps and pippins; the one well-cooked, delicious, the other cordial and restorative."

There is an old saying :

> Turkey, carp, hops, pickerel and beer
> Came into England all in one year.

Leonard Mascall's numerous books have expansive Tudor titles, very pleasant to the ear. His earliest volume—a very popular one, going into numerous editions for nearly a century after its publication in 1578—was a translation, called *A Book of the Arte and Manner how to Graft and Plante all Sortes of Trees, how to set Stones and Sow Pepins*. This was followed by *The Husbandlye Ordering and Gouvernmente of Poultrie*. After this came the *Book of Cattell; wherein is showed the Gouvernmente of Oxen, Kine, Caulfes, and how to use Bulls and other Cattell to the Yoake and Fells*. This book also treated of horses, sheep, pigs, and dogs. His last volume was *A Booke of Fishing*.

So it will be seen that Mascall was an industrious country gentleman, for he not only wrote of these things but practised them himself. It is pleasant to think of him engaged in these peaceful and satisfying rural pursuits—though as the local squire he would no doubt have an eye also to the proper readiness of the local beacons on the heights of the Downs against that vaunted Armada of Spain.

Anyone who journeys to Lewes from the eastward by that lovely twisting road under the Downs, just before reaching the Half Moon at Plumpton, will pass Mascall's old flint-built house. By the side of it is the delightful Mill House, in spring set in sheets of water and of daffodils. Mascall's Plumpton Place shows little from the road save a chimney or two among trees, and a glimpse of the not wholly congruous additions in red brick of Sir Edwin Lutyens. But Plumpton Place, with its moat and its gardens, lying so close under the Downs, so near to the main road, yet so secluded still and so beautiful, is an abode where it is easily possible to imagine that good countryman Leonard Mascall engaged happily about his rural business.

8

Andrew Boorde's is a name that belongs notably to Sussex annals, and his career is certainly one of the strangest and most varied that ever happened in the county. Among other things he was a physician, and all his countrymen's hearts will go out to him for one golden sentence, in which he declared that "water is not wholesome, sole by itself, for Englysshe men."

Perhaps that one sentence by itself is sufficient to justify his claim to be a Sussex worthy in a county where beer has always been properly appreciated.

But there are several other parts of his tale which deserve recording, and the first one is peculiarly interesting and strange from the historical aspect. Mark Antony Lower, in his *Worthies*, set it down. It takes one back to the days of Domesday, still lingering on in slow Sussex in the year 1511, when "George Neville, Lord Bergavenny, enfranchized Andrew Boorde, son of John Boorde, his *nativus* or villein, belonging to his manor or lordship of Ditchling in the County of Sussex, and him, the said Andrew, made free from all bondage, villeinage, and servile condition; so that neither he, the said lord, nor his heirs, nor any one else on their account should for the time to come have any right in or upon the said Andrew, nor on his goods and chattels."

That is curious reading for the century which was to see Shakespeare, But actually, so late as the second decade of the seventeenth century there were three persons in the Manor of Falmer in Sussex who were unfree. They are believed to have been the "last of the villeins," not only in Sussex, but in the whole of England. It shows how late and lingering was custom in the county of the South Saxons.

Borde Hill, in which Andrew Boorde is believed to have
been born—though Pevensey makes a claim to that event—
is in the parish of Cuckfield, to which the Manor of Ditchling
extends.

From his small beginnings Andrew Boorde leaped to curious heights. He obtained some kind of education at Winchester and Oxford though he did not take his degree. Then
he became a Carthusian monk—but found the monastic discipline too much for him. "I am nott able to byde the rugosite
off your relygon," he wrote to a Somersetshire Prior, though
declaring he was devoted to the Order, but wished to be
allowed to do what he felt inclined—a statement very typical
of Boorde, with his "rambling head and inconstant mind."

He returned to Oxford to study physic, and for a time
was actually a suffragan bishop—the Bishop of Chichester
being at that time eighty years old. There is an extraordinary
inconsequence about Boorde's career. He travelled exten-
tively abroad, and brought back with him all kinds of con-
tradictory reports as to the state of feeling on the Continent
in regard to England. In one of them he declared, "Few
frendys hath Ingland in theys part of Europe." He visited
Scotland—then a very foreign country—and advised Cromwell, "Trust you no Skott."

When the Dissolution of the Monasteries came, Boorde
was much upset, and pleaded with Cromwell for his friends
—he still considered himself enough of a Carthusian to suffer
a short imprisonment for his faith in the Tower, but very
soon gave it up, and wandered off in his curious irresponsible
way, finally ceasing to call himself a Carthusian at all. After
this he was appointed one of the King's physicians, but in
spite of his Court position turned up at Pevensey, where he
attended local fairs and markets, selling his medicines and
recommending them with all sorts of quips and tales. He was
to have many followers at country fairs for at least three
centuries. Mark Antony Lower considered that it was while
he was at Pevensey that Andrew Boorde brought out his
Merry Tales of the Wise Men of Gotham, which attained
such a widespread and prolonged popularity.

He was the author of another book, ribald and curious,
and also of some medical treatises, hardly less curious to the

modern mind. But he himself was more curious than any of his works—a strange fantastic figure to flit across the Sussex scene; born in the county, and for a time associated with Pevensey (Pevensey still makes capital out of the connection), but most of his life was spent elsewhere, and he died in the Fleet Prison.

In this Tudor period of Andrew Boorde, Sussex must not fail to claim what appears to be her only link with Shakespeare. Philip Henslowe, author of the famous *Diary*, and partner of Edward Alleyn, was born in Sussex at Lindfield, his mother being a Sussex woman, and his father Master of the Game in Ashdown Forest. Lindfield even to-day still retains so many lovely examples of Tudor building that it is pleasant to imagine Shakespeare on a visit to Henslowe in his native village admiring the Sussex scenery with that keen countrymen's eye of his—but it is to be feared there is no foundation for such a dream.

9

The winnowing-fan of time blows away much chaff, but, in the case of a poet, if but a few golden grains remain, immortality is assured. This is true of that Sussex poet, William Collins, who lives and will live, by virtue simply of his *Odes*. He, like the greater Shelley, is definitely Sussex-born—Shelley at Field Place, near Horsham; Collins at Chichester.

Sussex has other poets than Shelley and Collins. Otway, for one, and the much-forgotten Hayley, whose *Triumphs of Temper* was such a success in its day, though it has now lost all interest save as a period piece; and the melancholy minor muse of Charlotte Smith, who was born at Bignor Park, and whose verse is so typical of the weeping willow order, though it reflects a genuine love for her native Sussex scenery. But she, the least important of them all, is the only one who carries any Sussex stamp upon her verse—the others, though born in Sussex, and in the case of Collins, dying there, are only Sussex men by accident.

But Sussex has several diarists of quality, and the most

outstanding of these is William Turner. He kept a grocer's and mercer's shop at East Hoathly, where he sold a great abundance and variety of things, including groceries, drapery and haberdashery, clothes—including of course that admirable garment the Sussex round-frock—hats, ironmongery, drugs, gloves, stationery, and finally, Mr Turner would undertake to bury the customer. Of all these things he tells us in his *Diary*, and when he has had a good day in his shop thanks the Almighty with a kind of unctuous simplicity that is distinctly pleasing.

His own character comes out very clearly in this *Diary*. He is an odd mixture of gravity—greatly given to the reading of sermons and other theological discourses, a regular attender at church and a Communicant—but also a great reveller and drinker, though all the while innocently shocked at his own regrettable and frequent lapses from sobriety. There is more than a touch of Pepys in this attitude of his— Samuel, like William, was always piously resolving not to give way to certain vices (among which he regretfully reckoned attendance at the Play) and always surprised to discover that he had!

Turner was a schoolmaster before he became a haberdasher and from that calling he probably acquired his taste for sermons and other heavy reading.

His house at East Hoathly is a pleasant substantial Sussex dwelling, with a considerable span of roof, and pretty brick-and-tile work at the end. He inhabited the whole of it, but after his time it was considered spacious enough to be converted into three separate abodes. Turner married young, and did not get on very well with his mother-in-law, who had, as he said, "a very great volubility of tongue for invective, and especially if I am the subject." But what was more serious, he did not get on very well with his wife, and there are many complaints in the *Diary* as to his marital troubles. "How miserable must they be," he says, "where there is nothing else but matrimonial discord and domestic disquiet! How does these thoughts wrack my tumultuous breast and chill the purple current in my veins! Oh, how are these delusive hopes and prospects of happiness before marriage turned into briars of thorns."

To add to the domestic troubles, Mistress Turner suffered from bad health. "My wife a good deal indisposed," he wrote on one occasion, "with the pang in her side, and an ulcer on one of her legs. Oh, heavy and great misfortune!" However, he adds piously, "But let me not repine, since it is the will of the Almighty." It is a little doubtful if such resignation to her woes would have been very grateful to his wife. She was not an imaginary invalid, for she died quite young, and when she was gone her husband began to see her as a repository of all the virtues and bewailed her loss.

But when she was alive it is evident that they got on but ill together, and her scolding tongue may have been one of the reasons for his constant resort to liquor—though this habit was very general among Turner's acquaintances, from the parson downwards. The ladies also were quite unable to walk home after their potations at the local parties, and had to be carried on the backs of the less intoxicated gentlemen. A curious picture.

On one of those occasions Turner wrote that they came home from a festivity, "I may say, quite sober, considering the house we was at, though undoubtedly the worse for drinking, having, I believe, contracted a slight impediment in my speech, occasioned by the fumes of the liquor operating too furiously in my brain."

They not only drank, but ate. "After tea we went to supper on four boiled chickens, four boiled ducks, minced veal, sausages, cold roast goose, chicken pasty and ham."

It is amusing to find Turner writing on one occasion: "The too-frequent use of spirituous liquors, and the exorbitant practice of tea-drinking has corrupted the morals of people of almost every rank."

Another bit about drinking must be quoted, for it is so characteristic of this Sussex diarist. "We drank," he says, "a great many loyal toasts. I came home after eleven, after staying in Mr Porter's wood near an hour and an half, the liquor operating so much in the head that it rendered my leggs useless. Oh, how sensible I am of the goodness of the Divine Providence that I am preserved from harm!"

There is a priceless Pepsyian candour in one of his entries: "This being Christmas-day, myself and wife at church in the morning. We stayed the Communion; my wife gave 6d., but they not asking me I gave nothing. Oh, may we increase in faith and good works, and maintain and keep the good intentions that I hope we have this day taken up."

But Turner's *Diary* is not only valuable for the revelation of his own character. It throws much light on ordinary day-to-day existence in a very quiet and secluded Sussex village during the years between 1754 and 1765. It was written in a very clear hand in one hundred and sixteen "stout memorandum books," and descended to his son, and then to his grandson, through whom it first became publicly known. Mark Antony Lower and R. W. Blencoe first edited the *Diary* for the Sussex Archæological Society's *Collections*, and then in 1925 it was published as a small book under the editorship of Turner's great-great-granddaughter, Mrs Charles Lamb.

The great merit and value of the *Diary* is that it gives us an authentic and firsthand picture of a middle-class tradesman's life in Sussex at that period—a class of whom in general not much is known, as they were not usually articulate.

An interesting and curious custom is described by Turner when he went to a sale at Lewes in 1756, in which the method of sale was that the last bidder while a lighted candle burned was the purchaser. In this sale the candle was lighted at four o'clock and burned till eight, while property worth £420 was being disposed of. There is a curious *Alice Through the Looking Glass* air about such a proceeding, but it is an old custom, and a century earlier Pepys had been present at just such a candle-sale.

A glimpse of another ancient survival is given when Turner mentions how he and his wife and the maid and the two shop boys all dined together at the same table—in farmhouses and out-of-the-way rural places this custom, relic of the old communal life, survived till quite recent years.

Such statements of ways and manners of living, put down quite casually and without any thought, are what make old diaries valuable, even if they are otherwise dull. But William Turner's *Diary* is in no way dull, and he is a man we come to like, in spite of his weaknesses. His *Diary* ends with his second marriage, and though he says with his usual candour that his second wife was undoubtedly plain, we hope at least that she was kind, and made him happy.

10

The foundation of all life in Sussex, as everywhere else, is in the land, and Sussex has produced some notable farmers and improvers of the land, as well as some "labourers in husbandry" who have risen above their lowly circumstances to a place in the annals of their county—especially among the race of shepherds.

The shepherds of John Ellman must have been proud of their master, for Ellman's claim to fame is that he so improved the race of Southdown sheep as almost to have *invented* them, in Mark Antony Lower's words. "This able and persevering gentleman," he goes on to say, "sprang from a stock of Sussex yeomen." His father was a farmer of Hartfield, and there John Ellman was born on 17 October 1753. When the boy was eleven years old he moved from Hartfield to Glynde, near Lewes, and it was the Glynde farm that John Ellman was to make so famous when he took over its control. He farmed for more than fifty years, and there, again in Lower's words, he was "a model of a South Down gentleman-agriculturalist, exercising in every relation of life all the virtues which should be studied and imitated in such a sphere."

The sheep predominate to such an extent in Ellman's life that we do not get a very clear impression of his personality, except that he was generous and helpful to all engaged in his own pursuit and passion of farming. When his sheep gained such an unchallenged position at agricultural shows that no other competitor had a chance of beating him he often refused to compete at all, lest others should be too much discouraged. Arthur Young was greatly interested in Ellman's improvements in sheep-breeding. In 1786 the Earl of Sheffield and John Ellman founded the annual wool fair at Lewes. The Sussex Agricultural Association for the improvement of cattle and "the encouragement of industry and skill among the

Charcoal burners in Charlton Forest

labouring poor," was another effort of Ellman's to improve the conditions of rural life and of farming.

In the eighteenth century the great landed proprietors, people like the Duke of Bedford and the Earls of Sheffield and Egremont—the great Duke of Norfolk having led the way—were keen agricultural improvers, and they recognized Ellman's merits by presenting him in 1800 with a silver cup. That great agricultural duke, the Duke of Bedford, also presented him with a silver vase.

John Ellman did not confine his "improvements" exclusively to the breed of sheep, but also laboured for the welfare of his fellow-men. He was interested in bettering the navigation of that sluggish but useful river, the Ouse, and of Newhaven harbour. He did much for his charming adopted village of Glynde, set amidst the soft curves of the Downland, where his sheep flourished exceedingly, and helped to make it "the happy seat of rural plenty, industry and content."

Many men whose names sound louder in the world's ear have less claim to honourable remembrance than that true son of Sussex, John Ellman.

11

After the farmer comes the shepherd—and among a notable race of men the Sussex shepherd John Dudeney stands out. His is an idyllic story, yet has a solid pedestrian merit, with more than a touch of Smiles's *Self-help* about it. He was born among the Downs "in what is now called Plumpton Cottage," which was his grandfather's property, in April 1782.

Dudeney is an old Sussex name, and this John came from a long line of shepherd ancestors. In past days there was a real pride of heritage in all the rural crafts—a shepherd's son became a shepherd, a thatcher's a thatcher, a blacksmith's a blacksmith, and there can be no question but that skill, as well as the tradition, an inherited skill of hand and eye, was handed down from father to son. "The child is father to the man," as Wordsworth, who knew about these things, said. A shepherd's child who had tumbled about on the cottage

A shepherd's crook made at Pyecombe, near Brighton.
The smith is now over 90 years old and his son is seen
here. These crooks are used all over the world

hearth with a hand-reared lamb, and as a lad helped his father, and perhaps his grandfather, in hurdling sheep, would know instinctively how to handle a flock. And the skill was not all on the paternal side. John Dudeney said, "My mother sometimes tended my father's flock while he went to the sheep-shearing. I have known other shepherds' wives do the same; but the custom, like many others, is discontinued. I have not seen a woman with a flock for many years."

Another thing likely to be inherited from such parents besides skill was that calm and quiet disposition the shepherd needs—the disposition which is content to spend long days slowly moving with the sheep as they feed, with no entertainment save that provided by his own mind, the needs of his sheep, the sky above him, and the turf at his feet.

John Dudeney himself described how his days passed on the hill : "I have sometimes been on the hills in winter from morning till night, and have not seen a single person during the whole day. In the snow I have walked to and fro under the shelter of a steep bank, or in a bottom or coombe, while my sheep have been by me, scraping away the snow with their forefeet to get at the grass, and I have taken my book out of my pocket, and as I walked to and fro in the snow there, read to pass away the time. It is very cold on the Downs in such weather. I remember once, whilst with my father, the snow froze into ice on my eyelashes and he breathed on my face to thaw it off."

One of the strangest things in Sussex to-day is the disappearance of the sheep from the perfect pasturage of the Downland turf. Not more than a quarter of a century ago the Downs were dappled with white slowly moving flocks, and the quiet flat sound of the sheep bells could be heard far off on a still day.

"Why are there no sheep now on the Downs?" I asked a farmer a few years ago. "Because there are no shepherds," he answered.

In the days when there were a few shepherds left, I once met one whom I have never forgotten. I was walking in a remote part of the hill, and as I came round a fold of the Downs I found myself in the midst of a flock of sheep, accompanied by the most magnificent shepherd I have ever beheld.

He was an old man with a flowing white beard—rather like Blake's idea of the Almighty—very tall, and he carried the authentic Pyecombe crook. He wore a wide floppy felt hat —broader brimmed than the shepherd's "chummy"—and was swathed majestically in a great faded blue-cloth cloak. He gave me a "good-day"—I was too awed by him to do more than respond, any trivial feminine remarks seemed quite out of place—and moved slowly onward with his dog and his sheep. So might Wordsworth's "Michael" have looked.

Shepherds in Sussex used often to be called "perusing men," which did not mean that they were great readers, but that they slowly and carefully thought over the things they knew, and the things they saw. In John Dudeney's case it literally meant a reader. He became a shepherd at eight years old, and found the life to his taste as it gave him long hours of solitude in which he could study. All his earnings went to buy books—he had a kind master who allowed him to keep a sheep, whose lamb and wool were his own and worth about fifteen shillings a year. With this money he bought himself the needed books. When he was seventeen years old he became shepherd to a tenantry flock of fourteen hundred sheep at the lovely little village of Kingston, near Lewes. His wage was six pounds a year. To live contentfully on such a wage, working hard, and all the time acquiring book learning, has an idyllic air, a thought of Shakespeare's famous words :

> So many hours must I tend my flock,
> So many hours must I take my rest;
> So many hours must I sport myself;
>
> Ah! what a life were this! how sweet! how lovely!
> Gives not a hawthorn bush a sweeter shade
> To shepherds looking on their silly sheep
> Than doth a rich embroidered canopy.

With his savings out of his small wage John Dudeney bought his books. These books he carried with him to the Downs, and he dug a hole in the turf, with a large stone to cover it, where he kept the volumes he was studying and his slate and pencil. He studied astronomy and mathematics and geography, and got some knowledge of French. On Sundays he refrained from all secular books, and only read the Bible, which made him wish to read it in the original language; so he, all alone on the Downs, with one eye on his flock, taught himself Hebrew so effectively that later he was able to teach Hebrew to others.

The passion for books and for knowledge was so ingrained in this Sussex shepherd that in 1804 he gave up his sheep and went into Baxter's printing works at Lewes. After that, he, who was so entirely self-taught, became himself a schoolmaster. His gentleness, piety and simplicity of manners endeared him to his pupils and his friends. He continued to teach till a few weeks before his death in 1852, when he was seventy years of age. In W. H. Hudson's words in his *Nature in Downland*, it will be allowed that John Dudeney "was deserving of a place among the lesser celebrities of his county."

12

There is a Sussex man whom Lower included in his *Worthies*, not because he had achieved anything notable, but simply because his was a "good life," the type of life which is the foundation of a county's or a country's history. As Lower's monumental work is getting on for a hundred years old, probably only a few students of the past have any knowledge of the somewhat obscure history of William Catt concealed in its pages. The name Catt is a Sussex one, and any visitor to the little Downland church of Bishopstone will find in the churchyard many Catts inscribed on the tombstones, as well as the odd surname of Venus.

William Catt was the son of a small Sussex farmer, and was born in 1780. All the education he had was obtained at a dame school, and Lower says "He was not a particularly apt scholar : he hated his books—but loved cricket." In that being not unlike many a Sussex boy after him.

He married at the youthful age of nineteen, and, as Lower tells, "on the morning of his wedding day he went into a wood with his father's team for a load of hop-poles, was afterwards married in a white 'round-frock,' and returned to his usual work the next morning. . . . When settled in his little homestead, his household arrangements were of the simplest kind. One boy, one girl, and one horse formed his staff; yet he throve and prospered. And no wonder : for both himself and his young wife often rose at three in the morning : he to thrash by candlelight in his barn, she to feed and prepare her poultry for the market. His principle was— 'Earn a shilling and spend elevenpence,' and hence, no doubt. his subsequent success."

These habits of industry and economy enabled him in due course to become owner of the Bishopstone tide-mills, which he did much to improve and extend, as well as reclaiming a great deal of waste land between the mills and Newhaven harbour. William Catt was very proud of this piece of work, and said that to it he owed a large part of his success in life. He had eleven children, and his sons, as they grew up, shared in his work. He was a somewhat stern man—his face shows a very dogged jaw—but was devoted to his family, and took an honest pride in seeing his six sons, with their six wives, seated round his bountiful table when they visited him. He was wisely charitable to his dependants, and to the poor, and his servants stayed with him for most of their working lives. Lower records a pleasant little story : "On one occasion, at a harvest supper, one of those old dependants, being a little elevated with strong ale, thus addressed him : 'Give us yer hand, sir, I love ye, I love ye, sir; but I'm d——d if I bean't afeard of ye though !' "

13

That little village of Bishopstone, tucked away among the low Downs which slope gently to the Newhaven flats, can claim a somewhat more famous inhabitant than William Catt in its one-time vicar, James Hurdis, who was born there in 1763. He took the Church for his career, and after dwelling for some years as a poor curate at Burpham, he was made vicar of his native village. Eventually he became Professor of Poetry at Oxford. While he was at Burpham he wrote a long poem called "The Village Curate," which obtained the approval of Cowper, who wrote to Hurdis : "I have always entertained, and have occasionally avowed, a great degree of respect for the abilities of the unknown author of 'The Village Curate,' unknown at that time, but now well known, and not to me only, but to many."

When Cowper ventured into Sussex—and he wrote of this expedition : "I was daunted by the tremendous height of the Sussex hills in comparison of which all that I had seen elsewhere are dwarfs"—to stay with his friend William Hayley at Eartham, he begged Hurdis to come over there, as "it were a pity we should be in the same county and not come together." Hurdis went and Cowper found him congenial, telling Lady Hesketh that "You would admire him much. He is gentle in his manners and delicate in his person."

Hurdis's poem "The Village Curate" was written at Burpham, and the following lines describe his home there :

> In yonder mansion, rear'd by rustic hands,
> And deck'd with no superfluous ornament,
> Where use was all the architect proposed,
> And all the master wish'd, which scarce a mile
> From village tumult, to the morning sun
> Turns its warm aspect, yet with blossoms hung
> Of cherrry, and of peach, lives happy still
> The reverend Alcanor.

It is typical pleasant, uninspired eighteenth-century verse —the chaste and very minor muse so assiduously cultivated in many country places at that time.

Hurdis also wrote and published—"Printed at the Author's own Press, Bishopstone, Sussex"—another poem, the "Favourite Village." The village of that poem was his native one of Bishopstone, but the poetry is not, in consequence, any better.

Just before Christmas in the year following the publication of this poem, he died quite suddenly. He is buried in the peaceful churchyard of the place of his birth and of his parochial ministrations.

CHAPTER IX

LIFE ON THE LAND

1

WHEN I was a child I saw Sussex oxen ploughing at almost the last farm in East Sussex on which they were used. A child does not know the meaning of the things which it beholds—I did not know that those black, curly-polled oxen with the wide horns were the last of their kind, just about to disappear from the rural scene they had so long adorned and made. Still less did I realize that what I then beheld (with an admitted difference in the breed of the bullocks) would have been a familiar and normal sight to a Saxon child in the time of the Heptarchy, possibly on that very same parcel of earth. Such was the historical continuity of England up to the end of the nineteenth century—a continuity now unhappily broken.

As the plough is the fundamental implement of husbandry —which comes first, and from which all increase follows— so is the draught-ox the fundamental agricultural animal. His neat and cloven hoof, which has to be shod with two separate curved iron shoes, called ox-cues, was the hoof that first trod the furrow, and his were the powerful shoulders which first hauled the clumsy wooden plough through the resistant Sussex clay. Horses would have stood still, horses would have foundered in those early days.

So late as the end of the eighteenth century, oxen not only pulled the plough, but dragged the local squire and his lady to church in their coach along the morass-like roads for which Sussex was famous. This was apparently one of the sights that most amused the wits from London when they occasionally penetrated to the depths of "savage Sussex."

Timber was also hauled by oxen. Defoe saw an oak tree drawn on a tug by twenty-two oxen, but even with such a team declared it was sometimes two or three years before it reached the dockyard at Chatham from the Sussex Weald where it was grown and felled. In the time of Henry VIII the county was referred to as "Sousekes full of dyrt and myre."

For such a heavy and clogging soil as that of the Weald, the ox, with his neat hooves and solid shoulders, was the proper draught animal. He had other advantages over the horse—he was cheaper, his harness, grooming, and keep were all less expensive than that of the horse. And finally, though this seems a sad end for so good a labourer on the land, his flesh was food. The bullock-team, though slower than horses, ploughed deep, and their cloven hoofs had a kind of screwing tread that pulverized the soil and made a good tilth.

The strength and "pull" of oxen was shown at a farm near Saddlescombe some fifty years ago when a ten-ton steam threshing engine got sunk in a pond—a span of six oxen were yoked to it and proceeded calmly to pull it out.

Oxen could not be shod in the simple way horses are, by the blacksmith just lifting a hoof—they had to be thrown on their backs, the ox-herd then sat on their necks, and a kind of wooden tripod was placed over them to which their legs were tied for shoeing. It sounds clumsy, but the oxen very soon got used to it. At the forge at Pyecombe where the famous sheep-crooks were made, I have seen, laid across the open beam, one of those ox-tripods, and was told by the well-known old blacksmith, Mr Mitchell, who was then nearing his hundredth year, but as active as ever, of the numbers of plough-oxen he had shod by means of that tripod. He rooted about in a rough wooden box full of odds and ends —and there is no place like a forge for curious odds and ends of metal—till he found three of the kind of nails used for ox-cues, thin sharp nails with a flat head turned over. These he gave to me, with an air as if they were pearls. I quite felt they were—at any rate in these days they are more rare! Another thing now very seldom seen is the ox-yoke, that great double bow of wood which has not changed its shape since the same thing was depicted in the Luttrell Psalter. There used to be one hanging outside the blacksmith's shop at East Dean, but I believe it is now in a museum—a safer, though less natural place for it.

Plough oxen in the old days always had their own names, which they knew and responded to, and they were always paired with the same mate, and kept the same place in the ox-team. In the oldest agricultural records we have there is much wise advice to the ox-herd as to how he must keep his oxen happy—he is even advised to sing to them! The careful ox-man knew that if the ox is working his tongue must never hang out, as that meant he was being overdriven.

In the *West Sussex Gazette* for the year 1912, the sale is recorded of some plough-oxen which, the auctioneer said, were probably the very last he would ever bring under the hammer. Two pairs, named Frost and Fairman and Rock and Ruby, were bought by Mr H. Scrase for £46 and £41 the pair; while Mr W. Elphick bought Turk and Tiger and Lark and Linnet at £37 the pair.

It is interesting to note that the names of both purchasers of these oxen—so ancient in their use—Scrase and Elphick, are both very old Sussex names. Names and customs continue in Sussex long after the casual observer about the too popular sea-coast would imagine them vanished quite out of mind.

An old and noble custom connected with oxen has unhappily completely disappeared, as the oxen are gone. But in the old days the Sussex farmer who had used oxen at the plough was drawn to his burial in a farm wagon, with its big blue-painted wheels, by a slow team of oxen. How simply and yet stately was such a funeral—death linked to the natural increase of the soil.

And always we should remember how the ox and the ass —creatures so lowly—have their part in the Incarnation, and were present in that stable at Bethlehem—

> Where man was all too marred with sin,
> The ass, the ox, were bidden in.

It was an old belief in rural places that at midnight on Christmas Eve the creatures of the byre knelt down upon their knees in memory of that first Christmas. Hardy wrote a lovely little poem about it, called "The Oxen." James Kilvert in his most enchanting *Diary* (which has, unfortunately, nothing to do with Sussex) recalls it, and gives a perfect little conversation with a man who said: "I was watching them on old Christmas Eve and at twelve o'clock the oxen that were standing knelt down upon their knees and those that were lying down rose up on their knees, and there they stayed kneeling and moaning, the tears running down their faces."

Have we not lost much in losing the ox from the rural scene, where he had not only agricultural uses of the utmost importance but he was representative of many things in our history and legend?

2

The horse is an animal with a less ancient agricultural lineage than the ox. The ox and the pig tramp right through Domesday Book—land for ploughs and pannage for pigs are continually inquired after.

The history of the horse in Sussex is much the history of the horse elsewhere. But according to a statement in *Sussex Notes and Queries*, which I venture to quote, and which I believe was written by the late Miss Mary Holgate, to whom Sussex archæology owes much, there was a Sussex horse. She says :

"I well remember seeing one in the fields of Ardingly some 35 years ago. I was walking with an old uncle born in the twenties of last century, who had spent his whole life in Sussex. He called my attention to the horse and told me to remember that I had seen a real Sussex horse, which even then was rarely to be found. He was a good-sized beast, somewhat short-backed, but without the 'roly-poliness' of the Suffolk or the weight of the Shire. The colour was that peculiar dun brown shade known as sepia, and the remarkable thing was the contrasting pale flaxen mane and tail. The tail was very flat and carried close to the body, with an edge of little flaxen curls. Such is my remembrance of a true Sussex horse."

Till I read Miss Holgate's account I did not realize that I also had seen a true Sussex horse. When I was a child, a farmer near my home in East Sussex had one. I often saw it ploughing with two ordinary brown horses, and remember it because the light, bright flaxen colour of the mane and tail stood out in the sunshine. Wooden toy horses used sometimes to be adorned with manes and tails of that surprising blond shade.

3

The Sussex Downland was manifestly made by nature to be the home of sheep. There is not in England—and therefore not anywhere in the world—a finer, sweeter turf. It is from this turf that the flavour of Southdown mutton comes, and also, as I have been told, from the number of tiny brown and white snails (said to have come over with the Romans) which the sheep crunch up with the grass. The Downs also provide the wide wandering spaces and absence of alarms so essential to the welfare of a flock.

So perfect was the scene in the old days, of the slow-moving sheep—looking at a distance like clouds dropped from the sky above them—that a shepherd to match, a Corydon with fluttering ribbons at his knee, should have been piping on his recorder, sitting in the scant shade of a hawthorn or juniper bush, that perfect melody of Bach's, "Here sheep may safely graze."

But our Sussex shepherds have always been a sturdy breed, not much given to recorders or ribbons at the knee. Their proper garment was the smock—so protective against all weathers—and a great enveloping cloth cloak, a relic, I believe of old Waterloo and Crimea army cloaks, which when those wars were ended came to more peaceful uses, and the "chummy," the shepherd's round low-crowned wide-brimmed felt hat. And, of course, his hook or crook—the Pyecombe crook in most parts of eastern Sussex. As time went on, the older and more admirable garments slowly disappeared with that inevitable cheapening of quality which seems overtaking all aspects of our civilization, whether it is building, food, or garments. The iron-hard and indestructible linen from which smocks were made is no longer woven, and so too, one may suspect, no longer are the firm and patient fingers which stitched it. I have seen a shepherd's smock that had been worn and washed, exposed to sun and wind, for full sixty years, and not a stitch had given, and not a thread of the texture was worn thin. The only change that time had wrought was a slight softening of the original stiffness of the fabric, and a fading to a lighter shade from the original dark iron-grey colour. Many smocks, of course, were cream, but that blackish-grey was also much worn. The close gathering of the smocking on the shoulders and chest was impervious to the most driving rain—that was probably its original reason, and the decorative stitching but an afterthought.

The modern shepherd, where he still endures, wears the ordinary rural labourer's clothes; often corduroys, tied at the knee, a loose-hanging waistcoat, usually unbuttoned in warm weather, a nondescript coat. But even in these every-day garments there is often a touch of grace and freedom about him that comes of his calling. He may be slow in move-ment—those who dwell with animals are never hurried—but he has not the heavy-footed movement of the ploughman, his feet are not clogged with the clays of the Weald.

4

There is an account of the shepherd's important position on the farm in a little book published in 1862 by Richard Lower (uncle of Mark Antony Lower), an eighty-year-old schoolmaster of Chiddingly, called *Stray Leaves from an Old Tree*. By hearsay and personal knowledge, his memory of Sussex shepherds went back twice seventy years, and he said that the shepherd of the farm was "decidedly the chief ser-vant and generally, from generation to generation, a kind of heirloom to a farm. For, whatever changes occurred, the shepherd was still a fixture there. As for parting with a shep-herd, Master Giles would almost as soon have thought of separating from his good old spouse."

Among Richard Lower's earliest acquaintances, he says. was a shepherd named, very suitably, David, "about as fine a specimen of the true Anglo-Saxon as could well be con-ceived, six feet in height was he, and a 'proper man' in his proportions, while his lungs were stentorian. His whistle might be heard a full mile, and as he lay ensconced in his favourite bush on some lofty eminence, he would sing by the hour . . . he always sang Psalms, in the version of Sternhold and Hopkins. . . . David attended to his 'shepherding' until nearly the end of his life, which he closed at the advanced age of ninety years, regretted and respected by all who had known him."

David was a Sussex shepherd who went back in his heyday to the eighteenth century, and we know of him by hearsay. But of a shepherd of our own time we have an account direct from his own lips, as it were, in a marvellous bit of untouched autobiography which first appeared in the pages of the *Sussex County Magazine* in the year 1931—that most admirable publication founded and run for many years by the late Mr Arthur Beckett—to whose present Editor I am much indebted for permission to make these extracts.

The shepherd's name is Arthur Duley, and the photographs which illustrate his "Story of a Southdown Shepherd" in the *Sussex County Magazine* show him as a tall, lean man with a shock of white hair, a bush of grey beard under his ears and chin, humorous mouth and keen eyes. He is an East Sussex man, born in the Down country at Firle. His father was shepherd at Plumpton Place, and with one brief exception all Arthur Duley's shepherding has been done in the country round about Lewes.

The reason he had leisure to take up the pen to such good effect was a long and serious illness. I should like to quote the whole of his narrative, it is so rich and individual, but as that is not possible I will pick out characteristic bits here and there.

Duley was put early to shepherding by his father, and records that "There was an old shepherd came along with his sheep and he ask me what lettle man I was; he said very small to have all those sheep to mind. When I told him who I was he told me to tell my father that I had seen an old shepherd from Glynde; he said he will know who it is. His name was Mr Charles Tuppen."

The shepherd's pay was small in those days, and the rabbits were plentiful. The result was inevitable, the rabbits were poached: "Father use to wear a round frock, which was a fine thing to hide them."

Remembering the days when he was the "lettle man" upon

the hill, Duley says : "I felt very lonely up there all day by myself. It use to be a very good hill in those times; it was kept down more than it is now. My wages was 3/6 a week. My father use to let me have his watch, but if I see any one I use to ask them the time just to start a yarn. . . . I am very fond of dogs. I had some good and some bad. When you get a good one it is company when you are on the hills by yourself."

Even in the south country there are spells of severe weather. "In 1881 there was a big snowstorm. Our sheep was over the hill, and when we got to them they were nearly covered in." After rescuing the sheep, the shepherd and his son started to return : "My father tied a cord round his waist and I held on to it; that is how I got home. When I got home I was nearly done. My mother laid me down by the fire and rubbed me and got me round."

In his youth, he says, "there use to be a lot of lads about the same age; what one did not know the other did, but times are different now; lads won't stay in the villages. And there were old men too; they use to mow the grass and corn; that is done now by machine. My mother use to go cutting corn and bind it up into sheaves. I think the last she done she was paid 20/- an acre. It was hard work for a woman."

When Duley started on his own he went as under-shepherd at Firle : "The money was not very big : 13/- a week, 1/6 to keeping my dog, 6/1½ once a quarter for my club, 2/6 for lodgings, tea and sugar. I use to buy a loaf of bread a day and a pound of beef made into a pudding lasted Sunday and Monday, and a little piece of bacon; sometimes a rabbit for the rest of the week. I manage to get a glass of beer sometimes. . . . When I was at Firle the postmaster said to me one day, 'Young man, if you have a shilling to spare bring it to me and I will take care of it for you'; so I use to take him a shilling a week; it was not much, but it mounted up in time."

The valour of this saving out of such a wage is equalled by the courage with which he embarked on marriage. He moved to a new job, and 'After I had been there a few month I thought I would get married, as there was a cottage for the shepherd."

In rural life the cottage is generally more difficult to find than the girl.

Duley gives a picture of a certain type of farm foreman in these words, "plain Sussex; you could understand what he said; he did not wrap anything up."

Then here are some bits of shepherding experience and knowledge : "They say when you see the shepherd with his hat well back they have got something pretty good, but if it is over his eyes times are not very good. . . . I know the time when I use to meet at Rodmell as many as 11 shepherds at the Pub to have a chat and a drink of beer and a sing-song together. There is not many that will sing and tell a pretty good tale now."

He goes on to say a few things about sheep. "When I was at Beddingham my sheep got out on a piece of wheat one night and it looked like loosing a lot of them, but I kept them from water and that was how I saved them. . . . If you want some good lambs fed them well, and allso their mothers; that is where a lot of it lays; the more milk the mother gives, the better for the lamb. If you get a little linseed cake that will make their eyes shine and a little piece for the old ewe will help to get it back in wool. . . . The finner the wool the more money you can get. Chalk is the best ground for wool."

"A shephard life is not a bed of roses," concludes this fine specimen of his class, grown old. "I have had some good places and some bad; when one begins to fade they look at you as much as to say you are getting to old; I must have a younger man; but some of the old ones do more work now than the young ones can."

With increasing age and his long illness Shepherd Duley had to give up the work he had done all his life, and was grateful to the farmer who gave him a job at weeding the corn at sixpence an hour, saying he could do as much or as little as he had strength for. "I did not know who was going to be master," said Duley, "me or the work, first off, for it went very hard with me. The tale is you had better be born lucky than rich."

At the end of his narrative—in its vividness and simplicity such an achievement for an "unlettered" man—he says : "I have been reading in a book that the inhabitants of Firle, Alciston, Selmeston, are Saxon folk descended strait from King Alfred's rustics without a drop of mixed blood in their veins, so I feel quite proud as I was born at the Bean Stock, Firle."

5

There is an old Sussex shepherd song which is as charming as anything from the idyllic days of Phyllis and Corydon. These native rustic songs seem to alternate between a rural charm and delicacy and a medieval broadness which somewhat abashes the present age.

This is the song, which used to be sung at sheep-shearings, and also at Christmas :

Here the rosebuds in June and the violets are blowing,
The small birds they warble from every green bough;
  Here's the pink and the lily,
  And the daffadowndilly,
To adorn and perfume the sweet meadows in June.
'Tis all before the plough the fat oxen go slow;
But the lads and the lasses to the sheep-shearing go.

Our shepherds rejoice in their fine long fleece,
And frisky young lambs, which their flocks do increase;
  Each lad takes his lass
  All on the green grass,
  Where the pink and the lily
  And the daffadowndilly, etc.

Here stands our brown jug, and 'tis filled with good ale.
Our table, our table, shall increase and not fail;
  We'll joke and we'll sing
  And dance in a ring,
  Where the pink and the lily, etc.

When the sheep-shearing's over and harvest draws nigh,
We'll prepare for the fields, our strength for to try;
  We'll reap and we'll mow,
  We'll plough and we'll sow;
  Oh ! the pink and the lily,
  And the daffadowndilly,

The Old Water Mill at Fittleworth
Washington. Looking to the village from the east

To adorn and perfume the sweet meadows in June.
'Tis all before the plough and the fat oxen go slow,
But the lads and the lasses to the sheep-shearing go.

Very simple, a little clumsy, but full of the natural country
feeling, is that sheep-shearing song.

6

Sheep fairs—there was a big one on the wide common at
Lindfield, and another at Findon, as well as at Lewes and
Steyning—and sheep-shearings were great rural festivals in
Sussex. The two harvests of the living sheep are lambs and
wool—mutton being the final act of beneficence on the part
of that simple animal on whom so much of England's greatness in the past was founded that even to this day the Wool-
sack is a seat of high honour.

To see a sheep shorn by hand with the clippers—a rare
enough sight in these times—is to see the deftness of a traditional skill. So unwieldy is the heavy-woolled sheep, so awkward in the handling, and yet she is turned and twisted, and
half-sat up on her tail, and clipped with such swiftness that
before her slow apprehensive mind has half-taken it in, she
is put right side up and sent off with a slap, leaving her complete winter dress on the ground behind her. One would think
the shearer was equipped with four hands instead of two—
one to hold the ewe, with the aid of a knee, and the other
the shears. And if the blade slipped now and again, though
that was not often with a good shearer, there was the tar
boy with his pot to put a dab on the cut against infection.
Sheep are most unfortunate creatures in the infections to
which they are liable—the foot rot (it's a sad sight to see a
sheep kneeling on its front legs to feed), and the liver-fluke
and what all. The careful shepherd is always mending and
doctoring his charges.

When it was time to shear the sheep, teams of men under
a self-chosen captain used to go about the country to the
different flocks. They were competent men who knew their
job and also knew their value, and demanded certain rights

from the farmers who employed them. Their work was hard and thirsty, and one of their customary demands was that they should "light up," which meant pause for a drink, twice during the forenoon, and twice during the afternoon's work. In the morning they were to be allowed a pint of ale on each occasion to each man. For their breakfasts they were to be given meat pies and a pint of ale; for dinner boiled meat, or meat puddings, as much small beer as they liked, with half a pint of strong beer; for supper cold meat and bread and cheese (and in those days both the bread and the cheese were the real staff of life, not "processed" away into nullity) with a quart of ale and a pint of strong beer for every man. Hearty health and hearty fare went together. How strenuous was the work is shown by the record of one sheep-shearing gang who in a month sheared 11,000 sheep in the parishes of Patcham, Falmer, Stanmer, Saddlescombe, Westmeston, Standen and Blatchington.

In a letter from Ringmer, written on 9 April 1773, Gilbert White had something interesting to say about the Sussex sheep of his day:

"One thing is very remarkable as to the sheep: from the westward till you get to the River Adur all the flocks have horns and smooth white faces, and white legs, and a hornless sheep is rarely to be seen; but as soon as you pass that river eastward and mount Beeding Hill, all the flocks at once become hornless, or as they call them poll-sheep; and have, moreover, black faces with a white tuft of wool on their foreheads, and speckled and spotted legs."

The shepherd's trade needed few tools. First his dog, then his crook (and the shepherd in Sussex liked to own one of the famous "Pyecombe hooks," or a crook made at Kingston-by-Lewes, or at Falmer), his sheep bells and his horn lantern for use in the lambing pens by night.

The sound, the curious, metallic and yet unearthly sound of those bells coming from the slowly moving flock seemed the natural voice of the Downland. It is no longer heard. In certain states of the weather the sound of the sheep bells appeared to hang in the air *above* the flock.

The canister bell, a square-shouldered iron bell, was the one most commonly used in Sussex; but there were other types in use, as the clucket, and a latten bell, and what was called the Lewes bell. The bell was fitted to a slightly arched wooden yoke by two leather straps fastened in place by lockyers, little carved latches made, usually, of yew wood or bone. The shepherd often cut out these little lockyers in his spare time.

I have an old Sussex canister bell, which is a decorative and interesting object, hanging by its red-painted (most of the red worn off) wooden yoke from an old beam. The bell is just over four inches high and three and a half inches wide, and gives a pleasant note when struck. Sometimes brass was hammered into the iron to improve the tone. The lockyers of my old bell are very carefully shaped out of bone. Somebody enjoyed making the tackle for that bell.

The other type of bell which was in common use in Sussex was the cluck or clucket—the shoulder of this bell is wider than the mouth, and the note it makes is not so melodious as that of the canister; the sound is flatter, more of a clack. But a good clucket will carry far, and that is the first object of a sheep bell to the shepherd, for sudden mists often come down on the hill, and the flock may disappear in great swathes of sea-fog, white and dense.

Before parting from the Sussex shepherd let us remember the old folk custom when a shepherd died. The sheep have to be cared for on Sundays as well as week-days, and therefore the shepherd has few opportunities for attending church. So, just to remind the Almighty that he did not deserve reproach for his absence, a lock of sheep's wool was laid on the shepherd's breast before he was enclosed in his coffin.

And the shepherds had a lovely toast which typifies them and their way of life :

> If I had store
> By sheep and fold
> I'd give you gold;
> But, since I'm poor,
> By crook and bell
> I wish you well.

Shelter on the Downs there is little, especially on the eastward Downs, where a mere handful of trees, as at Black Cap, near Lewes, is a landmark for miles. In the west beech and yew holts and hangars grow like folded wings here and there on the chalk slopes. But great stretches of the Downs bear nothing taller than patches of gorse and scattered bushes—very gnarled and twisted with fighting the everlasting wind—of juniper and hawthorn. A bush a few feet high may be very old, for growth is slow in such stark conditions.

The Downland flowers, also, take refuge in lowliness and lie close to the chalk if their growth is solid enough to give a grip to the wind. It is only the light and airy things, like the devil's bit scabious and the exquisite little blue harebell, which dare to raise their flowers aloft. But the wild thyme, "which smells like dawn in paradise," grows in spreading cushions; the honey plantain is a rosette; and that enchanting little flower, bird's-foot trefoil, in its bright yellow coat touched with brownish red, rambles very close to the ground. The dwarf thistle is aptly named, as its largish head has so obviously adapted itself to a discouraging world by growing so short.

In May the full tapestry of the Downland flowers begins to spread to the sun. Milkwort is there with its little fringed flowers of blue, and mauve, and pink, and white; ladies' fingers, and the almond-scented vetch; squinancy wort with its waxen flowers; madder; tormentil; centaury; eyebright; and dropwort—minute and jewelled flowers of the Downs. There are scores of others, and certain stretches of the Down country abound in cowslips, especially in old pastures running up into the hill, and the scentless violet. To see the violet growing in great patches in the sun's unshaded eye is always rather surprising. Primroses prefer the quiet lanes and little spinneys. I remember once motoring down a Sussex lane that had surprisingly wide grass verges on either hand. The road was very bad and full of ruts, it looked as if nothing came there but an occasional farm-cart. And because of this the grass verges were covered with tufts and clumps and families of primroses, so thick that it was impossible to lay a hand on the grass without covering them. A truly heavenly sight. On one side of the lane was a copse of young oak trees, and the ground there was rich with primroses amid the brown curled leaves, and there were mysterious little rills of water which seemed to run from nowhere to nowhere. It was one of those strange bits of forgotten Sussex that the lover of the county encounters now and again—but where it is I have no intention of telling. I am not even sure that I could find it again myself, there is something very elusive about these places, as I have discovered when I have searched for them.

8

There is a plant which grows on the Downs that has been christened the Pride of Sussex, and that is round-headed deep blue rampion. There is also another rampion, the white spiked rampion, which perhaps more justly deserves the title, as it grows only in Sussex, and only in the eastward parts of the county, where in a stretch of about thirty square miles it may be found fairly abundantly, especially in woods which have been recently cut down.

An enchanting race of flowers to be found—but, it is prayed, not plucked—on the Downs are the wild orchises. In all England there are about fifty different species of wild orchids, and nearly thirty of these live in Sussex. Of these the lizard orchis is almost entirely confined to Kent and Sussex. Not all these orchises are confined to the Downs, some of them like the edges of woods and swampy places, but a great many appreciate a chalky soil and flourish on the Downs. The tway-blade, so called because of the two spoon-shaped leaves at the base, is very easy to know, with its spire of greenish flowers. In the lady's tresses, which flowers in September, the flowers grow spirally round the stem. The dwarf orchis and the pyramidal describe themselves. The early purple orchis, with its spotted leaves, is one of the most abundant and easiest to find, while the fragrant orchis betrays itself by its scent.

Of course the most exciting orchises to discover are those

that copy other forms of life, like the man, the bee, the fly, the lizard, the spider, the frog. The lizard is rare, but I remember as a child finding the bee and the fly orchises in quantities, and—I regret to say—gathering them in handfuls, though in mitigation of that unconscious crime I may say that I never left them to perish without water. They were so furry and sweet that I could no more have hurt them than the bee or fly they so amazingly resembled.

But in the responsible grown-up it is quite definitely a crime to pick these flowers at all. If a spike or two cannot be resisted it must be cut, not pulled, for pulling destroys next year's baby bulbs.

They are very fascinating flowers, and in some strange way, in spite of their slightly exotic quality, seem perfectly at home on the bare Downland, while a bowlful of the fragrant orchis will scent a room in an almost overpowering manner. Of course one should not have a bowlful of any wild orchis in one's room, as I had once. But I was not guilty of the plucking. They were brought to me by a Sussex farm labourer, who, owing to certain small kindnesses given him, displayed an almost feudal devotion to me and my family. This man knew the local countryside like the palm of his hand. He knew where all the wild flowers grew best and where every wild animal and bird lived in hole and hedge. He was also a bit of an archæologist—had a very sharp eye for a "worked" flint, and gave me some good specimens, which he would pull out of his capacious pocket, saying "Looks as though Somebody 'as been 'aving a go at these 'ere!" He was more than a bit of a poacher, and amazingly accurate and deadly with a catapult. But it was unsafe to ask him for anything; he had no sense of restraint—his nature was lavish, and he loved giving.

One Christmas I asked him to get me a little holly with berries on it, and was startled to have him arrive the next evening with a whole holly tree. I never could find out where it came from, it was obviously one of those well-grown straight trees which adorn the hedgerows here and there.

I had a primrose bank in my garden—he did not think it well enough stocked, and one day brought me a whole sackful of primrose roots—to my conscientious horror and secret delight!—and put them in for me, and he had a "green finger." It was his way of paying for such small things as we did for him—he was independent and proud, and would not take unless he could give. "The kindnesses we done each other," he said one day, stuffing some of the tobacco I had given him into his pipe. That is the attitude of the old-fashioned country man or woman.

9

The great variety of geological strata in Sussex makes for a great variety of flowers and herbage. The chalk has its own special tapestry—including patches of wild strawberries and raspberries; the sandy heaths another and a more monotonous one; while the river valleys and half-marshy places like Amberley Wild Brooks have their own rich and characteristic flora.

But the wild flowers are only a gracious adornment of rural life, on which the thoughtful shepherd may meditate, if he feels so inclined, and by them tell the passing of the hours and the seasons. But while the Sussex shepherd watched with his flock upon the hill, a great deal of strenuous and unceasing work was going on at the farmsteads in the Weald. From the northward slope of the chalk a marvellous picture is spread out of the chequered fields, brown, green, yellow, or purplish, according to crop—the vital patchwork quilt of Ceres. And at different points on the quilt, like little clumps of embroidery, are groups of farm buildings, the warm red roofs covering the homes of the farmer and his cattle. In that wide-spreading view the ungainly roof of a Dutch barn, a shed mended with corrugated, instead of thatch or tile, are hardly noticed in the embracing graciousness. Even clutches of building estates, so raw and red, lose their worst horrors in the beneficence of that wide and distant prospect. The scene, even in this our day, is predominantly agricultural. But this is only true when looking from the northward slope of the Downs—from the southern side it is a different and a sadder tale. If we find the change too despairing, we must recall the scene as Robert Bloomfield, author of that classic, "Farmer's Boy," beheld it:

... the famed, the brave South Downs,
   That like a chain of pearls appear;
Their pale green sides and graceful crowns
   To freedom, thought, and peace how dear.
To freedom, for no fence is seen;
   To thought, for silence smooths the way;
To peace, for o'er the boundless green,
   Unnumbered flocks and shepherds stray.

As our early ancestors lived their lives principally on the Downs, so our later ones lived theirs on the farmlands they dug out of the forests of the Weald. We think of these forests as being largely oak, as the Wealden clay is a happy home for oaks. But it is interesting to know that it has been found from analysis of the ashes found in Bronze Age graves that the trees which grew in Sussex in those remote days were not only the oak, but the ash, elm, horse-chestnut, whitebeam, and guelder-rose. Happily they grow here still.

Farming in Sussex in the past was much like farming in other parts of England at the different periods of history, and there is no need to go into it in detail. But there are certain Sussex peculiarities which are interesting to record, some of which lingered on in this backward and enclosed county—for so it was before the railway, and even the railway's services are mostly confined to north and south, anyone who desires to travel by train east and west in Sussex has a long, complicated and slow journey—for a remarkably long time.

The late-continued use of oxen for ploughing and other farm-work was marked in Sussex, and the continued use of the old wooden plough called the turn-wrist or turn-wrest plough. This is a two-wheeled plough, with a high wooden structure over the wheels supporting the plough beam. It is an ancient implement, particularly useful for ploughing the sloping Downland fields. It has almost passed out of use, but, ancient as it is, I saw it a few years ago being used at a farm at Streat for trenching.

One of my cherished possessions is a beautiful little model of the old turn-wrest plough, about a foot long, made for me by an East Sussex blacksmith and wheelwright. It is a beautiful bit of work, made by one of the real old village craftsmen—both spiritually and materially the most valuable of England's citizens—but we are killing them off as fast as we can; they are "not economic." We have forgotten our Shakespeare's words :

> There is a history in all men's lives,
> Figuring the nature of the times deceased.

10

The visible relics of the old life on the land in Sussex are all beautiful. The old farmhouse and cottages, the tithe barns, the massive brick-built dovecots, the windmills—so many of which have vanished away and so few of which are any longer in use—the watermills, one or two of which still grind flour, and as watermills are much older than windmills, so it is good that they have held out longer against disuse and decay.

Any eye can see the homely, honest beauty of these buildings, and any mind may vainly wonder why our forefathers built with such natural grace and sense in a way we can no longer achieve. Perhaps the answer is that they lived with more sense than we do.

From old records, old customs, old accounts, old diaries, we get glimpses of how our ancestors lived out their lives under these mellow roofs.

Their first necessity of food was of course home-grown in early times, and even in later ones there was a stubborn resistance to the "far-fecht and deare bought." A typical Sussex tale is told of the chapel people of Little Ote Hall, near Wivelsfield. In the fashion of the day the whole congregation drank beer when at work and at play, with the exception of one family which ventured on the new beverage of tea. When he heard of this backsliding, the minister turned them out of the congregation of pious beer-drinkers. It was only when the erring family promised to reform and go back to beer that they were once more permitted to enter the fold.

Like most other counties Sussex has her traditional dishes —and they are of a substantial nature fitted to the appetites of what was a largely rural and Saxon population. Having so long a sea coast, fish (after St. Wilfrid had taught the inhabitants how to fish) naturally had a place in the diet of the people. It used to be said that Sussex was celebrated for seven good things to eat—one of them was that little Downland bird, the wheatear, called the Sussex ortolan, but the other six were fish; the Selsey cockle, the Chichester lobster, the Arundel mullet, the Amberley trout, the Pullborough eel and the Rye herring. John Evelyn, who lived for a time in Sussex, praised the fishponds there. That famous lady, Mrs Beeton, said the inhabitants of this county "were noted for their savoury puddings." There is a Sussex eel pudding, and almost anything can go into these puddings, rolled in a suet blanket and boiled in a cloth. One favourite and very good one is made of bacon and herbs.

Wheatear pies used to be a famous Sussex dish. The wheatears were caught in hundreds on the Downs, largely by the shepherds, who looked upon the wheatear harvest as part of their exiguous income. They used to get a penny for each bird. That native Sussex poet and parson, James Hurdis, displayed a doubly humane feeling—he used to walk on the Downs, releasing the little birds from the turf traps, but remembering the shepherds' poverty always put a penny for each bird he set free.

A wheatear pie is supposed to have saved a high sheriff of Sussex who was suspected of working for the restoration of the exiled Charles II. Cromwell sent his men to search his residence at Eastbourne, Bourne Place. They arrived at dinner-time, and there was a large wheatear pie upon the table, of which the sheriff's wife invited them to partake, her husband being at the time laid up in bed. The Roundheads found the pie so good that while they were eating it time was given to the sheriff to destroy papers which would have incriminated him, so that when the house was searched nothing was found.

Lamb and mutton, it is needless to say, are dishes appreciated in Sussex, the small Southdown mutton being the best in the world. The use of cucumber sauce with mutton has quite disappeared, but it was eaten in the past, and at the Sussex village of Yapton there is an inn with the curious name of the Shoulder of Mutton and Cucumber.

Of the classic apple pie Sussex has its own version, and a rich one it is. To start with it is made in the ordinary way with apples and short pastry, cloves, and the juice of half a lemon, with a syrup made from the apple cores and peelings and sugar added before the crust is put on. Then the beaten yolks of two eggs and half a pint of cream are slowly cooked, and when the pie comes out of the oven the crust is lifted and the egg and cream mixture is poured in.

Pond pudding is another specimen of rich fare which used to be much favoured in the county. Suet crust with currants was filled with half a pound of butter and half a pound of brown sugar rolled into a ball, the crust closed round it and then boiled in a cloth for three hours.

Many kinds of cakes are made in Sussex which are not peculiar to the county, but lardy Johns, plum heavies and flead cakes have an authentic Sussex flavour, while a hefty concoction called coger cakes was made by the cottage wives of flour, fat of salt pork, sugar and currants, and baked into cakes for their menfolk to take to the field.

The bullace, a small round green plum, used to be much grown in Sussex, and made into cheese, and most farmhouses had a damson tree against the wall, whose tart, richly flavoured fruit was made use of in the same way.

As to home-made wines, almost everything that grew in the county was turned into wines and cordials, from the elderflower and elderberry, cowslips, dandelions, parsnips, potatoes, sloes, hawthorn berries. Mead was also made. When properly made and matured these wines were delicious—and surprisingly potent, as the incautious sipper discovered who thought the term "home-made" was equivalent to "non-alcoholic"—particularly as the cottage dame offering her own brew of cowslips looked so innocent of anything so fiercely alcoholic.

11

When we think how narrow was the old agricultural labourer's wage and how restricted, in consequence, was his diet, we forget one thing. His bread, which was truly his "staff of life," was made from whole wheat which still re-

tained the germ, and had not been doctored or mishandled
in any way. The corn had probably been grown in the parish
and ground at the local mill. The labourer's wife would herself glean enough ears after the harvest to keep the family
in loaves for some time. When the bread was made it was
baked in the brick oven, and the result was a loaf which in
flavour and health-giving quality was incomparable. Such
bread, with beer or milk, was a meal in itself, and with the
addition of a bit of cheese or bacon, a feast. With a pig in
the sty, vegetables and soft fruit, as well as an apple tree, in
the garden, you have the "cottage economy" Cobbett advo-
cated with such ardour. Well-being cannot be judged simply
in terms of money.

On the whole Cobbett approved of the state of things in
Sussex as he found them in the course of his rural rides, and
Sussex people may well feel pleased to have won the approval
of this great Englishman.

Writing from Singleton Cobbett said :

"There is besides, no misery to be seen here. I have seen
no wretchedness in Sussex; nothing to be at all compared to
that which I have seen in other parts; and, as to these villages
in the South Downs, they are beautiful to behold. . . . There
is an appearance of comfort about the dwellings of the
labourers all along here that is very pleasant to behold. The
gardens are neat and full of vegetables of the better kinds.
I see very few of 'Ireland's lazy root'; and never, in this
country, will people be base enough to lie down and expire
from starvation under the operation of the *extreme unction* !
Nothing but a *potato-eater* will do that ! As I came along
between Upwaltham and Eastdean I called to me a young
man, who, along with the other turnip-howers, was sitting
under the shelter of a hedge at breakfast. He came running
to me with his victuals in his hand; and I was glad to see
that his food consisted of a good lump of household *bread*
and not a very small lump of *bacon*. I did not envy him his
appetite, for I had, at that moment, a very good one of my
own; but I wanted to know the distance I had to go before
I should get to a good public house. In parting with him I
said, 'You do get some *bacon* then?' 'Oh, yes ! sir,' said he,
and with an emphasis and a wag of the head which seemed

to say 'We *must* and *will* have that.' I saw, and with g
delight, a pig at almost every labourer's house. The ho
are good and warm; and the gardens some of the very b
that I have seen in England. . . . No society ought to exi
where the labourers live in a hog-like sort of way."

12

Cobbett, when he rode about Sussex, would see an abundance of windmills—so naturally at home on the breezy chalk
hills and on the rising ground and little eminences that
diversify the Weald. Most of these windmills have now
tumbled down from disuse and neglect, or succumbed to their
natural enemy, fire. But, happily, the most famous, because
the most prominent, pair of windmills in Sussex still survive
to adorn the scene—they are known throughout the county as
Jack and Jill, most appropriately as they have certainly gone
up the hill, though the pails of water have to be fetched to
those who dwell in them. These two mills are so admirably
sited on the crest of the Down as to be almost as important
in the landscape as the Ring on Chanctonbury's head. It is
long since they did any work, and for a time they were in
peril of the fate of many other Sussex windmills, but they are
now in good hands and have become the twin guardians of
what must be the most breezy and elevated dwelling in the
country, set in untouched Downland and commanding amazing views from the topmost story of Jack, the black tower-
mill. The variety of shape in the two mills which stand so
friendlily together adds to their enchantment—there is a
touch of fairy-tale about them, as though they had walked
there from some mysterious region for the love of Sussex.
Jack is a black tower-mill, and Jill is a white post-mill.
Adjoining the tower-mill Jack is the round house, all that
remains of a little tower-mill, found too small to draw full
benefit from the powerful winds, which Jack was built to
replace. This round-house is all that remains of one of the
oldest mills in Sussex, and is supposed to be something like
three hundred years old.

An interesting bit of Jill's history is that she is that rare

ig, a travelled windmill. She was built on the Dyke Hill
ove Brighton in 1821, and was later moved all the distance
across the Downs to the elevated site above the retired little
village of Clayton, where she now spends an honoured old
age. This removal was accomplished by an immense team of
oxen, and must have been a notable sight.

In *Sussex Notes and Queries* for 1886 there is an account
of the moving of another mill : "In 1797 a miller at Brighton,
in the presence of many thousand spectators, removed his
windmill whole, and literally as he worked her, with the help
of 36 yoke of oxen and a number of men, across the plains
to a brow near Withdean, a distance of more than a mile,
where he fixed her without the smallest accident. The above
mill stood to the westward of Brighton, very near the edge
of the cliff, and had long been complained of as a nuisance
which caused the removal. The neighbouring farmers accom-
modated him with their oxen for the purpose, gratis."

Not very far away from Jack and Jill above the village of
Clayton, on that sudden eminence called Lodge Hill, which
runs down to Ditchling, is another white post-mill, that has
had its sails restored and has become a protected object.
One cannot but feel that these poor pensioned mills of an age
which has no use for the true stone-miller's art and mystery,
would so much prefer to be doing their proper job. They
were not made as objects to adorn the landscape, but to produce the whole-wheat flour to make man's bread. The beautiful natural sequence of the growing corn to the cottage loaf,
in which the mill played an essential part, is broken.

One of the post-mills that is still working—though not to
grind flour—is at Cross-in-Hand. And almost in the very
centre of Sussex, on high and breezy Chailey North Common, is one of the prettiest and most shapely white smock
mills in the whole county. Beside it stands a large pointed
clipped yew tree, which looks as though it had come from a
gigantic Noah's Ark—indeed, both the white mill and the
everlasting green tree have the look of enchanting outsize
toys. The mill is, happily and suitably, in the hands of the
Chailey Heritage Craft Schools, which are doing such
marvellous work for crippled children.

From this well-cared-for mill it is a long stretch to the

derelict old St. Leonard's mill at Winchelsea. When I last saw this mill it had the most completely haunted air—it was evident that the saint, who used to keep watch over Winchelsea, had long forgotten his poor mill. But old though the mill is (it was built about 1760) that is a date long past the great days of Winchelsea. But it is very old for a wooden post-mill, and makes it definitely an historic relic, so it is good to know that this ancient mill has now been restored to life.

A certain number of windmills in Sussex have been saved from complete extinction, even if sometimes considerably altered in appearance, by being made into dwelling-houses. There is one hidden away up Pipe's Passage in Lewes, and another at West Chiltington, which is a black smock-mill, still retaining its shutterless sweeps and fantail, both of which are painted white, so that it keeps much the appearance of a working windmill. There is something very fascinating about a windmill house, and always great views from the top story.

But the vital working windmill is a sadly diminishing object in the Sussex countryside. The Reverend Peter Hemming, in his valuable book on *Windmills in Sussex*, has made a list (which he does not claim is complete, but is eloquent enough of windmill history to-day) of active, disused and completely vanished mills in the county. Of post-mills there are two in use, sixteen disused, and forty-seven vanished away. Of smock-mills, in the same order, there are two, twelve and nineteen. Of tower-mills there are two, nine and five.

It is a sad tale, for the windmill, like the watermill which is historically so much older, is associated with one of the fundamental needs of mankind. And it is the one building raised by human hands and rooted in the ground which yet seems endowed with some vital life of its own. There was a recognition of this, as well as the old religious feeling which linked the fruitful earth with the God "from whom all blessings flow," in what was called "the miller's pride"—when, at the end of the day's good work, the four sails were placed in the shape of the Cross.

From an old Sussex windmill there comes this simple rhyme :

The windmill is a curious thing
Completely built by art of men,
To grind the corn for man and beast
That they alike may have a feast.
The mill she is built of wood, iron and stone,
Therefore she cannot go aloan,
Therefore, to make the mill to go,
The wind from some part she must blow.

13

Horace Walpole said of Sussex: "The whole county has a Saxon air. . . . Sussex is a great damper of curiosity."

We may well be thankful for the "Saxon air" which for so long kept change and "improvements" at bay, which retained—and still retains in many of the remoter parts—the old and fundamental quality of the county.

One of the small things which shows how self-contained was Sussex is what appears to modern travellers, who can move about with ease and speed, the perversity of Sussex place-names. It might be thought that East and West Chiltington would be fairly close together, but they are separated by more than half the county; West Blatchington belongs to Brighton and East Blatchington to Seaford; Upper Beeding is on the marshy ground on the banks of the River Adur, while Lower Beeding is high up near Cowfold; and there are four confusing "I" names: Ifield, Isfield, Iford, and Itford, the last two being on opposite sides of the Ouse. The truth of the matter is that these names were not given for the convenience of travellers—Sussex did not expect or particularly want travellers from "furrin" parts. The natives knew where these places were, and that was sufficient for them. They did not travel much themselves—like the celebrated Sussex man who having gone a matter of fifteen miles or so from his native place came home with satisfaction, saying he did not care for "furrin parts, Old England was good enough for him."

Country names are old names, and they change, if at all, very slowly—place-names and earthworks being the oldest

240

historical script that we possess. Field names are still waiting for fuller study; their meanings are often very difficult to decipher. But they are intriguing to the mind, even when their meaning is unknown or only guessed at. Words wear down in the course of centuries, just as coins do, and the apparent meaning of a name may be completely remote from its real origin. At one place in Sussex one may come upon the curious names of Miss Meadow, Miss Wood and Little Miss, and might puzzle indefinitely as to their origin—which after all is quite simple, for in the fourteenth century those lands belonged to a certain Nicholas le Mist. Another place called Barley Beans took its name from a long-past owner called Parlebien, who came over with Norman William.

Certain names carry their meaning obviously enough, as Pook Pit—there are many Puck names in Sussex—Twisly Wood, Fright Farm, Wolves Farm, and Wolveslond, which last dates back to 1306. There is a Lampelands at Steyning which paid for the upkeep of the church lamps. Another village in Sussex has a little holding called Gospels, while close by is Epistles—a little bit of unravelled church history. Both odd and pretty—they range from Slugwash to Bo-Peep —are the names of fields and farms and places in Sussex. If anyone could tell us why and when they were first christened and how the names have changed in the slow course of time, on the slow lips of the South Saxons, we should know a good deal more of Sussex domestic and agricultural history than we do now.

14

Owing to its isolation till comparatively late times, super-stitions lingered on in Sussex till quite late times, and it would not be safe to say that even now, in remote corners, the belief in witchcraft and "ill-wishing" has quite faded out. In the *Sussex County Magazine* in 1935 there was a letter from Miss Amy Sawyer, the artist and dramatist, who lived most of her long life in the village of Ditchling, from which I quote a portion because of its first-hand interest :

"I had a girl of 15 to work in the mornings. She had a tale of a witch who lived on Ditchling Common in a cottage

The Old Mill, Cross-in-Hand
The Little White Church, Falmer

called Jack o' Spades. This witch could stop the wagons and they could not go on till she let them. She also went out at night in the form of a hare, and one evening some men waited for her with dogs. The next morning the girl's grandmother was called in to plaster up a bite on the witch's leg where the dogs had caught her as she jumped through the window.

"The second story I had from an old man who has lately died at the age of ninety. He said he once lived in a thatched cottage (now pulled down) between the Half Moon and Plumpton village. Here at one time a witch had lived who played the same trick on wagoners : 'An' the men 'ud beat the hosses an' they'd pull an' they'd tug, but the wagon wouldn't move an' the ol' witch 'ud come out a-laughin' an' a-jeerin' at 'em, an' they couldn't get on till she let 'em. But there wor a carter what know, an' he guessed he'd be even wid the ol' witch, so he druv he's wagon before her door an' then it stopped, an' the hosses they tugged an' they pulled an' they couldn't move it nohow, an' he heard the ol' witch a-laughin' in the cottage. Then this carter what knew, he took out a large knife an' he cuts notches on the spokes, an' there wer a screechin' an' a hollerin' inside, an' out come the ol' witch yellin' and sloppin' blood, an' for every notch on the spokes there wor a cut on her fingers.' "

It was a Sussex belief that one of the most infallible ways to discover a witch was to get her into a room where a cauldron of water was boiling on the fire, then manage to snip off a bit of her hair and throw it into the pot—as the hair touched the boiling water the witch would give a loud scream.

It is extremely dangerous to eat or drink with a witch, for that will give her power over you. Another belief was that a witch could never die till she had passed on her power to someone else.

There were other creatures who had uncanny powers besides witches, hounds and headless horses, and suchlike. It was reported so late as 1935 that "witch-hounds" had been heard near Ditchling Beacon. There is at Chichester a white bird which is supposed to foretell the death of the reigning bishop.

Most of the old local superstitions and omens are more concerned with bad luck than good. Evil will befall those who kill a cricket, remove a swallow's nest from their walls, or cut down a house-leek from the roof. "Hauntings" of a house or other building may often be traced to the smugglers who were so active in Sussex and preferred to keep certain places to themselves. But the story of the ancient oak on the Downs by Broadwater has obviously an older origin than smugglers—on Midsummer Eve a number of skeletons would appear and, forming a ring, dance round the tree till cock-crow. A generation or so ago there were a number of villagers who would testify to having seen this awesome sight with their own eyes.

It is considered extremely unlucky to bring the first snow-drop of the year into the house singly, or of the "rathe prim-rose" fewer than twelve for the first time. This is less well-known than the perilousness of bringing blackthorn in flower into the house at all. But to set against these unlucky omens it should not be forgotten that in Sussex if you find nine peas in the first pod you gather you will have an abundance of good fortune. It was necessary to keep a wary eye on nature in one's walks abroad, which was only to be expected, as all these are rural beliefs, and the country was there before the town.

Finally, here is a charm against the toothache—to make it efficacious this charm had to be written in a Bible or prayer-book :

"As Peter sat weeping on a marvel stone, Christ came by and said unto him, Peter, what hailest thou? Peter answered and said unto Him, My Lord and my God, my tooth aketh. Jesus said unto him, Arise, Peter, and be thou hole; and not the only, but all them that carry these lines for My sake shall never have the toothake."

15

The belief in fairies—though few of the old Sussex people would dream of using such an "outland" word, it is as pharisees they are known—also continued late in the county, and it was no belief of children, but solemnly held by old countrymen, shepherds and ploughmen and suchlike people, and old cottage grandmothers who went piously to church with their prayer-books wrapped up in a clean handkerchief into which a sprig of mint or lavender was tucked.

Getting on for a hundred years ago, Mark Antony Lower (so indispensable to all who write of past Sussex) published from St. Anne's House, Lewes, a book which contained some very interesting examples of then-existing beliefs. On the subject of fairy rings one old countryman said : "It's very hard to say how them rings do come, if it's not the pharisees that made 'em. Besides, there's our old song that we always sing at harvest supper, where it comes in— 'We'll drink and we'll dance like pharisees!' Now, I should like to know why it's put like that 'ere in the song, if it an't true."

Then there is a delightful story given by a certain Will Fowington. It is not only an excellent story, but an admirable example of the old Sussex dialect, one of the peculiarities of which is that "th" becomes "d," thus emphasizing its Saxon origin.

"When I was a liddle boy," the tale begins, "and lived with my gurt uncle, old Jan Duly, dere was an old place dey used to call Burlow Castle. It wa'n't much ov a castle— ouny a few old walls like—but it had been a famous place in de time when dere was a king in every county. Well, whatever it had been afore, at de time I speak on, it was de very hem of a place for pharisees, and nobody didn't like to goo by it ahter dark, for fear on 'um. One dee as Chols Packham, uncle's grandfather, was at plough up dere, just about *coger* time [Sussex for "elevenses," for which the coger cakes were made] he heard a queer sort of a noise right down near de groun' dat frightened him uncommonly surelie. 'Hullo,' says Chols to his mate, 'did you hear dat, Harry?' 'Yakes,' say Harry, 'what was it?' 'I reckon 'twas a pharisee,' says uncle's grandfather. 'No, 'twa'nt,' says Harry, 'dere a'n't no pharisees now. Dere *was once*—at Jerusalem; but dey now full-growed people, and has been dead hundreds o' years.' Well, while dey was a-talkin' Chols heard de noise again. 'Help, help!' Chols was terribly afeard, but he plucked up heart enough to ax what was wanted. 'I've bin a-bakin,' said de liddle voice, 'and have broke my peel and I dunnow what upon airth to do,' Chols, being a tender-hearted kind of chap dat didn't like anybody to be in trouble, he made answer, 'Put it up and I'll try and mend it.' No soonder said dan done; dere was a chink in de groun, for de season was dryish, and sure enough through dat chink dere come up a liddle peel not bigger dan a bren-cheese knife. Chols couldn't hardly help laughin', it was such a monstrous liddle peel, not big enough to hold a gingerbread nut hardly ... but he knowed of old how dahngerous 'twas to offend any of dem liddle customers. So he outs wud a tin-tack or two as he happened to have in his weskit pocket and wud de help ov his coger knife for a hammer, and his knee for a bench, he soon mended de peel and put it down de chink again. Harry was back-turned while dis was a-goin' on, and when he come back Chols up and told him all about it, but Harry said 'twas all stuff, and he didn't believe a word consarnin' aut, for Master Pettit, de parish clerk, had tole him 'twas all a galusion and dere wa'n't no pharisees nowadays.

"But howsomer he proved to be wrong more ways dan one; for de next dee at coger time when Harry was back-turned agin, Chols Packham heard de voice as afore a-comin' up out of de chink and a-sayin', 'Look here!' Well, Chols turned roun', not quite so much frightened dis time, and what should he see standin' close agin de chink but a liddle bowl full of summut dat smell a hem-an-all better dan small beer. 'Hallow!' thinks Chols to himself, 'dis is worth havin',' he thinks. So he tasted it, and at last drunk it all up; and he 'llowed dat of all de stuff *he* ever tasted dat was de very best. He was a-goin' to save de liddle bowl to show Harry dat dere certainly *was* fairies, but whilst he was a-thinking about it, all of a sudden de bowl slipped out of his hands and dashed itself into a hundred pieces, so dat Harry onny laughed at him, and said it was naun but a cracked basin. But howsomever, Harry got served out for bein' so un-believin', for he fell into a poor way, and couldn't go to work as usual, and he got so tedious bad dat he fell away to mere skin and bone, and no doctors couldn't do him no good, and dat very day twelmont he died, at de very same hour dat de pharisee was fust heerd, and dat he spoke agin 'em.''

So close to our own time could have been found some Sussex country-people to link hands with Chaucer :

> Al was this land fulfild of fayerye,
> The elf-queen, with hir joly companye,
> Daunced ful ofte in many a grene mede,

Though it must be sadly admitted—

> But now can no man see none elves mo.

But Sussex has one old woman left whom she is unwilling to give up—the Old Woman of Hefful Cuckoo Fair on April 14, who lets the cuckoo out of her basket, and so brings spring to Sussex. She is very punctual, and on that date the voice of the cuckoo is heard in the land, that voice which so unfailingly makes the heart leap up. But one wet spring the old woman and her cuckoo were late, and an old Sussex gardener said : "It do be time as de cuckoo come to clear up de mud—I don't hold with she being laäte."

16

In a few of the old churches in Sussex the ancient oak pews still survive, and the interest of this survival is increased when, as at Shermanbury, the names of the local farms are inscribed on the sittings in the pews in white letters adorned with little curlicues—such names as Sakham and Abbeyland. In this tiny church the pews are lit by tall three-branched candlesticks fixed in each pew. In West Grinstead Church the pews are likewise adorned with the names of the adjoining farms, names that carry local history in their syllables : Little Champion, Clothalls, Sunt, Pin Land, Copy Hold, East Rith, Priors Bine.

It is easy to imagine the Sussex equivalent of Hardy's "Farmer Ledlow, late at plough," sitting in those solid pews on Sunday, red-faced and slightly somnolent after his week-day labours—especially if he was what used to be called in Sussex a "round-frock farmer," meaning one who himself wore the smock and laboured in his own fields—accompanied by his wife and numerous offspring. He sat in the same seat his father occupied before him, and maybe his grandfather before that.

According to a curious note of Mark Antony Lower's in *Sussex Notes and Queries* for 1854, the mortality among Sussex farmers' wives was much greater than among their husbands. He quotes from an unspecified work on Sussex published in the eighteenth century :

"Many farmers and other natives of the aguish and unhealthy parts of this county marry women born in the Uplands, who when they are brought here soon lose their health and die in a few years; by which means some of the Sussex men (as well as others in Essex and Kent, where the air is similar) have been known to have had seven or eight wives successively. One of these, who had a knack of rhyming, wrote the following lines on his various nuptials, a copy of which we obtained when in Sussex :

My first wife (nam'd Peggy) was noisy and rude;
My next was a coquet; my third was a prude;
My fourth was so-so; and my fifth was precise;
My sixth was but silly; my seventh mighty wise;
But the air of the county deprived them of life,
And left me without either trouble or wife.
So now I'll contented a widower die,
Nor more matrimonial experiments try.

It must be added that Mark Antony Lower does not vouch for the authenticity of these reflections on the lethal quality of the Sussex air, or the callousness of the Sussex husband. On the whole there seems plenty of evidence that the Sussex goodwife was quite capable of holding her own, and keeping her husband from "spannelling" all over her clean kitchen in his dirty boots.

If a man and his wife notoriously quarrelled and the husband beat his spouse, a hint of village disapproval was sometimes given in the old days in Sussex by laying straw and chaff before his door to indicate that domestic threshing was not approved. On the other hand there was a famous Sussex whistling song, sung at harvest suppers and similar occasions, the singer being accompanied by a chorus of whistlers. It began :

There was an old farmer in Sussex did dwell,
And he had a bad wife, as many knew well.

Then Satan came to the old man at the plough—
"One of your family I must have now,

"It is not your eldest son that I do crave,
But 'tis your old wife; and she I will have."

"O! welcome, good Satan, with all my heart;
I hope you and she will never more part!"

But Satan found that the old woman made Hell a most uncomfortable place—she knocked the imps about, and when she "spied seven devils all dancing in chains she up with her pattens and knocked out their brains." Satan began to fear that she might even murder him, so he bundled her up on his back and took her along in a great hurry to her husband, crying

"I've been a tormenter the whole of my life;
But I ne'er was tormented till I took your wife."

17

For amusements the Sussex people had their own version of the Christmas Mummer's Play, played by the "Tipteers" of West Wittering, near Chichester. It had eight characters, who were Old Father Christmas, Prince Feather, the Noble Captain, King George (really St. George), the Turkey Knight, the Valiant Soldier, the Doctor, and his little boy called Jupiter Pills. The play is the usual fandango of old traditional stuff, garbled and half-forgotten, with much later additions. There are people still living, I believe, who have seen it acted, but it belongs now quite definitely to the "bygones."

Happily this need not be said of cricket—and though cricket does not belong exclusively to Sussex the county has taken an important part in the history of the game. It is played with great ardour on village greens, and though nowadays everybody, from the squire to the chimney-sweep, is correctly attired in white flannels, and there is no longer the fearful joy of seeing the brawny blacksmith in fustian trousers and his braces, advancing menacingly towards the wicket, the game is just as good, and the interest of Sussex youth just as keen.

I shall never forget scoring at a village cricket match in Sussex, where all the conditions (including the wicket) were primitive, but the "swiping" and excitement were tremendous. Sixes were as common as ducks—a sort of "death or glory" game. Scoring was extremely difficult, as I had to score on my knee, with a permanent wreath of small boys round my neck. This was a great contrast to another cricket match I once attended at Burpham on that high fantastic field, where there was—so different from the little boys, but just as full of love for the game—a row of very aged men, with serene pink faces and scanty beards, sitting solemnly with their hands on their knees, an occasional high cackle of appreciation issuing from their toothless gums. There were the "forefathers of the hamlet" who had kept the spirit of cricket alive in Sussex since the game first began.

Nyren, most famous of the "Hambledon Men," was taught his cricket by his uncle, Dr Richard Newland of the village of Slindon, so there is some justification for Sussex regarding itself as the nursery of cricket. In his *History of Cricket* H. S. Altham says: "The richest vein of cricket talent [in Sussex] lay at Slindon, and when that parish played the Londoners in 1742 and thereby suffered their second defeat in 44 matches, we may suspect that they were really equivalent to the county."

Noah Mann, another of the great names of the Hambledon club, was a Sussex man. It is recorded that he once made ten runs for one hit, which suggests a very rough outfield. Nyren wrote of Noah Mann: "He was from Sussex, and lived at Northchapel, not far from Petworth. He kept an inn there, and used to come a distance of at least twenty miles every Tuesday to practice. . . . He was a fine batter, a fine field, and the swiftest runner I ever remember. . . . He was a most valuable fellow in the field; for besides being very sure of the ball, his activity was so extraordinary that he would dart all over the ground like lightning."

In the Sussex Archæological Society's *Collections* for the year 1878, the editor of the volume indulges in an article on "The Archæology of Sussex Cricket," with a certain amount of apology for applying so learned a word to a game. But there is really no reason why the beginnings of cricket should not interest archæologists. It is probable that Neolithic Man played some sort of game with the equivalent of a ball.

This article is illustrated by a charming lithograph of the cottage at West Hampnett where Lillywhite was born—a pleasant-looking place, with a good roof and creepers on the walls. Lillywhite, whose name shines so brightly in cricket records, used to bowl to the writer of that article when he was a small boy, on his private ground with perfect turf at Brighton, where Montpelier Crescent now is. The modest sum of five shillings gave the subscriber the privilege of being bowled at by Lillywhite, or caught by his colleague "little Wisden." Lillywhite had a "steadfast look, thick-set build and determined air," and always wore a black broad-brimmed hat whatever the weather.

The cradle of cricket in Sussex, as in the other cricketing counties, was the village green and the village clubs. Some of the members of these clubs would think nothing of walking twenty miles a day to get practice with good players. From the end of the eighteenth century to 1815 there was a very strong club at Oakendene at Cowfold. The most prominent members of this club were a William Wood and his two brothers, a Marchant from Hurstpierpoint, a Bower of Ditchling, and a Voice of Hand-Cross. William Wood was considered the best bowler of his time in Sussex. He was a farmer, and carried a ball with him on his walks about his fields, and practised bowling at any likely object; he had a dog which he had trained to return the ball to him. Body-bowling was not unheard of in those days—"frightening" the batsmen out. There was a half-gipsy Sussex bowler who played in village matches who was so fierce and fast that the wicketkeeper always had a sack stuffed with straw fastened on his chest.

Sussex can claim to be the real originator of round-arm bowling, through Lillywhite and Broadbridge. Forty years earlier it had been tried, but forbidden by the Hambledon club. It was owing to the skill of Lillywhite and Broadbridge in the new style of bowling, after it had been officially countenanced, that Sussex won that prominent position in county cricket which has been hers ever since. In 1827 Sussex played three great matches against All England at Sheffield Park, Lord's and Brighton, and won two out of the three.

On one historic occasion that perfect batsman Fuller Pilch had sixty balls bowled to him by Lillywhite from which he could not score a run; with the sixty-first ball Lillywhite clean bowled him.

In the records of Sussex cricket it must not be forgotten that the Prince Regent gave Brighthelmstone cricket ground on the Levels, by the parish church, in 1791. He also occasionally played cricket himself, in a "condescending" manner. Presumably the bowlers and fielders took care that nothing occurred to disturb this condescension.

Life on the land in the old days was like a good solid cake. There was the plain dough of hard work, growing things, making the things of daily need, from a plough to a barn or dovecot, a wooden buttermould or a child's cradle; ploughing, thatching, mowing—this for the men. The women cooked and scrubbed, milked the cows and fed the poultry, made butter and made bread. In those days the women also spun, and, as the rector of Maresfield, the Reverend Edward Turner, one of the early members of the Sussex Archæological Society, records : "Rarely did you pass a cottage door without hearing the agreeable hum of one or more spinning wheels in full operation, and if you entered a farmhouse for the purpose of having a little chat with the farmer's wife, no sooner had she greeted you and placed a chair for you, than if otherwise employed at the time, she would desist and sit down to her spinning wheel and continue to spin merrily on so long as the conversation lasted."

This was all part of the careful economy of a life where nearly all necessities were home-made. Candles were often made with rushes for wicks, and that Sussex lady, Miss Maude Robinson, who was born and bred on a good Quaker farm at Saddlescombe among the Downs, and who knows more about Sussex farmhouse life than most people, says that these rush candles were sometimes called "fried straws." She also remembers an old man who died in the workhouse at Cuckfield who contrived to "light his pipe with the aid of his knife, a flint picked up in a field, and a tuft of thistledown." It seems hard that such delicate economy and rural skill should end in the workhouse. Another thing Miss Maude Robinson recalls is how the wool of the perhaps only black sheep in the flock was kept separate to be woven into "tuck aprons," which were worn for the roughest work.

The life was hard, without doubt, and the labourers in husbandry very poorly paid in cash, but they had other compensations, both material and otherwise. As Dr Nathanial Blaker says in his *Sussex in Bygone Days*, "It was not an unusual thing for men to work all their lives on one farm, and in it and all that belonged to it they took the deepest interest, regarding it almost as their own property and speaking always of 'our' cows, 'our' sheep, 'our' wheat; and their great object and ambition was to do their work, ploughing, mowing, etc, well, and to have the crops and animals under their care to look a little better than their neighbours'."

The plums in this rural cake were the seasonal festivals, which were derived, little as people after the Reformation may have remembered it, from the holy days of the Church or, much earlier back, from pagan festivals :

> A Christmas gambol oft could cheer
> The poor man's heart for half a year.

The round of daily life was in itself full and satisfying—it did not breed a restless desire for change. It was a life that had roots, and these roots, partly owing to the physical nature of the county, were nowhere deeper than in Sussex.

CHAPTER X

FAREWELL TO THE DOWNS

MANY of the English counties have some special feature of landscape or building which is their pride—the "symbol at their door" of all that the county stands for in the hearts of those who dwell there. The symbol of all things Sussex is the Downs, the range of chalk hills, and it is a symbol that in an extraordinary manner can be seen from all over the county. Near or far, the Downs are there, and the little bits of tucked-away country from which the Downs are invisible can hardly be called authentic Sussex.

Even the day tripper to Brighton who toils up the steep road to the station to catch the evening train is walking on the Downs, little though he may realize it under that dreary coating of bricks and mortar—it seems an inescapable law in England that all station approaches partake of the sordid.

When Sussex was divided into the six Rapes which portion it out, all but one Rape claimed a share of this Downland. From the west the Rapes are those of Chichester (the only ecclesiastical Rape), Arundel, Bramber, Lewes, Pevensey and Hastings. The Rape of Hastings is without any Downland, for the Downs come to an end at Beachy Head.

At one time it was thought these Rapes were pre-Conquest, but most historians now regard them as being established after the Conquest. They stretch from south to north, running right up the county, and therefore include a portion in each Rape, save Hastings, of Downland, Weald and forest. Also the idea of each was to contain a river, with a castle to guard each river gateway.

The full length of the Downs can be walked comfortably in a week, descending each evening at nightfall to some little village at the foot for food and sleep. There are no hamlets on the Downs themselves much above the two hundred feet level, with the exception of Telscombe—a charming little place with its early church, tucked away in a narrow combe—Pyecombe, and Up Waltham in the west, where the number

253

of farms, cottages, and population has hardly changed since Domesday. Height, and the difficulties of water, have happily preserved the South Downs from the perils of building. Great stretches of them remain as they were a thousand years and more ago. They are the great treasure of Sussex, and the chief justification of Belloc's words when he wrote of "that centre of all good things and home of happy men, the county of Sussex." It was in continued view of the Down Country that his "Four Men" made their memorable pilgrimage, of which Belloc wrote a book which is one of the few perfect tributes to the county of Sussex. What Sussex heart but will echo Grizzlebeard's words : "I see before me the Weald in a tumbled garden, Wolstonbury above New Timber and Highden and Rackham beyond, and far away westward I see under Duncton the Garden of Eden, I think, to which we are bound. And sitting crowned in the middle place I see Chanctonbury, which, I think, a dying man remembers so fixed against the south, if he is a man from Ashurst, or from Thakeham, or from the pinewoods by the rock, whenever by some evil fortune a Sussex man dies far away from home."

The great feature of the Downs, and their great distinction, is that they have so few features—they are lines, curves, folds, of a noble and satisfying simplicity. Their very bareness is part of their beauty and makes them unrivalled in the display of changing light and racing cloud shadows. So subtle and so constant are these changes that it is as though these hills of chalk breathed and moved gently as if in sleep. Those who live in sight of the Downs will never give assent to this statement made in the *Victoria County History of Sussex* : "The Downs are dead. Their flowing outlines and winding valleys point to bygone conditions which can never recur till the climate again becomes arctic."

But the Downs are not dead, whatever the geologists may say. That is a heresy of science, and a contradiction of the vital truth that the Downs are the mother of innumerable flowers and grasses, and, when man had not walked contrary to his natural path, the mother also of innumerable flocks. When sheep grazed the Downs, it was as though white chalk, to prove how far from dead it was, had taken to itself white wool and four legs, to roam and feed upon that Downland turf which also is a child of the chalk.

If we in Sussex are inclined to take chalk as a commonplace, it must not be forgotten that in reality this soft limestone is a rare deposit in the world, and particularly rare in the thickness and depth which form our Downs. It is a sea-made substance, and it has the peculiar property of taking something of the flowing curves of the waves of the ocean. "Our blunt, bowheaded, whalebacked Downs," Kipling has called them in his lovely and often-quoted poem; while to another poet, Edmund Blunden, they are "huge images of creative calm." But perhaps Belloc's words are the best : "And along the sky the line of the Downs so noble and so bare."

W. H. Hudson, who knew the Sussex Downs well, said : "Here are no inviting woods and mysterious green shades that ask to be explored : they stand naked to the sky, and on them the mind becomes more aerial."

In tune with this thought of Hudson's is another of Charles Vince's from his *Wayfarers in Arcady*, where he says that the Downs stand like a great green wall, "and the little chalk roads that go up them are like tall and slender ladders, from which a man, if he ever climbed them, would step straight into the sky."

But there is one error of observation here—the Downs are not green in any accepted sense of the word, as when we say green leaves. They are an indescribable colour, that is not green and is not brown, and is not gold, yet is a little of all these. It is a colour that very few painters ever succeed in catching. And to express the softness of the Downs painters are too fond of a smudged horizon line—in any but misty weather the line of the Downs against the sky is always delicately sharp and clear.

The mists that suddenly arise on the South Downs are most erratic—sometimes the southern slopes are shining in sunshine when the northern scarp is almost invisible in fog. so that to cross the width of the Downs is to go from November to April.

In these sudden mists that come down it is possible to get completely lost. It is dangerous walking on the hill when you cannot see, for in places there are unsuspected steep chalk quarries, unfenced, or with fencing so old and rotten that it is no protection.

Mists or sea fog are regarded as infallible weather-signs in Sussex. All over the county you find the little clumsy couplets and folk-rhymes that are weather-warnings. In the west people look up at Chanctonbury and say :

> Old Mother Goring's got her cap on,
> We shall have some rain.

In the east the inhabitants round Lewes say :

> When Beddingham hills wear a cap,
> Ripe and Chalvington get a drop.

Then a little further eastwards it is :

> When Firle hill and Long Man has on a cap
> We at Al'ston get a drap.

Another sign that almost infallibly means rain is when the Downs are very hard and clear and close, almost as though they were stooping over the Weald. In that good Sussex book, *Lonewood Corner*, John Halsham depicts this aspect of the hill :

"In days when the air is dead still and clear for coming rain, the Down seems to come up to the garden bounds, a dun-green bank, hard-edged and massive, showing every plane in relief, making out every gorse tuft and chalk pit and white track up the Beacon, and the dusty ploughed fields on its flanks."

To the natural majesty of the South Downs—"majestic" was Gilbert White's word, and no exaggeration—is added a solitude that is quite astonishing so near to the population of the coast. It is a real solitude where there is no sound save the voice of the "viewless wind," the song of the ascending lark, the cry of a seabird. For miles upon miles there is no sign of mankind—no sign at all except the sign of his death, in the barrows which rise here and there like smaller swellings of the Downland itself. Indeed, to the unarchæological mind they will often appear nothing more than that, there are so many of them—something like a thousand scattered

South Downs, near Steyning

about the Downs, of the round barrows, though the long barrows are much more rare. This link with our forerunners on the Downs is a very deep one, unbroken by all the centuries of change that have gone over the bones of the sleepers in the barrows—and the memory of it adds immeasurably to the solemnity of the Down country.

When we think of the immeasurable toil with which Early Man, with his scant tools, raised these perdurable monuments to his dead, we cannot but believe that he meant us—of an age incredibly remote from his—to see and salute them. It was imagination in action; it was faith in futurity, even if but a future upon this earth. And he wrote something else upon the Downs for us to read when he cut the vast outline of the Long Man of Wilmington upon the chalk. Of all the fantastic ideas that historians ever invented, one of the most fantastic is that the Long Man of Windover Hill—and also the giant Cerne Abbas, so crude and threatening—were made as an idle amusement by the Benedictine monks who in both cases had monasteries at the foot of these superhuman figures. The most elementary knowledge of monastic life and ideals would contradict this idea. Such figures are plainly pre-Christian, even if they are not prehistoric.

Local folklore has a tale to account for the Long Man which is quite different from that of the archæologist. Once upon a time there were two giants, one of whom lived on Firle Beacon and the other on Windover Hill. These giants had a quarrel, and the giant of Firle threw a great boulder at his brother of Wilmington and killed him. In proof of this, there he lies to this day, on the northern face of Windover Hill above Wilmington.

It has been thought that the Long Man is the sun god opening the doors of the dawn, or that he is simply a colossal farmer with a rake in one hand and a scythe in the other—the cross-teeth of the rake and the short-bladed Saxon scythe, as they are represented in a drawing in the Burrell manuscripts, having been obliterated by time. It has been suggested also that the Long Man is a representation of a Roman surveyor with his sighting rods.

To each Sussex man or woman there is, according to the

place of habitation, some particular group of the Downs that
holds the heart. The whole long range of fifty miles or so is
full of changing beauty. To some it is the marvellous slopes
of Duncton Hill, where that boy whom Belloc has made
immortal sings :

> He does not die that can bequeath
> Some influence to the land he knows,
> Or dares, persistent, interwreath
> Love permanent with the wild hedgerows,
> He does not die, but still remains
> Substantiate with his darling plains.

To others it is the incomparable panorama of Bury Hill,
with the woods and the chalk pits and the river unfolding
with every ascending step. And there are Rackham and
Bignor Hill, crowned Chanctonbury, Cissbury, with its encircling view, Truleigh Hill and Wolstonbury, Firle, and the
noble promontory of Mount Caburn—and many, many
more.

But to me it seems that there is an incomparable magic in
the Downs that lie in the middle of the range, between west
and east—there they seem to turn, and shed their woods,
like a cloak slipping off their shoulders, and become most
truly typical of all that is meant by the South Downs. The
colour changes, becomes less green, has a paler tinge, as
though a little moonshine has mixed with the light of day.
There is a certain spot where one can stand and behold in
full effect the swing round for the eastward march of those
great hills. In my mind this aspect of the Downs is the most
significantly Sussex of all—far more so than where Arundel's
lovely woods sweep across the curving shoulders of the chalk.
Then further eastwards there is a fresh aspect of this range.
In the admirable words H. J. Massingham wrote in his
English Downland : "On the dullest day, the wonderful forms
of the Downs, curving out from Firle Beacon, and the way
their spurs and bays and bosses shape into a kind of intri-
cate pattern against the chequered floor of the Weald, are a
sight whereof the resurrected dead in the barrows, watching
through forty centuries, could never tire. But when these con-
tours flush to warmth under a sky of interchanging sun and

cloud, and the valleys between are suffused in amber mist, and the little river slips in folds of silver into a grey-blue sea, soft as the flocks of cloud, earth has nothing to show more fair."

To all who dwell in Sussex the Downs are the background of their lives, for we no longer exist, as in the remote past, upon the crest of the chalk. But if background in the literal sense, they yet remain "a presence that is not to be put by." As Belloc has said with so much truth : "Sussex is Sussex on account of the South Downs. Their peculiar landscape, their soil, their uniformity, give the county all its meaning."

Ditchling
January 1944—*January* 1945

BIBLIOGRAPHY

Sussex Archæological Collections relating to the History and Antiquities of the County, vols 1 to 83.

Sussex Notes and Queries.

Sussex County Magazine.

The Archæology of Sussex, E. Cecil Curwen (Methuen).

Prehistoric Sussex, E. Cecil Curwen.

Earthwork of England, A. Hadrian Allcroft.

Sussex Geology, E. A. Martin (Archer & Co).

The Sussex Coast, Ian C. Hannah (Fisher Unwin).

The County of Sussex, Hilaire Belloc (Cassell & Co).

The Four Men, Hilaire Belloc.

Story of King Edward and New Winchelsea, F. A. Inderwick (Sampson Low).

History of Winchelsea, W. Durrant Cooper.

A New History of Rye, L. A. Vidler (Combridge, Hove).

Off the Beaten Track in Sussex, A. S. Cooke (Combridge, Hove).

Windmills in Sussex, Peter Hemming (C. W. Daniel).

Highways and Byways in Sussex, E. V. Lucas (Macmillan).

Our Sussex Parish, Thomas Geering (Methuen).

Shepherds of Sussex, Barclay Wills (Skeffington & Son).

Downland Pathways, A. Hadrian Allcroft (Methuen).

Sussex Folk and Sussex Ways, J. C. Egerton (Methuen).

Glimpses of Our Sussex Ancestors, Charles Fleet (*East Sussex News*, Lewes).

The Worthies of Sussex, Mark Antony Lower.

Castles, Mansions and Manors of Western Sussex, D. G. Cary Elwes (Longmans).

Bodiam Castle, Lord Curzon of Kedleston (Cape).

History and Antiquities of Lewes, T. W. Horsfield (J. Baxter, Sussex Press).

Some Sussex Byways, Viscountess Wolseley (Medici Society).

Spirit of the Downs, Arthur Beckett (Methuen).

Lonewood Corner, John Halsham (Smith, Elder).

Old Standards, John Halsham (Smith, Elder).

English Downland, H. J. Massingham (Batsford).

INDEX

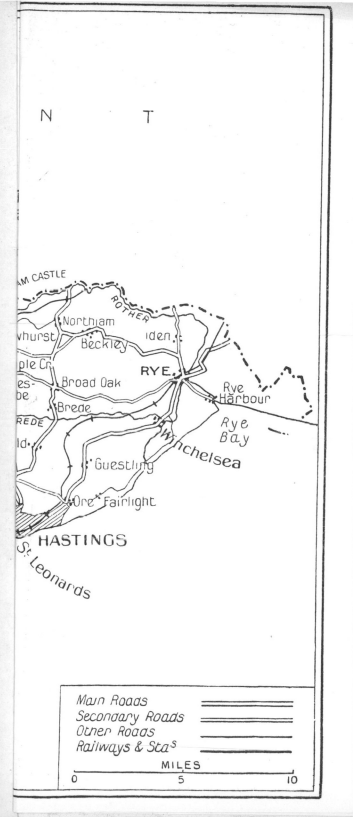

N   T

AM CASTLE

ROTHER

Northiam

vhurst   Beckley   Iden

ple Cr

es-   Broad Oak   RYE

be   Brede   Rye Harbour

REDE   Rye Bay

Id   Winchelsea

Guestling

Ore Fairlight

HASTINGS

St. Leonards

Main Roads
Secondary Roads
Other Roads
Railways & Sta^s

MILES

0   5   10